Susie!
Here's to staying
drama free!

This book is smart, practical, funny, and revolutionary. Patti has combined decades of expertise, a fresh voice, and cutting-edge academic research to create an indispensable guide.

—Alexandra Bodnar,
Deputy General Counsel, Volt Information Sciences, Inc.

My work involves advising corporate leaders, including directors, on issues related to ethics, compliance, and corporate governance. In *The Drama-Free Workplace*, Patti Perez identifies root causes of lapses in these areas and offers real-life, actionable solutions that will help any company not only achieve compliance, but also achieve corporate health. This book should be on your reading list if your job involves any of these areas.

—Angelica Espinosa,
Vice President, Compliance and
Governance and Corporate Secretary, Sempra Energy

Patti's ability to weave academic research findings with practical experience and real-life examples is the perfect blend for anyone who wants to better understand why issues such as sexual harassment and bias still plague our workplaces. *The Drama-Free Workplace* is an authentic, no-holds-barred collection of Patti's 25 + years of experience providing real-world solutions to these important business challenges.

—Carla Boren,
General Counsel and Head of Human Resources, Otonomy, Inc.

This book could not have come at a better time. HR professionals have continually struggled with the critical question posed in this book: "Can we really eliminate drama at work?" The emergence of the #MeToo movement has elevated the need for real life practical solutions that can be adopted in the workplace. Patti offers many business-savvy solutions throughout the book that are grounded in legal knowledge and experience. Her ability to eliminate legalese, pose solutions in easy-to-understand English, and go beyond compliance will serve as a valuable reference guide for HR practitioners, and ultimately contribute to making the workplace healthier, more productive, and more profitable.

—Debora Burke,
Vice President, Human Resources, General Dynamics NASSCO

The Drama-Free Workplace is packed with keen insights about what causes workplace conflict. More important, it's filled with practical solutions for how to resolve drama, how to increase employee trust and engagement, and how to create and maintain a healthy and productive workplace culture. This is a must-read for any business leader who intuitively understands the link between the lack of drama and business success, but needs tools to implement a plan to address it. The result will surely be an increase in your business value.

—Pete Leddy, PhD,
Board Member, Chief People Officer

Tension, anxiety, and conflict at work all fuel what is known today as "drama" in the workplace, causing loss of income, productivity, and profit to all involved parties. Finally, help is available.

Highly respected attorney and consultant Patti Perez has written an easy-to-read manual offering step-by-step instructions for addressing the issues, diagnosing the problem, and implementing a resolution.

Ms. Perez offers, in everyday language, a guide to climbing the workplace-culture pyramid to achieve goals for improving and enhancing a satisfying work environment. Her "Roadmap for Creating and Maintaining a Drama-Free Culture" offers simplified checklists for conducting investigations and creating workplace policy.

This real-world guidebook belongs on the shelves of enlightened supervisors, managers and business leaders everywhere.

—Donna M. Dell,
Former Labor Commissioner for the State of California

The Drama-Free Workplace is a much-needed solution to the people challenges that keep executives up at night. Whether you define drama as ethics lapses, harassment, unconscious bias, resistance to change, or lack of accountability, Patti Perez tackles these issues and more head on. Better yet, her roadmap solutions for creating and maintaining a drama-free culture are practical and relevant, no matter what industry, company size, or geography you find yourself in. Make this mandatory reading for your leadership team and in your MBA classes!

—Paul Falcone,
HR executive and bestselling author, *101 Tough Conversations to Have with Employees* and *101 Sample Write-Ups for Documenting Employee Performance Problems*

This is a first-of-its-kind book—it leverages Patti's deep expertise and gives leaders and HR practitioners a robust toolkit to help them build their own authentic, drama-free workplace. When we're faced with tough workplace situations, it's great to have a toolkit of sound, proven methodologies to rely on to help us navigate the situations and emerge with a return to harmony in the workplace. This is a must-read for all HR practitioners … I'll be issuing this out to my team!

—Tonya Cross,
Senior Vice President, Human Capital, Lytx

The Drama-Free Workplace is a forward-thinking manual on how to foster the workplace of the future. Patti's thought leadership and years of in-depth workplace problem-solving experience are brilliantly woven together in a manner that provides readers with the practical tools to generate a healthy workplace culture. Leaders focused on moving beyond compliance and toward talent growth and workplace success should include Patti's book in their library.

—Mishell Parreno Taylor,
Shareholder, Littler Mendelson

The Drama-Free Workplace is sure to become a text that will be read by HR professionals, employment attorneys, executive coaches, and really anyone in the modern workplace who wants to do their part to reduce unnecessary conflict. As a lawyer who has seen the drama up close, both as in-house advisor and as outside counsel dealing with the aftermath, I welcome this type of direction for my clients. Too often, companies fail to prevent or address drama because their focus is not genuinely rooted in making the workplace better for all but is instead focused on avoiding lawsuits. Patti's methodical explanation of the root causes of drama, combined with her no-nonsense, practical solutions make *The Drama-Free Workplace* an easy read that users can go back to repeatedly for ideas and guidance.

—Nestor Barrero,
Senior Counsel, Costangy, Brooks, Smith & Prophete, LLP.
Formerly Vice President–Employment Law, NBC/Universal

Patti Perez understands the American workplace. She is a seasoned employment lawyer, an investigator of countless workplace harassment claims, and is a woman who can easily slide into the shoes of the lowest-level non-manager *or* the CEO. In *The Drama-Free Workplace,* Patti taps into her deep understanding of the law and people, and uses plain language and real-life tales of workplace woe to deliver an analysis of where workplaces go wrong. She provides bold yet practical prescriptions for creating a workplace that is goal-focused, fun, productive, and, yes, *drama-free.* Spoiler alert: skittishly striving for mere legal compliance won't cut it; you need to define, create, and maintain an actual culture. I'll be sending copies of *The Drama-Free Workplace* to clients and friends.

—Mike Cramer,
Employment Law Shareholder, Ogletree Deakins, Chicago

For many companies, glossy brochures market a culture of inclusivity, fairness, and respect. However, for many of those same companies, all that fancy marketing masks a drama-filled, toxic culture that is anything but inclusive, fair, and respectful. But toxic workplaces can be fixed, and even better, they can be avoided altogether. Relying on the basic tenants of authenticity and trust, Patti Perez applies commonsense principals, solid research, and years of experience to demonstrate how drama in the workplace can effectively be managed out of existence.

Patti Perez rejects the hyper-legalized and reactionary policies that have been shown to stifle effective workplace communication and increase workplace drama. Instead, the book offers a fresh, holistic approach to creating a vibrant and respectful workplace culture. Patti Perez shows how companies can take a page from the workplace safety playbook and encourage employees to work together to identify, address, and resolve challenging issues related to sexual harassment, microaggressions, and implicit bias. Gone, says Patti Perez, are the lengthy policies that police employee conduct; and gone are the disingenuous zero-tolerance policies and selective enforcement. Instead, *The Drama-Free Workplace* offers an alternative approach to conflict prevention and resolution—one that reduces policing and increases engagement and trust.

If your organization is looking for a practical and effective tool to reduce workplace drama and foster a healthy culture, you would do your organization a great service by taking the journey with Patti Perez in her new book, *The Drama-Free Workplace*.

—Dawn T. Collins, Esq.,
Employment Lawyer, Co-founder and Partner, CollinsKim LLP

Patti Perez is a well-known industry expert on the topic of workplace drama—how to identify it, how to prevent it, and how to fix it. This book compiles her decades of experience and is a must-read for anyone who wants to address workplace strife in ways that are proven to be effective.

—Diego Arp,
In-house counsel

the drama-free workplace

the drama-free workplace

HOW YOU CAN PREVENT UNCONSCIOUS BIAS, SEXUAL HARASSMENT, ETHICS LAPSES, AND INSPIRE A HEALTHY CULTURE

patti perez

WILEY

Published by John Wiley & Sons, Inc., Hoboken, New Jersey.
Published simultaneously in Canada.

For general information on our other products and services or for technical support, please contact
our Customer Care Department within the United States at (800) 762-2974, outside the United
States at (317) 572-3993 or fax (317) 572-4002.

Wiley publishes in a variety of print and electronic formats and by print-on-demand. Some material
included with standard print versions of this book may not be included in e-books or in print-on-
demand. If this book refers to media such as a CD or DVD that is not included in the version you
purchased, you may download this material at http://booksupport.wiley.com. For more information
about Wiley products, visit www.wiley.com.

Library of Congress Cataloging-in-Publication Data

Names: Perez, Patti, 1967- author.
Title: The drama-free workplace : how you can prevent unconscious bias,
  sexual harassment, ethics lapses, and inspire a healthy culture / Patti
  Perez.
Description: Hoboken, New Jersey : John Wiley & Sons, Inc., [2019] | Includes
  index. |
Identifiers: LCCN 2018055956 (print) | LCCN 2018058851 (ebook) | ISBN
  9781119546443 (ePub) | ISBN 9781119546436 (ePDF) | ISBN 9781119546429
  (hardcover)
Subjects: LCSH: Personnel management. | Employee morale. | Problem employees.
  | Organizational behavior. | Corporate culture.
Classification: LCC HF5549 (ebook) | LCC HF5549 .P4164 2019 (print) | DDC
  658.3/12--dc23
LC record available at https://lccn.loc.gov/2018055956

Printed in the United States of America.
V10008318_021919

To my mami *and* papi,
my first and best teachers on living drama free

Contents

Foreword

Times have changed. The old way of managing (but not solving) employee conflict doesn't work anymore. Social media has increased transparency in every organization and our changing demographics make it more important than ever to be authentic and promote a healthy workplace culture.

The #MeToo movement is the culmination of employers taking the wrong approach to solving conflict, and it was during the unfolding of this movement that Patti joined our team at Emtrain.

This watershed moment created an instant bond between us—two California employment lawyers who understand that intentions drive results, and that the intent should always be to create a healthy culture, not mere legal compliance. Patti and I are both on a mission to educate people on workplace issues and ensure we solve problems in a more authentic, effective way. *The Drama-Free Workplace* is Patti's latest effort in this mission and her practical guidance and strategies are invaluable for any leader who wants a healthy, drama-free workplace.

As you'll read in *The Drama-Free Workplace*, that doesn't mean taking actions that might increase your risk for claims. It means widening your view and treating the workplace in a more integrated, holistic way, rather than narrowly focusing on the symptoms (claims) of an unhealthy workplace culture.

You'll learn about the root causes of workplace drama and, especially relevant for today's climate, you'll learn in detail what is most likely to give rise to sexual harassment at work. Given that we find ourselves in the middle of a cultural transformation about the definition of appropriate and inappropriate conduct at work, the topics covered in this book are a must-read for any business leader, emerging leader, or employee who wants to learn how to keep drama out of the workplace.

Janine Yancey, Founder and CEO

Emtrain

Acknowledgments

While my name appears as the author of this book, *The Drama-Free Workplace* would have never come to fruition had I relied solely on my own abilities. It took more than a village to write this book—it took a family of committed and giving people who were always willing to help.

First, my deepest thanks to my friend and colleague Paul Falcone, who recommended me to the Wiley family. His generosity is indescribable and I'll be forever grateful to him for trusting me enough to recommend me.

Next, my two main points of contact at Wiley have been incredible. Richard Narramore believed in the book concept from the beginning and had a vision for making this book come to life. My editor, Vicki Adang, has been my life raft. From her gentle first message ("That was good, but not quite right") to the ones that followed ("Yes, you've got it!"), I couldn't have done this without her guidance. Her abundant patience and kindness kept me going when I thought I'd never be able to quite articulate what I was thinking. And her encouraging words helped propel me more than she'll ever know. Thanks, Vicki!

Writing a book while working full time is no easy feat, so I'd also like to thank my wonderful teammates at Emtrain, especially Janine Yancey, who serves as equal parts mentor and cheerleader. And to the rest of the Emtrain team, thank you for your understanding and unwavering support while I wrote this book!

I need to thank more friends than can be mentioned here, but I'll start with the guy who has been my brother since freshman year in college. Ray Nieto not only read and edited several versions of the book, but he also helped me with ideas for how to get the word out about the content.

Thanks, Ray, for always being there for me! My other BFFs, especially Joyce Magsarili, were, as always, only a phone call away when I was panicked about a deadline or about whether my content would resonate. Joyce, for 30-plus years you've been my "ride or die" girlfriend, my third sister, and truly my best friend! And to the rest of my friends, those who helped me flesh out concepts, those who encouraged me in real life and in the virtual world, and those who promised to read and share the book—thank you, thank you, thank you.

While this book is dedicated to my parents, humble immigrants from El Salvador who gave up everything to give their kids a better life, it's really a tribute to my entire family. My parents, Maria and Francisco Chavarria, taught my sisters, brother, and me that love and family are what it's all about. They had the most drama-free marriage of any I've known, and raised us in a loving environment where each one of us learned to keep our lives as uncomplicated as possible. Thank you, Annie Chavarria, Margie Esquivel, and Edward Chavarria for being the best siblings anyone could ever ask for! And thanks to my brother-in-law Tomas for putting up with us for almost 40 years and for giving me the best niece and nephew I could ever imagine. Tommy and Karlita, I love you and thank God for making me your *tia*.

I was fortunate enough to have been born into a big, fat Salvadoran family, and became even luckier when I married into an equally crazy and loving Philly Italian family.

My husband, Tom Scutti, has been my rock throughout this process and I thank you, sweetheart, from the bottom of my heart. I know the "I'll get to that as soon as I finish my book" refrain got old, but you never showed that you were tired of hearing it. Your love and commitment to me and to our kids are inspiring. Thank you for supporting me through this process, and through every other crazy idea I've had. My life doesn't work without you in it.

And thanks, too, to the other Scuttis in my life—my two fabulous bonus kids. Nick, I love your beautiful heart and your dedication to your craft. Thanks to you and Katie for always listening to my crazy rants, about my book and other topics. Christina, your passion—for your family, your work, and your sports teams—is infectious. Thanks for being my test audience for many of my theories about how to live a drama-free life.

And finally, to my baby boy (who isn't a baby anymore, but . . .), Tony Perez, you are my love, my rock, my passion. God gave me the greatest privilege when He gave me you to raise. Looking at you now, a young man starting his journey into adulthood, I see that the legacy of your *abuelito* Paco lives in you and I'm grateful for any part I've played in making you who you are today. Words aren't enough to describe the immense love and pride I feel, but I think you know.

To everyone who has heard me advocate for doing all you can to keep your life (including your work life) drama free, thanks. I'm so grateful for everyone's help along the way. This book couldn't have happened without each of you touching my life in some way.

About the Author

Born in El Salvador, Patti Perez began living as a compassionate sharp-shooter early in life. Patti and her family moved to the United States when she was three, and throughout the next several decades, she lived in San Francisco; Los Angeles; Houston; Washington, DC; Mexico City; and San Diego. These experiences taught her to be flexible and open-minded—making diplomacy and communication key skills.

Patti has continued to hone these skills in her professional life. A graduate of UCLA and the UCLA School of Law, Patti began her career as an employment law litigator, but quickly learned that the life of a litigator was not her calling. Her post-litigation career included leading an international judicial education program in Mexico City, working as the head of HR at Skadden Arps in DC, and serving as a shareholder at Ogletree Deakins in San Diego. Patti also founded Puente Consulting and for 14 years she dedicated her career to helping prevent and address workplace drama, including conducting more than 1,000 workplace investigations, training thousands of professionals, and serving as an expert witness. During that time, two California governors appointed Patti to the Fair Employment and Housing Council, where she authored a number of regulations clarifying various aspects of the state's employment laws.

Patti currently serves as Vice President of Workplace Strategy for Emtrain, a culturetech company offering comprehensive online training programs, expert guidance, and insightful data analytics—all with the goal of creating healthy workplace cultures and eliminating workplace drama.

Patti and her husband, Tom, live in San Diego, where they spend their time enjoying the life of empty nesters but still miss their kids: Nick, Christina, and Tony.

Introduction

Companies are hungry to find ways to differentiate themselves, to become employers of choice, to present themselves as organizations that deserve to win the "war for talent." Cue the calls for a dynamic workplace culture as the secret weapon to make all this come true.

Workplace culture has become a familiar term in corporate America. But despite all the talk about how much culture matters, few companies actually do the work required to build and maintain a healthy and productive environment at work. Research validates the fact that a healthy culture drives business results, but little attention is paid to how to actually improve your culture and keep it healthy.

First, let's define the term. In short, workplace culture encompasses the beliefs, values, and behaviors that guide your company. There are many components that define and measure the health of a culture at work, including employee engagement, employee satisfaction, happiness at work, compensation, benefits, and other workplace perks. People confuse these individual elements with defining their culture. ("We have a great culture . . . our employee surveys indicate our workforce is engaged.")

As outlined in Figure I.1, a healthy and productive workplace culture has various components. Like Maslow's hierarchy of needs, you can't get to the top rungs without first satisfying basic needs.

A company that provides the basics—fair pay and benefits, and a generally safe workplace—has a mediocre culture. People come to work for their paychecks. There is little innovation and profits are flat. (Note: Companies that don't provide even these basics are cultures that are usually seen as toxic, and this toxicity eventually destroys the company's ability to succeed.)

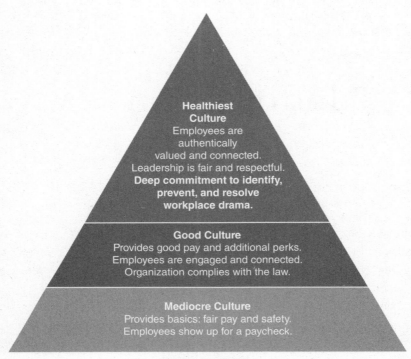

FIGURE I.1   The Healthy Workplace Culture Pyramid

A company that goes a step above and provides additional perks and takes steps to ensure an engaged and connected employee base has a good culture. Their employees understand the company's mission, they feel connected to it and to each other. In terms of employee relations, these companies focus on and follow the law.

Then there are the companies with fantastic workplace cultures. The secret to these companies' success is threefold:

1. They are intentional and relentless about planning and executing a strategy to put culture at the center of everything they do;
2. They have leaders who walk the walk and set the tone; and,
3. Because *culture* refers to the norms that govern how people approach problems and develop solutions, these companies also see preventing, managing, and addressing conflict (drama) as a vital part of their culture.

And the results are undeniable: a cohesive and collaborative workplace that leads to innovation and, as study after study shows, increased revenue and profit.

Think about a company that boasts about its engaged and satisfied employee base. Now think of how well this company fares if information comes to light about an executive who is allowed to remain on the job despite credible allegations of sexual harassment or some other ethical lapse. The weak foundation that holds up the fallacy of a great workplace culture collapses under the weight of the hypocrisy.

In today's post-#MeToo world, it is more important than ever to find groundbreaking solutions to address harassment, bias, and ethical lapses in the workplace. Without addressing these concerns—drama at work—a company's claim of an excellent workplace culture is incomplete.

While much has been written about topics such as employee engagement, climate surveys, and the introduction of Ping-Pong tables as tools to build a healthy culture, little attention has been paid to how critical conflict prevention and resolution are to a company's ability to provide employees with an environment in which to thrive. This book addresses that very topic and introduces an innovative and fresh approach to reducing or even eliminating workplace drama.

This book is for the leader, for the emerging leader, and for anyone who has to manage drama at work. A recurring theme throughout the book is that it will take each and every one of us to achieve the goal of a drama-free workplace.

The book is divided into three parts:

- Part One: Diagnosis Drama: What You Can Do to Identify, Prevent, and Fix Workplace Drama. This section gives the reader an overview of the root causes of drama and practical solutions to rid the workplace of it, followed by detailed chapters on the three most common types of drama at work: sexual harassment, bias/diversity, and ethics lapses.
- Part Two: "Hiking" to the Top of the Healthy Workplace Culture Pyramid. Using the metaphor of hiking, this section provides some essential and easy-to-implement formulas for making your workplace healthier. It also draws from analogous fields (safety, emotional intelligence, persuasive communication) to provide cutting-edge solutions on how to become drama free.

- Part Three: A DIY Roadmap for Creating and Maintaining a Drama-Free Culture. In this section, I'll share my very practical, step-by-step roadmaps on how to write and enforce policies, how to provide effective training, and how to investigate and resolve workplace drama.

And one last note: Don't forget that a healthy culture is a fun culture. There is a misconception that in order to be drama free you have to erase all things entertaining and amusing. But who wants to work in that type of environment? A culture that is healthy, inclusive, and respectful can and should also be fun.

You can read the book from beginning to end, or you can turn to the chapter that has information about your most pressing need. The goal is to introduce you to a fresh approach to prevent and address drama at work so that yours can be an organization that is proud of its culture.

I'll use case studies and real-life examples throughout the book. I've collected these stories from my work as an employment attorney and HR professional, as well as my experience as a workplace investigator—a specialist in the field of drama prevention and resolution. This work has given me a bird's-eye view of how drama unfolds. More important, it has given me insight into how the need to prevent and fix workplace drama is a key ingredient in the secret sauce of creating and maintaining a healthy workplace culture.

Whether your organization is already on its way to the top of the Healthy Workplace Culture Pyramid or you're starting from scratch, this book will provide you with a roadmap to identify, prevent, and resolve workplace drama. And whether you're a leader, an emerging leader, or an employee who wants to stay drama free, the tips in this book will help you be a part of the solution we're all striving for—a workplace free of useless drama.

PART I

Diagnosis Drama: What You Can Do to Identify, Prevent, and Fix Workplace Drama

1

How to Blow Up an Organization (and Rise from the Ashes)

Chances are, you encounter drama in your workplace on a daily basis. My guess is that if you had a nickel for every time someone asked for advice because they'd been "harassed at work" or they have to deal with an employee who is "gaming the system," well, you'd have lots of nickels.

Some of the drama is subtle and nuanced, related more to perception than the actual facts of the story. Other times the stories you hear are blatant and in your face. These are the stories that make you cringe and ask yourself, "Did she really do that?"

The skills required to address these situations vary, but regardless of where the drama falls on the intensity spectrum, you need to do everything in your power to manage, if not eliminate, it. Will it really take blowing up your organization to identify, prevent, and fix workplace drama? *Yes* (but not literally!).

#WorkplaceDrama: Identifying Problematic Behavior

Workplace drama takes many forms, but all drama is rooted in conflict and heightened emotions. The drama might involve just a few people (at least initially). But like a progressive disease, the drama spreads if it isn't dealt with swiftly and effectively. And too often unchecked drama ends up infecting an entire department, division, or company. Identifying the problem is vital to ultimately figuring out how to prevent it and solve it.

So how does drama manifest itself at work? Here's a partial list:

- *"Harassment."* This word is in quotes for a reason; it's a word that is misunderstood and therefore misused. Too often, people use the term to describe behavior that is annoying or bothersome. While that is the dictionary definition of "harassment," the legal meaning is quite different. More than likely, you've had this conversation before. You've had to explain this distinction between the layman's definition and the legal definition, though hopefully you've made it clear that even behavior that is "less than" illegal is nonetheless problematic and needs to be addressed. Harassing conduct takes many forms and involves the entire gamut of personal characteristics, but the type of workplace harassment that is most often discussed remains sexual harassment. And of course, in the post-#MeToo world, it's taken on an additional urgency. In many instances, an employee complaining about "harassment" is actually referring to disrespectful, rude, or demeaning conduct, and, in more severe cases, workplace bullying. Having a respectful and civil workplace environment is vital to having a truly healthy workplace culture, but a problem can't be fixed if it is imprecisely stated. It requires a new plan and it is one of many ways that a company needs to blow up before it can rebuild.

Harassment: It's important to distinguish between exposure to annoying or bothersome behavior (the dictionary definition of harassment) and unlawful harassment, which involves a protected category and must meet other legal requirements, including unwelcomeness and either severity or pervasiveness. (See Chapter 3.)

- *Bias – conscious and unconscious.* You've seen bias, or at least allegations of it, every day, right? It may take the form of a boss who is playing favorites, inaccurately describing someone's performance, or making judgmental comments. Undoubtedly, you've also had discussions about unconscious bias—whether it involves African-Americans who are arrested for waiting for a friend at a coffee shop or women who say they experience "mansplaining" at meetings. The reality of unconscious bias and the ways in which it affects our decision-making is well chronicled, even if the average employee still doesn't understand it completely.

I'll use the term "unconscious bias" throughout this book. *Unconscious biases* are social stereotypes about certain groups of people that individuals form outside their own conscious awareness. Sometimes the term "implicit bias" is used instead of unconscious bias, particularly by academics. *Implicit bias* refers to the attitudes or stereotypes that affect our understanding, actions, and decisions in an unconscious manner. (For more, see Chapter 3.)

- *Perceptions of unfairness.* "I work just as hard as Sarah, but Joe always gives her a higher rating and a higher raise." "I just wish I knew the rules of the game so I could succeed at this company." "They tell us that there is a procedure to deal with this issue, but we all know rules are bent if you have the right title." "I honestly have no idea why my boss dislikes me and treats me so disrespectfully." Whether these examples ultimately uncover *actual* unfairness ends up being of little consequence. If employees have a reasonable perception that an individual or "the company" is treating them unfairly, you have workplace drama you need to deal with. (More on this in Chapter 5.)
- *Ethical lapses.* Many examples of ethical lapses involve a lack of thought and analysis. While there are certainly examples of employees embezzling money or committing other blatantly fraudulent acts, in many instances the ethical lapse is an employee receiving a gift from a vendor, a committee leader advocating for his friend's company during an RFP process, or a manager going against policy and hiring someone without going through the pre-established procedure. Regardless of whether the conduct is purposeful or is due to laziness, ethical blunders, and how the company deals with them, are a common source of drama at work. (More in Chapter 4.)

There are, of course, many other examples of workplace strife, but these examples of drama at work are the ones we see most often.

Root Causes of Workplace Drama

Just as important as identifying and recognizing drama (preferably early, when it can still be easily addressed), is recognizing its root causes. Any one of these examples—not to mention a combination of them—has the potential to devastate your company.

1. *Inauthentic leadership:* A lack of authenticity creates or perpetuates a belief that management is hypocritical, that they only talk the talk but don't walk the walk. In this environment, employees lose enthusiasm for their jobs, passion for what the company represents, and, most dangerous, they lose trust.

2. *Problem-solving deficit:* A lack of authenticity leads to inconsistency, usually seen in the form of the failure to implement solutions in an even-handed way. Over time, this creates *actual* unfairness (and also creates a strong perception of a lack of workplace justice).

3. *Persistent confusion: Unfair or illegal?:* Repeated inconsistency in dealing with conflict (e.g., ignoring misconduct, conducting sham investigations into claims of misconduct, uneven distribution of consequences when misconduct is proven) not only leads to the erosion of trust, but it also increases the probability that employees will perceive any level of misconduct not only as unfair, but also as illegal. This increases the chance that they will make internal or external claims of legal violations. If made internally, the company must go down the compliance route and conduct a formal workplace investigation. Or the employee might choose to file a lawsuit. And in today's social media–filled world there is another choice. An employee's grievance could end up on a blog, an employer review website, a social media site, or as an exposé on the front page of a national newspaper. Yesterday's biggest workplace fear might have been an employment lawsuit. Today, brand value is more easily lost with one press of a button . . . a button that says "post."

Imprecise use of legal terms

Similar to the misunderstanding about the term "harassment," employees (including managers) also use the terms "hostile work environment," "discrimination," and "retaliation" imprecisely. Each of these are legal terms of art; an employee must establish several specific elements to prove any of these legal violations. But these terms are often used in the workplace to point to behavior that is irritating, biased, or vindictive. Use of precise language—which then leads to an appropriate corporate reaction and resolution—is vital. But make no mistake, this is a two-way street. Just as it is important for employees to learn to precisely report their concerns, it is equally important that employers, especially managers and HR professionals, learn to establish an effective way to then address those complaints, regardless of whether the behavior is unlawful.

4. *Lack of transparency:* Long-standing fear of getting sued has, paradoxically, led to decisions that increase the chance an employer will be sued. (I discuss this in great detail in the "Fearlessness" section in Chapter 5 by walking you through the litigation-avoidance paradox.) A prime example is with the lack of transparency. Convinced that they are prohibited from sharing "confidential," "private," or "personal" information, companies create shrouds of secrecy. In some instances, it's inaccurate or incomplete information about why someone was disciplined or fired. In others, it's making large-scale corporate changes (reorganizations, selection of new leadership, etc.) behind an impenetrable wall, with no employee knowledge or input. No matter the specific secret, two lessons are clear: Employees know more than you think they know (so trying to pull the wool over their eyes is obvious to them) and you do more harm than good since employees know you're lying (employees have a very well-honed BS meter). Old-fashioned though it may sound, it really does pay to be honest.

5. *Communication gaps:* Confusion between unfair and illegal behavior, an uneven playing field (or the reasonable perception of one), and secrecy do not mix well. To make matters worse, employers

only teach employees "legal language" (that is, employees only learn about "harassment" and "discrimination"). This gives employees one of two messages. The first is: Don't come to me with a complaint unless it's one of unlawful conduct. When this happens, employers don't find out about problems until they reach crisis level. The second message is: When you do eventually report your concerns, do so by using charged legal terminology such as "hostile work environment" and "retaliation," rather than reporting facts and consequences. This then causes the company leader to go into defense mode rather than problem-solving mode. This merry-go-round of posturing makes it clear that we need to establish a common and productive language at work . . . one that actually has the goal of fixing the workplace drama problem.

Precision in reporting

Which of these "reports"—both of which essentially say the same thing—is most likely to decrease the temperature and prevent further drama?

"I need to report sexual harassment. Charlie is such a jerk. He's always calling us 'chicks' and 'babes' but never uses those types of nicknames for any of the guys. And, ugh, I hate that he talks about his dating life. It's so gross."

Or

"I'm having a hard time working with Charlie. I don't think he respects women. He calls us 'chicks' and 'babes' but never uses those kinds of nicknames for the guys—they're always referred to by their names or by 'chief' and 'bro.' And his constant talking about his dating life makes me think that he only sees women as potential romantic partners. I don't know if he realizes that all of this makes me feel belittled and makes it harder for me to do my job. Can we work together to help him understand how his words and actions are affecting me?"

6. *Increased division:* This confusion drives an us–versus–them mentality that causes even further division and mistrust. With increased division comes an erosion of empathy and self-awareness. It becomes nearly impossible to see the issue from the other person's perspective and to be self-aware and humble enough to admit mistakes. Viewed through this lens of suspicion and selfishness, actions are more likely to be negatively interpreted which makes drama inevitable.

7. *Culture of complicity:* The us–versus–them culture becomes permissive and tolerates bad behavior. And tolerance inevitably leads to even more egregious behavior (since the bad actor is emboldened by the tolerance). After all, in this type of culture, trouble is always blamed on the person on the opposite side. What results is a failure to view situations objectively and we instead view them through the expedient lens of quick blame. We hide behind "business decisions." Sure, Charlie is hard to take, but he's so valuable to the company. Yes, Jessica has made some decisions that push the bounds of ethics, but it's only because external factors make it nearly impossible for her to do her job effectively. Once you start making these types of excuses, you've crossed a dangerous line and drama will be ever-present.

Precision in response

Using the Charlie example, which of these responses is more likely to decrease the temperature and prevent further drama?

"I don't really see this as a harassment issue and it sounds more like Charlie's management style. You haven't said anything about him being sexual or making a pass at you. Maybe this is just his way of motivating his team. I guess I'll talk to him about the nicknames, but you're just going to have to learn to get along with him. I mean, he is the boss."

Or

"Thanks for letting me know about this. I can see why Charlie's behavior makes you feel as if he doesn't fully value your contributions.

I'm happy to talk with him, but before I do, I'd like to hear more details from you, and then I'll also talk to Charlie to get his perspective. My goal here is to make sure everyone's voice is heard and to make sure that everyone feels valued and included."

8. *Blind spots pop up:* As each side begins to think the other is out to get them, we develop blind spots, and our ability to anticipate and respond to drama becomes weaker. Of course moving someone to a lower position on the organizational chart during a reorganization will lead to hurt feelings and claims of unfairness, but reorg strategists think, "Hey, they're lucky to have a job." Yes, it's true the company has lost one-third of its female leaders in the past six months, but that's just a coincidence and says nothing about the company's commitment to diversity—unless you ask the remaining female leaders. The ability to anticipate and plan for drama is a critical skill that is unfortunately missing at most companies. (See Chapter 6 for more on how to take action in situations that are known to result in drama.)

9. *Wrong solution:* Since we aren't identifying root causes to the drama, we implement ineffective solutions or we overcorrect. In either case, we make an already difficult problem even worse. The most typical answer to drama in today's workplace is to "review our policies and procedures." More rules. There is a growing perception of HR and leadership as cops, thus making the drama worse, not better. Just as bad as implementing the wrong (read: not well-thought-out) solution is overcorrection. This too is rooted in a failure to think critically and creatively about what might actually solve the problem. Your diversity metrics show low numbers of underrepresented employees at your company? Clearly the answer is to begin hiring anyone and everyone who checks the "diversity box" without regard to qualifications. While this might solve your short-term numbers problem, it inevitably breeds resentment, hurts your business and does nothing to ultimately help with "diversity numbers" since you're setting the candidates up to fail. Drama, drama, drama.

10. *Unwillingness to admit wrongdoing:* The thought of apologizing in corporate America is unfathomable to many. But if we want to move the needle on culture, it's a key ingredient. We all make mistakes. We fail to anticipate problems. We fail to take the time necessary to make wise decisions. We ignore problems, hoping they will go away. Making the mistake is human; failing to admit and make amends is fatal. A company made up of leaders (or employees) who fail to admit wrongdoing is an inauthentic company, thus perpetuating the cycle of mistrust.

Unchecked, these triggers create a negative work environment and cause tangible (and detrimental) effects. Widespread mistrust leads to low morale and low productivity, high (and unnecessary) turnover, increased claims of unfairness, difficulty in recruiting and retaining top talent, legal claims, and, of course, damage to corporate brand.

A key question then is, how did we get here?

Legal Compliance: Friend or Foe?

Employment laws prohibiting discrimination at work have been around since the 1960s. Over the years those laws have expanded to include a prohibition of harassment, including sexual harassment and retaliation, among other types.

A review of the intent of those laws makes one thing clear: They were enacted to provide an important, but not exclusive, avenue for redress. They were never meant to be the sole way to solve problems at work. In fact, they weren't even meant to be the primary go-to for the elimination of workplace drama. At their core, these laws seek to provide a level playing field, a set of standards to ensure consistency in decision making, an avenue to address egregious behavior. They were certainly not established to increase animosity at work and were not meant to question every business decision or establish a way to keep track of daily behavior.

But a deep misunderstanding of the law has negatively impacted the way both employees and company leaders make decisions, and this has had an equally negative impact on workplace culture.

- *Misguided corporate reaction:* In terms of company leaders, the answer has been to wear legal blinders at all times—to make business decisions through the narrow lens of risk management. By doing so, leaders have lost sight of what actually creates a healthy, respect-ful, and inclusive work environment. Companies rely on "solid" legal advice: Approach conflict resolution with a fear-based, "I'll get them before they get me" mentality. While there are many law-yers who provide sound advice—advice that complies with legal mandates and also focuses on business success—too many attor-neys have convinced companies that being scared is the best way to avoid lawsuits. The irony? Over the years claims have gone up, not down. In fact, high-profile scandals have become an almost daily occurrence. Apparently, we're doing it all wrong. (See more on this in Chapter 5, where I introduce you to the concept of the litiga-tion-avoidance paradox.)

- *Misguided employee reaction:* Employees have been similarly brain-washed into believing that the only way to get justice is through the legal system. Gone are the days of wanting to participate in fixing what's broken but salvageable. Don't get me wrong, there are, unfor-tunately, many instances in which the legal system is the best and only way to resolve harassment issues (think Harvey Weinstein, both his behavior and the shameful failure by the corporation to protect his victims). But this isn't always the case. More often than not, sit-uations can be dealt with through precise reporting, an appropriate corporate reaction, and a mutual problem-solving approach. But it will take the re-establishment of trust, respect, and accountability to do so.

Two equally important phenomena, both based on a hyper-focus on the law, track the inevitability of the #MeToo movement:

1. *Focus on fear:* Fear-based and inauthentic decision-making leads to bad decisions. Blind spots created by that fear leads to a culture of complicity. In story after #MeToo story, targets of harassment speak of what is essentially double victimization. First, there is the sexual harassment itself. What's worse, the victims say, is working with lead-ership that turns a blind eye to what's right in front of them. What happens? Employees (both targets and bystanders) don't trust the system so they don't report problems when they can still be easily solved. Or worse, they report the problem and the company does

nothing. The employee leaves or sues. The fear-based mentality is reinforced: "See, all they wanted was to sue us." And so it continues.

2. *Taking your eye off the ball:* While the workplace was consumed with worries about the law, a brave new world emerged and no one noticed. This brave new world is largely fueled by social media. Employees are increasingly using social media as the channel to change the workplace power dynamic. They are reclaiming control of the employment relationship by using posts, blogs, and company review sites to vent their frustrations. And it's been incredibly effective. Media personalities have been removed not because of lawsuits or the threat of a claim, but because of detailed newspaper stories — stories where every gory detail of bad behavior gone wild and details of a complicit corporate culture are exposed to the world. Fast-rising tech companies have been rocked, not because of legal claims, but because of a single blog post gone viral. Employees are using social media to effectuate change and a company that ignores this reality does so at its own peril. Understanding and embracing this brave new world is vital for a company to maintain a healthy internal and external brand.

If we are serious about working together to revolutionize the workplace, then it's time to stop playing to not lose and begin playing to win. After all, doing the same thing over and over, expecting a different result, is what got us into this mess in the first place. This leads to one conclusion: The answer isn't to continue to operate with compliance blinders but rather to focus on trust, mutual respect, transparent communication, and, above all, authenticity.

The #1 Culture Problem in Organizations: A Lack of Authenticity

Of all the underlying reasons that drama creeps into our workplaces and ruins corporate culture, a lack of authenticity is the most serious.

We know the drill: Have a policy for everything, make employees sign acknowledgments for all those policies, draft a statement about your company's "commitment to diversity and inclusion" and post it on your company website. Defend every claim of unfairness with your standard statement that your company is "committed to an environment free of harassment" and that you are an "equal opportunity employer." I'm not necessarily saying any of these are bad, I'm saying they are rote responses that send a clear message: "We are an average company who implements average solutions." And what's worse is a company that says these things but means none of them.

I liken a company's promise of a "harassment-free" workplace to a restaurant that promises diners "poison-free" meals. I suppose a restaurant wants to make sure that diners know they won't get food poisoning when they visit, but isn't a better marketing strategy to promise them an excellent dining experience?

Similarly, promising a harassment-free workplace tells employees: "We promise to do the minimum" or "We promise to do what the law requires." A more effective approach is to promise a healthy and inclusive workplace culture. That necessarily means that the culture won't tolerate harassment, and it also means that employees will be respected, developed, and provided with opportunities to thrive.

Here's a common scenario:

Company: We have a zero-tolerance policy when it comes to sexual harassment.

Employee: My boss tells sexually suggestive jokes and makes sexually charged comments and at the last sales conference he invited me up to his hotel room. (Employee's inner-dialogue: *This is hard to do, but I want this to stop, and I'm going to believe the company's stated commitment to keep me safe.*)

Manager: Well, was he drunk? (Manager's inner-dialogue: *I have so much work to do, this is the last thing I want to deal with. And besides, this employee is complaining about a guy who brings a lot of money to the company.*)

Employee: I don't know? (Employee's inner-dialogue: *Is this person serious? What happened to zero tolerance?*)

Manager: Were you drunk? (Inner-dialogue: *I mean, it's a fair question.*)
Employee: No. (Inner-dialogue: *Well, I guess I know where this is going . . .*)
Manager: Okay, we'll look into it, but I'm sure he was joking. (Inner-dialogue: *I better not find that any of this is true . . . I can't lose this guy.*)
Employee: Um, okay. Thanks, I guess. (Inner-dialogue: *I should have listened to my coworker who told me to keep my mouth shut.*)

How do you create and maintain a culture that says what it means and means what it says? Try this three-step process: Define it. Live it. Color it in.

Define it: You can't "live your values" until you've defined what those values are. This involves more than putting a mission statement on your website. What does your company really stand for? Why do employees and leaders join and stay with your company? If your company's focus is on increasing revenue (for example, a start-up that will perish without showing profit quickly), then don't pretend to be a company that wants to retain employees for a lifetime. If you are a company whose passion is making the world a better place, say so and structure your culture to attract employees who buy into that philosophy. More than ever, culture matters to employees, often even more than compensation.

Live it: So now that you've found your company's true north, how do you make it real? First and foremost, walk the walk. Be radically authentic. All work on defining your culture will go to waste if your employees sense that it is simply lip service. If you've defined integrity as a core company value, then act in all instances of ethical lapses. All of them. If you say you believe in and value diversity and inclusion, then be a champion for a comprehensively and creatively designed and deployed D&I plan.

Color it in: Simply defining and living your values isn't quite enough. Be meticulous about linking your company culture to your company's purpose and passion. And do so in detail. Will you draft and distribute an employee handbook (yawn) or an inspirational guide that gives employees genuine guidelines about what to expect, and also tells them what is expected of them? Will you talk about your values during interviews, at performance meetings, during coaching sessions and even when an employee is exiting your company? If not, why not? Once you've made your company purpose clear, it's time to yell that message from the rooftops every chance you get.

Practicing profound authenticity is the first step on the path to a drama-free workplace.

The Courage to Be Different (and Therefore Effective): Focus on the Good

We know the problem—drama that appears in the form of harassment, bias, a perception of unfairness, or ethical lapses. We know the root causes for the drama: a lack of authenticity and transparency; failure to properly identify, anticipate and prevent strife; a perpetuation of a destructive us-versus-them mentality; and failing to properly fix problems once they've been identified.

Now comes the hard, but fun, work. Blowing up all preconceived notions about how to decrease or even eliminate drama from your workplace. Yes, it's necessary to identify mistakes and root causes of drama. But the most effective way to eliminate bad behavior is to study and focus on good behavior. What does that look like and how can we model our conduct, our policies, our practices after those positive examples? Whether your goal is to manage risk or to create a healthy environment, the old way of doing things simply doesn't work in today's workplace. It's time to blow up those tired solutions.

And definitely don't forget that "the good" also includes fun. A workplace culture that is boring, robotic, or dry is not one that has reached the top of the Healthy Workplace Culture Pyramid.

2 | Why Is Sexual Harassment Still a Thing and What We Must Do to Fix It

You've probably read at least one story this week involving allegations of workplace sexual harassment. From banking to entertainment, from media to tech and beyond, powerhouse men in almost every industry have been brought down because their workplace harassment was exposed. As we watch well-known figures fall, questions of "why" and "who knew what, when" swirl.

While the task of taking steps to prevent harassment isn't easy, too many companies have taken an approach that has made it infinitely harder than it needs to be.

In a nutshell, here is the drumbeat of "solutions" we've heard for decades: Review and distribute your policy prohibiting sexual harassment; republish your promise of zero-tolerance and a harassment-free workplace; slap together a compliance training session to "teach" managers about unlawful harassment; train managers to document everything, have a witness for everything they do, run every decision by HR; and . . . well, you get the idea.

These "solutions" have failed. Miserably.

It's time to explore new ways to solve the issue and reduce workplace drama.

Allegations of sexual harassment take many forms and include claims by men. However, the overwhelming majority of sexual harassment claims have two characteristics in common: they are brought by women, and the accusation is against a man in a position of greater power. For that reason, while recognizing that this is not always the case, I'll use pronouns that match up with what we know is the most common scenario when it comes to sexual harassment.

The Road to #MeToo

In 1991 the entire nation was gripped with the testimony of a law professor named Anita Hill. She previously worked with Clarence Thomas at the Equal Employment Opportunity Commission (EEOC), where Justice Thomas had worked as director and Professor Hill served as his assistant director.

Though other women made accusations of sexually charged conduct, only Professor Hill testified before the Senate subcommittee in charge of Justice Thomas's Supreme Court appointment. She testified about stories of Justice Thomas's alleged unwanted sexual advances, which, she said, included asking her out, talking with her about pornography, and having other sexually charged conversations at work.

Her testimony was considered then (and is considered now) to be a watershed moment in the fight against workplace sexual harassment. Many, especially women who had endured behavior similar to that reported by Professor Hill, hoped that awareness of this issue would result in organizations corporate, public, for-profit, nonprofit, in all industries—taking the issue seriously and in turn taking steps to prevent and address it.

Professor Hill's testimony had some impact. The most notable was the exponential increase in charges of sexual harassment filed with the EEOC. More companies developed policies prohibiting workplace harassment; harassment prevention training became a cottage industry (managers began to dread the reminder to attend the training session); and some women felt more comfortable with the idea of speaking up.

Unfortunately, it's now abundantly clear that these changes were cosmetic, not systemic. Over the next 25-plus years, companies relied on these cosmetic tools to stave off claims of sexual harassment. But by focusing on this window dressing, they missed the big picture—the importance of creating an actual culture of respect and inclusion, not just policies that said "no harassment." Many complaints were ignored, many men guilty of engaging in egregious conduct were allowed to get away with bad behavior (so long as they continued to be seen as valuable to the organization), and too many so-called unbiased workplace investigators conducted inquiries into allegations of misconduct to show that they "did something," even if everyone knew nothing would really change.

And then, on October 10, 2017, the floodgates were opened and the #MeToo movement began. In a lengthy, well-vetted, and impeccably researched article, Ronan Farrow described behavior by powerful Hollywood producer Harvey Weinstein that spanned several decades and included sexual harassment and sexual assault.[1] Over the next several months, more women came forward to describe the horrific behavior they suffered because of their contact with Weinstein, and also described decades of corporate complicity—colleagues and corporate leaders who knew about the behavior but did nothing to stop it. Also over the next months and into the one-year anniversary of the publication of this article, women felt empowered to speak about the harassment and abuse they'd suffered at the hands of powerful men in various industries.

During that time, corporate America responded differently than it did after the Anita Hill hearings. This time, many of the men faced consequences for the actions these women were able to corroborate and substantiate.

---

[1] R. Farrow, "From Aggressive Overtures to Sexual Assault: Harvey Weinstein's Accusers Tell Their Stories," *The New Yorker*, October 23, 2017. https://www.newyorker.com/news/news-desk/from-aggressive-overtures-to-sexual-assault-harvey-weinsteins-accusers-tell-their-stories.

Additionally, although Congress has yet to pass any legislation related to workplace sexual harassment, a number of states, most notably the country's two most populous states, California and New York, passed sweeping legislation sending a clear message to employers: Do all you can to prevent sexual harassment at work—or else!

There was, however, another side to the #MeToo movement. A small but growing number of men (and some women) began to express worry and confusion. Many began to worry about their contact with female colleagues or subordinates and we saw some of those men admitting that they were curbing their mentoring or other interactions with women. Although this phenomenon—men fearing the #MeToo movement has gone too far—is too detailed to discuss at length here, it is a reality that we saw in the contentious hearings in 2018 related to the confirmation of yet another Supreme Court justice, this time Brett Kavanaugh, who was accused of sexual assault by Dr. Christine Blasey Ford.

So the question is, where do we go from here? Can we take the energy created by all the attention on sexual harassment and harness it into ways to thoughtfully and methodically change our mindset and develop new and better solutions to prevent and fix this problem?

We can and we must.

Are We All on the Same Page? Key Legal Definitions and Clarifications

A crucial issue that has made solving the sexual harassment problem more difficult than it needs to be is confusion and misunderstanding about what "sexual harassment" means and what it doesn't mean. I'll look at it from both a legal perspective and a real-life perspective.

Legal Definition of Sexual Harassment

The Civil Rights Act of 1964 (the federal law that prohibits discrimination based on certain protected categories) did not identify sexual coercion as unlawful. Starting in the 1970s, courts began to recognize quid pro quo (Latin for "this for that") sexual harassment as a form of illegal gender discrimination.

Quid Pro Quo Sexual Harassment

While exploring every nuance of unlawful harassment is beyond the scope of this chapter or this book, the generally accepted definition for unlawful quid pro quo sexual harassment is: the loss or denial of a job benefit for refusal to cooperate sexually. That means that this type of harassment has a few distinct characteristics:

- It involves a supervisor/subordinate relationship (since the supervisor has the power to grant or deny some job benefit);
- It involves a boss asking for some sexual favor ("sleep with me or else"); and
- It involves the loss of some tangible employment benefit (the "or else" is "you'll lose your job," "I'll demote you," etc.).

In the 1980s, courts began to recognize a second type of unlawful sexual harassment. Legal arguments were made that women were sometimes exposed to offensive behavior by colleagues, that the behavior didn't necessarily involve a "this for that" request for sexual favors, and it didn't always result in a tangible job loss. Thus, the law was expanded to recognize a new form of unlawful sexual harassment: "hostile work environment" harassment.

Hostile Work Environment Sexual Harassment

Details might differ from state to state, but generally speaking, a claim for hostile work environment sexual harassment requires proof of various components, including:

- Unwelcome conduct of a sexual nature (though a plaintiff does not need to show romantic or sexual desire). The behavior could be physical, visual, or verbal.
- The conduct must be objectively and subjectively unwelcome (this means that the woman, at the time the behavior occurred, found the behavior offensive or unwelcome, and the behavior must pass the "reasonable woman" test, meaning that any women in the plaintiff's shoes would have found the behavior offensive).

- The behavior must be sufficiently severe (usually referring to serious physical conduct) or "pervasive" (occurs with sufficient frequency) that it unreasonably interferes with the plaintiff's ability to do her job.

Finally, it's important to define legal defenses since they are an important contributing factor to getting us to where we are today.

Defenses to Claims of Unlawful Sexual Harassment

Attorneys who represent "management"—that is, organizations or individuals who have been sued for violating sexual harassment laws—have various legal defenses at their disposal to either convince a judge to dismiss a case before it even reaches a jury, or to convince a jury that there is no legal liability.

These defenses essentially track the legal elements and include (among numerous others):

- "My client made some tasteless jokes but did not mean to make the plaintiff uncomfortable and he didn't mean them in a sexual way." This is meant to disprove the first requirement of a hostile environment claim, namely that the behavior was of a sexual nature. This is where the concept of "reasonable women" comes in – would a reasonable woman find the behavior offensive? If so, then while the man's intent isn't completely irrelevant (it will be evaluated in an analysis of whether the comments were reasonably interpreted as unwelcome), it is not the determining legal factor.
- "My client engaged in the behavior, but the plaintiff welcomed the conduct." Essentially, this argument attempts to refute the "subjectively unwelcome" requirement – yes, it's true my client made comments that most women would find offensive, but *this woman* found the behavior acceptable. She laughed right along, she didn't complain about it, she participated in it, and so on. While this legal defense works in some cases, the argument tends to fall apart if evidence exists showing that the plaintiff might have participated in the misconduct unwillingly—usually because the overall environment was such that "going along" was the only realistic choice she had.

- "Ladies and gentlemen of the jury, I have evidence showing that the plaintiff is of bad character," or "the plaintiff is simply making these claims because she is trying to get even or to distract you from her poor performance." Again, if evidence exists to support this defense, it could work. But in today's climate, shaming a plaintiff could backfire.

- "Your honor, this case shouldn't even get to a jury because there is insufficient proof that the behavior alleged was severe, and it only happened a few times." This is an attempt to undercut the "severe or pervasive" requirement and though it sometimes works with juries, it rarely works with judges who are asked to dismiss the case before it gets to a jury. And the issue here is that the definition of "pervasive" is fuzzy — there is no singular definition of how many times someone has to engage in misconduct in order to reach the "pervasive" level. Each jury will make that determination based on the totality of the evidence.

- "Yes, we admit to the behavior, but the plaintiff failed to let us fix the situation; she never complained and never gave us a chance to investigate and implement a solution." Again, there are certainly cases where this argument works since courts have said (generally) that it would be unfair to hold a company legally liable if it took reasonable steps to prevent the behavior from happening, and the organization has a history of taking complaints seriously. But there's the rub . . . this defense only works if the company can show that there is sufficient trust in the system so that the plaintiff's failure to use the company's complaint resolution procedure was unreasonable. The company must show more than the mere existence of policies, training, and complaint-resolution mechanisms. It must show it followed policies, provided a safe place for employees to raise concerns, and consistently investigated and resolved claims in an effective and even-handed way.

- "While it's true that the behavior occurred, the plaintiff has not presented evidence that it so strongly interfered with her ability to do her job that legal liability should be found." Basically, yes this plaintiff was subjected to bad treatment, but she was able to overcome it and hasn't shown us that it affected her so strongly that we should have to be legally liable. This is another interesting but dangerous defense.

This is an abbreviated discussion of a complex legal issue. However, if you've dealt with workplace harassment issues, you probably recognize some of these examples and now have a better understanding of why attorneys approach the issue from a purely legal angle. Too many attorneys, and now too many HR professionals and managers, focus exclusively on ways to avoid lawsuits, or begin developing defenses to a lawsuit, rather than focusing on creating a healthy culture. The irony, of course, is that this approach has done nothing to stem the tide of legal claims. (See more on the litigation-avoidance paradox in Chapter 5.)

In short, this summary paints a picture of what's going on in so many organizations. If the issue of harassment is viewed exclusively through a legal liability/risk reduction perspective, you can see that the incentive is to be in constant CYA mode.

Real-Life Definition

If you ask 100 average employees to define "sexual harassment" you'll get 100 different answers. My guess is that you won't get one that includes the legal definitions outlined earlier.

It's extremely unlikely that an employee (or frankly, even a seasoned manager) understands the nuances related to whether the behavior was "objectively and subjectively unwelcome," and whether it was "severe or pervasive." Instead, when we ask people to define sexual harassment, we tend to get answers that describe offensive actions and corresponding feelings: "It's when someone at work says or does something that is sexual and it makes you uncomfortable," "It's when someone at work hits on you, you say no, and now things are awkward," or similar statements.

Despite varying definitions, what is clear is that the public views "sexual harassment" as prevalent and problematic. In fact, research indicates that "anywhere from 25% to 85% of women report having experienced sexual harassment in the workplace."[2] A recent study by the Pew Research Center found that 6 in 10 women say they have been sexually harassed.[3]

---

[2] Chai Feldblum and Victoria Lipnic, "Select Task Force on Sexual Harassment in the Workplace," U.S. Equal Employment Opportunity Commission, 2016. https://www.eeoc.gov/eeoc/task_force/harassment/report.cfm

[3] "About six-in-ten women say they have been sexually harassed," Pew Research Center, 2018. http://www.pewsocialtrends.org/2018/04/04/sexual-harassment-at-work-in-the-era-of-metoo/sdt_04-04-18_harassment-00-05/

As will be discussed below, the differences in the legal and layperson's definitions of sexual harassment are vital to understanding and solving the issue. Too many companies have approached the issue through a legal lens, ignoring that it doesn't match what most people believe is problematic workplace behavior. And even worse, too many companies take the view that the problem doesn't require a response until it's reached the critical point of illegality. This misses the point—early intervention and early resolution not only shield a company from legal liability, but they also get to the real goal of creating a healthy culture.

Why the Behavioral Continuum Matters

Our failure to distinguish between the legal and layperson's definition of sexual harassment has also created a lack of distinction between bad behavior, worse behavior, and illegal behavior. All misconduct needs to be addressed, but the manner in which it is addressed will depend on a number of factors, including where the behavior falls on this continuum. Too many people have mistakenly lumped milder behavior into the same bucket as egregious conduct, making it harder to solve the problem.

This failure to recognize the varying severity of workplace conduct and the harm that it causes is displayed in the ubiquitous zero-tolerance policies embraced by so many companies. Without explaining nuances such as what behavior is not tolerated and what the consequences are for varying types of misconduct, these policies end up doing more harm than good. The implication is that the same price will be paid for one sexually tinged joked as for sexually charged physical conduct like sexual assault. In practice, this creates fear and confusion for men and women. Men think, "Will I be fired for making a joke or giving a compliment?" Women think, "I better not report the behavior since doing so might get that person fired [which is usually the implication in a zero-tolerance workplace]."

On the other end of the spectrum, failing to differentiate between bad, worse, and illegal behavior results in a decreased likelihood of addressing and resolving problems early. Sexual harassment often starts with milder behavior and escalates if no one stops it. Common precursors to workplace sexual harassment include sexist or misogynistic statements, a devaluation of women, behavior that shows gender bias, sharing offensive or sexually charged images or jokes, or milder physical contact (hugs, shoulder rubs). If companies aren't precise about the behavioral continuum and send a message that giving a compliment is the same as demanding sex, employees (targets and witnesses) are less likely to intervene at the mild end of the behavior spectrum. That leaves the door wide open for mild behavior to quickly escalate and eventually become unlawful sexual harassment.

The Law Is Your Friend

The irony about companies viewing legal principles as the enemy is that, when viewed correctly, the law provides a valuable framework that essentially amounts to a built-in methodology to simultaneously avoid legal liability and, more important, to create a healthy workplace culture.

With a few exceptions based on state law, organizations are generally shielded from legal liability if they can show they have taken reasonable steps to create an environment where employees feel safe reporting concerns, where those concerns are taken seriously and therefore investigated fully and fairly, and proactive and effective measures to stop any identified misconduct are taken. (For more on investigations, see Chapter 11.)

That means that taking a big-picture approach insulates companies from lawsuits not only because happy employees tend not to sue their employers, but also because companies are not legally liable if they have an environment in which employees are given tools to resolve issues before they escalate, are provided with a number of avenues to raise concerns if they need help solving issues, trust the system to investigate allegations of misconduct, and know their company deals with proven cases of misconduct in an even-handed way.

Viewed this way, the law actually provides employers with a road map for preventing lawsuits. In fact, the law provides an almost foolproof early intervention system that should encourage employers to welcome complaints of misconduct. Here's how:

- Teach employees and witnesses how to safely and effectively intervene early (this requires learning a new language that is precise and also involves emotional intelligence—knowing when and how to speak up). (For more on techniques to communicate precisely and persuasively, see Chapter 8.)

- Teach employees to be empathetic and get a better understanding of how their words or actions might be perceived as hurtful or demeaning. Give them an incentive to listen and do better.
- Establish a culture of trust and truth-telling where every employee knows HR and the rest of management is available and will provide an avenue to be truly heard (this is more than just saying you have "an open-door policy").
- Develop systems that are actually fair and also inspire trust and a perception of fairness. Follow the systems you've developed.
- Fix problems. Really. No matter who is involved. This means putting ethics and integrity above all else.

Consider Making an Early Intervention System a Formal Program

For companies that are ready to do away with compliance blinders and instead focus on culture, consider making an early-intervention system a formal part of your workplace.

As outlined above, the law essentially provides built-in guardrails. Take advantage of those safeguards. Establish authentic methods to prevent misconduct and establish ways to make sure misconduct doesn't rise to the level of illegality. Ever. If you know about misconduct, don't turn a blind eye to it. Address issues early by teaching employees to resolve conflict on their own when possible, but make it clear that management is there to help when that's not possible. If you do find out about misconduct, through observation or a report, address it. Investigate it and fix it if you find a problem. And fix it every time and in an even-handed way. Re-read this paragraph. This is what the law says you must do. And if you take these steps, you've complied with the law. Even better, if you do these things, you're guaranteed to make your culture healthier, and you'll drastically reduce workplace drama.

If you're ready to establish a formal early-intervention system, simply take those requirements and flip them around:

- Rewrite policies to focus on the prevention of behavior that demeans or excludes so that it never reaches the level of unlawful harassment.

- Provide training that includes legal definitions and examples, but also identifies behavior that might not be unlawful, but still needs to be addressed and fixed. Provide education on how employees can resolve this low-level, early conflict on their own. Establish a way to help if your employees are uncomfortable or unable to resolve the issues alone.
- Encourage and welcome reports. Take each report seriously.
- Develop a two-track system for reports. If you determine the report is one that requires a formal investigation, refer that to your investigation unit (see Chapter 11 for ways to conduct effective investigations).
- If, however, the concern doesn't warrant an investigation, send that concern to your second track. This could be a system of restorative justice, perhaps led by an ombudsperson or a workplace mediator.
- If the concern is on the formal investigation track, make sure you implement effective remedial measures that address the misconduct; measures that seek to stop the behavior. Also use forward-looking accountability principles (see a discussion on this in Chapter 7). This means that, in addition to disciplining the person who engaged in misconduct, use each investigation as a learning lesson to make it less likely that the misconduct recurs.
- If the concern is on the second, less formal track, develop a way to fix the problems found, and again use both backward-looking and forward-looking accountability principles.

It's time to stop viewing sexual harassment law as an enemy or something companies must endure. Instead, take advantage of the roadmap the law provides so that you not only eliminate the risk of liability, but you also eliminate drama along the way.

Leading Predictors of Workplace Sexual Harassment

There are numerous root causes of workplace harassment, but research and experience tell us there are three in particular that correlate strongly to the presence of sexual harassment at work.

A Culture of Complicity

A comprehensive study of workplace sexual harassment confirms what practitioners have known for decades: The strongest predictor of organizational sexual harassment is a corporate culture that tolerates the behavior. In other words, a company that accepts, enables, or encourages misconduct will have a sexual harassment problem.[4]

A landmark 2018 report summarizes leading research on the topic and finds that harassment is less likely to occur in organizations that take it seriously. Specifically, a healthy culture:

- Acts as a deterrent against misconduct and
- Encourages employees to speak up about the misconduct.

These are critical points and worth reiterating.

In an organization that is serious about creating a culture of trust and respect, bad actors are less likely to misbehave.

In an organization that is serious about creating a culture of trust and respect, employees feel safe speaking up about misconduct, whether it's targeted toward them or others.

If we're serious about stopping harassment in its tracks, it's time to change the corporate mindset from compliance and complicity to courage and compassion.

Male-Dominated (or Male-Only) Leadership

The second most potent predictor of sexual harassment identified by the 2018 study is whether men outnumber women at an organization, especially if that gender disparity occurs at the top of the organizational chart.[5]

---

[4]E. Peck, "Want to End Sexual Harassment? Landmark Study Finds Ousting 'Bad Men' Isn't Enough," *Huffpost*, June 16, 2018. https://www.huffingtonpost.com/entry/sexual-harassment-ousting-bad-men_us_5b23f8c3e4b0f9178a9cd6f5.

[5] Ibid.

Having too few women, especially in leadership, means the issue of harassment is viewed through a one-sided lens. Men and women view issues related to harassment differently. Not better. Not worse. Just differently.

> I have a vivid recollection of an SAT question that discombobulated me when I took the test in high school. It was back when the SAT had word analogies as part of its vocabulary section. The question was: "running is to marathon as rowing is to ____." All four choices might as well have been written in Greek (the right answer, I found out later after looking it up, was "regatta").
>
> I'm in immigrant from El Salvador who grew up mostly in the inner city, so it goes without saying that there were no regattas in my 'hood.
>
> This example perfectly captures the problem with assuming that we all understand the same things. While I'd like to think that the majority of male corporate leaders have good intentions and do their best to discourage sexual harassment, it would, simply put, be immensely helpful to have women (plural) in the room to give the context and nuance that male leaders typically do not have the life experience to understand, just like I didn't have the life experience to know about regattas.

In a first-of-its-kind study, Emtrain partnered with In the House to survey in-house counsel on issues related to workplace sexual harassment. One key finding was that there is a gender divide when it comes to identifying harassing or offensive behavior, and an equally wide gulf between perceptions of whether women suffer negative repercussions as a result of objecting to unwelcome conduct.

"Simply put: men and women do not see eye-to-eye when it comes to the presence of sexual harassment." The data showed that "[W]hile *zero* percent of men [surveyed] perceived sexual harassment as being 'very prevalent' at their company, 3% of women did. At the other end of the spectrum, while 23% of men [surveyed] said sexual harassment was nonexistent in their organization, less than half as many—only 10%—of women believed this was the case."[6]

---

[6]*Emtrain and In the House Survey: Sexual Harassment Prevention in the Age of The #MeToo Movement*. San Francisco, CA: Emtrain, 2018.

The gender divide was most prominently displayed in a side-by-side comparison using both internal and external research data:

Whereas *6 in 10 male* respondents in the Emtrain/In the House survey said sexual harassment rarely or never occurs in their workplace, a 2018 study by the Pew Research Center found that *6 in 10 women* say they have been exposed to sexual harassment in the workplace (see Figure 2.1).[7]

These statistics came to life in the survey comments. The striking contrast between the perception of the prevalence of behavior that might be called out as "harassing" was highlighted in two divergent comments:

1. Male respondent: "The male owner of the company would sometimes have consensual sexual relationship with female employees who worked for the company. The women did not object to these affairs, and there were no overt threats if the women refused sexual advances."
2. Female respondent: "Women are scared to reject men because they think it can impact their job."

Beyond the issue of whether harassment is prevalent, survey participants were asked about the effectiveness of their companies' reporting, investigation, and resolution systems. Taking just one data point on this topic, many more women (27%) as compared to men (12%) reported that employees *did not* feel comfortable reporting misconduct.

[1]Source: Pew Research Center Study

Figure 2.1   The Difference between Men's Perception and Women's Perception of Sexual Harassment in the Workplace Is Striking[8]

---

[7]"About six-in-ten women say they have been sexually harassed." Pew Research Center, 2018. http://www.pewsocialtrends.org/2018/04/04/sexual-harassment-at-work-in-the-era-of -metoo/sdt_04-04-18_harassment-00-05/.

[8]Reprinted with the permission of Emtrain.

One woman shared her experience. Her comment illustrates one important reason for the underreporting: "When I reported behavior [involving]
4.5 years' worth of incidents, the investigation took less than 24 hours, I was
put on a PIP [performance improvement plan], then laid off the next week
with *no severence*. And, this [was in] big oil."[9]

In fact, a significant percentage of in-house attorneys responding to
the survey pointed to working in male-dominated industries or companies.

The research on the topic of the gender divide points to the same
conclusion—women must be equally represented at the table of influence
that determines the best ways to prevent and address workplace sexual harassment. Organizations that are making decisions on the topic based only
on their male leaders' view of sexual harassment are missing a critical voice
in that decision-making.

Frank Dobbins, a Harvard professor known for his groundbreaking
research on issues of harassment and diversity, put it this way:

> Male-dominated management teams have been found to tolerate, sanc-
> tion, or even expect sexualized treatment of workers, which can lead to a
> culture of complicity. People may chuckle over misbehavior rather than
> calling it out, for example, or they may ostracize harassed women, privately
> ashamed of not having spoken up. Reducing power differentials can help,
> not only because women are less likely than men to harass but also because
> their presence in management can change workplace culture.[10]

Compliance Blinders

The combination of a culture of complicity and a male-dominated leadership creates an environment that could give rise to workplace sexual harassment. An additional ingredient that creates an even stronger likelihood of
sexual misconduct at work is leadership that views issues through a narrow
compliance lens.

[9]*Emtrain and In the House Survey: Sexual Harassment Prevention in the Age of the #MeToo Movement*. San Francisco, CA: Emtrain, 2018.

[10]Frank Dobbin and Alexandra Kalev, "Training Programs and Reporting Systems Won't End
Sexual Harassment. Promoting More Women Will." *Harvard Business Review*, November 15,
2017. https://hbr.org/2017/11/training-programs-and-reporting-systems-wont-end-sexual
-harassment-promoting-more-women-will.

Anyone who has attended a compliance workshop has heard phrases such as "document everything" (which becomes code for "we want to have documented evidence for the inevitable lawsuit"), "always have a witness and get things signed" (which becomes code for "we don't trust our employees . . . they will almost certainly call you a liar at some point"), and my favorite "if it isn't in writing, it didn't happen" (which becomes code for "judges and juries lose all common sense when making decisions and will see you as a liar if you don't write everything down").

Just how preposterous is the most-often given legal advice of "document everything" and "if you didn't document it, it didn't happen"? Let's put it in a different context.

Imagine Maria Portokolas telling Toula the night before Toula's big fat Greek wedding, "You know, Toula, the key to a happy marriage is to assume your husband will cheat and lie. My advice? Save all email exchanges and document your conversations with Ian so that when your attorney litigates your divorce, you can take Ian to the cleaners because of all the great evidence you've saved."

Crazy, right?

So why do we listen to the same silly advice when it comes from an employment attorney? Regardless of the underlying nature of a relationship, when one or both parties enters it with a sense of inevitable gloom and doom, the self-fulfilling prophecy cycle kicks in and you can expect to hit the skids faster than Gus Portokalos can whip out a bottle of Windex.

Rather than sending a message of: "We trust our employees and strive to treat them respectfully, share information with them transparently, and provide a safe and inclusive environment," companies with this outlook send the opposite message: "We are paranoid about getting sued by our employees and therefore will give lip service to wanting to create a healthy culture, but what we really mean is that we will take defensive measures to keep you in your place."

That's hardly the message that a company striving for a healthy and inclusive culture—and a reduction of workplace drama—wants to send.

Other Factors That Contribute to Sexual Harassment

The causes of sexual harassment are complex, and while identifying the three big-picture predictors of workplace sexual harassment is vital, it is important to understand the parts that individuals play.

The Harassers: Why They Harass and Who Is More Likely to Harass

There are a number of issues that research and experience show influence a harasser's decision to misbehave. They include:

- A perception of high worth, with minimal accountability;
- Toxic personality characteristics; and
- Power imbalances that are exploited.

Perception of High Worth, Minimal Accountability

Abraham Lincoln said, "Nearly all men can stand adversity, but if you want to test a man's character, give him power."

A reality that impacts the frequency and severity of sexually harassing behavior at work is whether the harasser sees himself as so powerful that he is above the rules, essentially untouchable.

Many of the men accused of sexually inappropriate conduct, especially the ones featured in high-profile news stories, have (or had) immense power. For these industry powerhouses, the temptation to (ab)use that power is apparently so strong that they find themselves flexing their corporate muscle far beyond the board room. And in many instances, the men featured in headlines are not only sexual predators, they're also notorious for overly aggressive behavior, exhibiting a strong taste for intimidation tactics to satisfy their hypercompetitive egos.

For example, when asked how he could assault women so easily, Harvey Weinstein said, "I'm used to that."[11]

---

[11] Tufayel Ahmed, "Full Transcript: Harvey Weinstein Accuser Turns Down His Advances 12 Times in Two Minutes in Chilling NYPD Audio," *Newsweek,* October 10, 2017. https://www.newsweek.com/full-transcript-harvey-weinstein-accuser-tried-turn-down-his-advances-12-times-681711.

Toxic Personality Characteristics

But why is it that only a percentage of influential men abuse their power to the point of engaging in sexual harassment? Is it possible to identify behavioral red flags? And if so, can they be spotted early so that problematic conduct can be dealt with swiftly and effectively?

In fact, research by Zeigler-Hill et al. (2016), uncovers a "dark triad" of personality traits linked to sexual harassment. The three identified psychological characteristics of a "typical" sexual harasser are narcissism, psychopathy, and Machiavellianism.

The study defines narcissism as "malevolent behaviors associated with grandiose identity," psychopathy as "malevolent behaviors associated with impulsivity," and Machiavellianism as "malevolent behaviors associated with long-term strategies." The results suggest that this "dark triad" of traits is associated with a propensity to engage in sexual harassment.[12]

If referring to the "dark triad" is too abstract, try taking a page from Bob Sutton who wrote the book, *The No Assholes Rule: Building a Civilized Workplace and Surviving One That Isn't.*[13] Though Sutton is a Stanford University professor and organizational psychologist, he presents his theories in a no-nonsense way that makes it no wonder that his book is a best seller. He makes an important distinction between "temporary assholes" and "certified assholes" and uses the following questions to put people into the right category:

1. After talking to the alleged asshole, does the target feel oppressed, humiliated, or belittled?
2. Does the alleged asshole aim his or her venom at people who are less powerful than they are?

If the answer to both these questions is "yes," Sutton says, then you are officially a "certified asshole." In fact, Sutton created a test he calls the

---

[12] Virgil Zeigler-Hill, Avi Besser, Judith Morag, and W. Keith Campbell, "The Dark Triad and Sexual Harassment Proclivity," *Personality and Individual Differences* 89 (2016): 47–54. https://www.researchgate.net/publication/282701745_The_Dark_Triad_and_sexual_harassment_proclivity.

[13] Robert Sutton, *The No Assholes Rule: Building a Civilized Workplace and Surviving One That Isn't.* Reprint, Ed. Business Plus, 2010.

Asshole Rating Self-Exam (ARSE), which uses 24 nonscientific questions to help people determine where they fall on the spectrum.[14] A testament to the amount of work we have to do in this area, as of 2017, more than 400,000 people had taken the test.

Does this mean that high-powered men who exhibit even some of these traits will engage in harassment? No, but they are red flags. And if most companies are honest, they are usually able to distinguish between a strong and decisive leader, and an abusive one.

Power Imbalance

These realities become more potent when the workplace includes a power imbalance. To the extent a powerful man abuses or harasses a woman, he most often exerts that power toward women in a less powerful position, often reminding the woman that he has the power to make or break her.

The bottom line is that most harassers harass because they can. This begs the question: How can we flip the script so that it is clear that they can't?

A commitment to a "harassment-free" workplace or even a commitment to a diverse and inclusive one isn't enough—company leaders must develop a systematic approach to ensure accountability.

While looking at issues related to the bad actors is important, it's equally important to explore issues related to the victims of harassment and witnesses of the misconduct to get a complete view.

Issues Related to Targets: How Prevalent Is Harassment and How Frequently Is It Reported?

Despite laws prohibiting harassment, decades of companies focusing on creating "zero-tolerance" policies, and lawsuits exposing distressing examples of workplace misconduct, we have failed to do away with workplace harassment. A fact brought to light by the #MeToo movement is that sexual harassment is widespread. Many, including those of us who have been in

---

[14] Robert Sutton, "Are You a Certified Asshole?" Electricpulp.com. https://www.electricpulp.com/guykawasaki/arse/

the business of workplace drama for decades, know that the examples high-lighted by #MeToo are only the tip of the iceberg.

The 2016 EEOC report explored the issue of the prevalence of work-place harassment, the differing definitions of harassment, and the phenomena of severe underreporting of the misconduct. As noted earlier, various metrics put the percentage of women exposed to harassment or sexually charged or gender-biased behavior at work at anywhere between 25% and 85%.[15] The Pew study previously cited puts that percentage at 60%.[16]

Unfortunately, the vast majority of misconduct is not reported. In fact, the evidence is overwhelming: Most misconduct involving sexually charged or gender-biased behavior is never reported internally (through employer-sanctioned complaint systems) or externally (through govern-mental enforcement agencies or in the court system). The EEOC report cites data indicating that "roughly *three out of four* individuals who experi-ence harassment never even talked to a supervisor, manager, or union rep-resentative about the harassing conduct."[17]

The report also cites research exploring the reasons for the failure to report. In short, the researchers conclude, "employees . . . fail to report the harassing behavior or to file a complaint because they fear disbelief of their claim, inaction on their claim, blame, or social or professional retaliation."[18]

Issues Related to Bystanders: Does It Affect Them and Do They Intervene?

Bystanders are individuals who either observe misconduct firsthand or hear about the misconduct from someone else. This includes both "passive" bystanders (those who take no action) and "active" bystanders (those who take action to prevent or reduce the harm—often referred to as upstanders).

---

[15]Chai Feldblum and Victoria Lipnic, "Select Task Force on Sexual Harassment in the Work-place," U.S. Equal Employment Opportunity Commission, 2016. https://www.eeoc.gov/eeoc/task_force/harassment/report.cfm.

[16]"About six-in-ten women say they have been sexually harassed," Pew Research Center, 2018. http://www.pewsocialtrends.org/2018/04/04/sexual-harassment-at-work-in-the-era-of-metoo/sdt_04-04-18_harassment-00-05/.

[17]Feldblum and Lipnic, "Select Task Force."

[18]Ibid.

An approach most cutting-edge workplaces are taking is to focus on helping witnesses go from passive bystanders to active upstanders.

Upstanders can, individually or collectively, have a tremendous impact on workplace sexual harassment—preventing it, stopping it early so that it doesn't escalate, and helping to fix it if it does occur. Upstanders have opportunities to help by reporting the problem on behalf of the target, supporting the target in making a complaint, offering support or advice to the target, or directly confronting the bad actor (as the conduct occurs or afterwards).

It's helpful to outline the general ways in which bystanders can and must play a role to achieve our goal to prevent and address harassment. One important issue is exploring what motivates a bystander to act. There have been numerous studies looking into "bystander apathy." The studies that specifically look into the issue at work have identified several factors that influence a bystander's decision whether to act, including:[19]

- *Identification with the target:* Observers who perceive themselves to be similar to the target of the injustice and, therefore, identify with them are more likely to act. This means that focusing on an inclusive workplace—one where people feel connected no matter their gender, race, ethnicity, political views, upbringing, or work style—is key. Employees who are working together toward a common mission and who therefore feel connected to each other are more likely to speak up on behalf on someone they see is being exposed to misconduct.

- *Perception of injustice:* In addition to the issue of connection, witnesses who identify with the target are also more likely to perceive the behavior itself as an injustice and are therefore more likely to act. Studies also show that witnesses will look to the reaction of the target—is that person showing signs of discomfort? If so, the bystander is more likely to act. This means that in addition to providing a means of connection, the organization must make clear to those targeted that it's okay to express discomfort . . . that simply going along is not the expected behavior.

---

[19]Paula McDonald, "Bystander Approaches to Sexual Harassment in the Workplace," Australian Human Rights Commission, 2012. https://www.humanrights.gov.au/sites/default/files/content/sexualharassment/bystander/bystander_june2012.pdf.

- *Organizational climate:* When an injustice is perceived, an observer's decision to respond is largely influenced by the organizational environment. This means that bystanders are exponentially more likely to become upstanders if they work in an organization that says what it does and does what it says. If a company is open to receiving and fairly resolving complaints and if bad actors are subject to consequences, a bystander will feel safe to intervene.

In short, an observer's decision about whether to intervene (individually or collectively) depends on the perceived costs and benefits of speaking up.

Companies would be wise to educate everyone on ways in which they can become responsible upstanders to stop bad behavior before it escalates.

How Corporate Complicity Factors into This Reality

Every one of the issues related to individuals, while important, only serves to highlight the importance of the overall corporate climate. Even if an employee (or leader) with a propensity to harass joins a company, the chances of harassment actually occurring are minimal if that company has an authentic culture of respect and inclusion. In a healthy culture, these employees will either temper their behavior once they get the message that it's unacceptable, or they'll be stopped in their tracks by brave employees who know their company has their back (or the bad actor will opt to leave the company if he isn't allowed to do what he wants).

Sexual Harassment: The Cure

A few themes emerge from a careful review of the various causes of workplace sexual harassment. Each one provides insight and ultimately gives us a road map to create actionable solutions to prevent and address workplace sexual harassment:

- Promote a culture of precise communication.
- Develop a culture of courage.
- Cultivate a culture of truth-telling.
- Foster a culture of equity and inclusion.
- Create a culture of continuous learning.

Promote a Culture of Precise Communication

Communicate your values clearly and persuasively. Begin with an authentic message that your company stands for respect, civility, and belonging. Define, live, and color that message in. Tell your employees and your leaders what you expect in terms of behavior, integrity, and ethics. Be very specific—without specifics, people will interpret "harassment," "inappropriate," "unprofessional," and "civil" in varying ways.

Communication is a two-way street; do your part as a corporate leader to communicate precisely and persuasively, especially on complex and sensitive issues like workplace harassment.

Here are some tips on using communication skills to effectively identify, prevent, and stop harassment:

- Replace "we promise a harassment-free workplace" with: "We are committed to being a world-class company that values respect and inclusion. It goes without saying that we do not tolerate unlawful harassment, but that's the floor, not the ceiling. We strive to do much better than the minimum that the law requires from us."
- Replace "we have zero tolerance for harassment" with "rest assured that we will not only investigate claims of misconduct, but that we will take swift and even-handed action that is commensurate with the level of misconduct our investigation uncovers." (For more on investigations and remedial measures, see Chapter 11.)
- Don't just write a policy that prohibits unlawful harassment, write one that says: "Here is the definition of unlawful harassment. While it's important that all our employees understand what unlawful behavior looks like, what's more important to us is that you understand that we're committed to far more than just following the law. We want to create an environment where employees feel safe to speak up when they hear or see something that goes against our core values of respect, civility, and inclusion. We'll provide you with tools to intervene yourself if you're comfortable doing so. But if you're not, then we are committed to providing you with channels through which you can raise your concerns, knowing that they will be taken seriously and that we'll view them as an opportunity to make the workplace better for everyone." (For more on how to write clear-cut and strong policies, see Chapter 9.)

- When you provide harassment prevention training, don't focus about what employees and managers *can't* do; instead talk about what they can and should do. Provide realistic (preferably real life) examples of nuanced behavior so that everyone is not only on the same page about what is acceptable and unacceptable, but also so they can practice the skill of using their best judgment when they encounter a difficult situation where the answer isn't clear cut. (For more on how to provide great training, see Chapter 10.)

Develop a Culture of Courage

Advertise something unique: your company's early-intervention system. Make everyone comfortable with early intervention. This means employees and bystanders. It also means HR, the legal department, and members of the C-suite. A courageous culture equals a proactive culture. A proactive culture is always one step ahead of misconduct.

Despite myths and legends that have convinced many workplace leaders to see the law as the enemy, be audacious enough to view legal principles about sexual harassment as your best friend and your best defense against a lawsuit.

How do you do this? You follow the early-intervention system that the law has laid out for us, but that no one has bothered to engage.

- Empower everyone to speak up. Teach them how to do so respectfully but firmly. This doesn't mean you make your employees into members of the civility police. If they have a deep and clear understanding of your company's core values, they'll be able to distinguish between good-natured comments and those that have the potential to create workplace drama.
- Make sure departments like HR, risk management, finance, and legal are on board with these concepts. Use your best powers of persuasion to help them see that an early-intervention system is not only the best way to avoid getting sued, but it will also improve loyalty, retention, and, yes, profitability.
- Rework policies, practices, and training on issues related to reporting, investigating, and resolving concerns about harassment. Reject

the idea that not hearing any complaints about harassment means there must not be a problem. It might mean that. Or it might mean that there is a problem, you just don't know about it. This is probably because employees are too scared to speak up, or they have no trust in the system.

Cultivate a Culture of Truth-Telling

Encourage reports. Really. View reports as your best opportunity to deal with workplace drama early. Before it becomes too big to solve.

Be a champion for a culture of truth-telling: Reinvent corporate attitudes toward reporting workplace concerns. Employees are talking—and what they're sharing often isn't pretty. If they're not sharing stories at work, they're posting on employer review sites, sharing on social media, or writing blogs: Employees will get the word out. Today's reality means that ignoring the problem of sexual harassment in your workplace doesn't make it go away, it only robs you of the opportunity to control the narrative.

It pays to be proactive—and to encourage employees to do the same. If you become aware of issues related to overly aggressive, wholly unprofessional, or harassing conduct, deal with it. Quickly. Fairly. Employers who take this type of proactive stance are almost always able to address issues before they become impossible to fix. Think of the time, energy, and money you'll save by nipping issues in the bud. And imagine the brand reputation you'll create as a result.

Foster a Culture of Equity and Inclusion

Don't just pay these concepts lip service. Do more than develop an employee resource group or expand your recruitment efforts to attract diverse candidates. Hold people accountable—for doing good and for behaving badly. And make sure your practice of accountability is fair, consistent, and even-handed.

If you're worried about pay equity, then be proactive and courageous—take a page out of the Salesforce playbook. When two brave members of Salesforce's executive team (both women) took their concerns about possible pay equity to the company's CEO, they hardly expected that he would not only agree to conduct an audit, but that he'd be willing to fix any gaps they found, that he'd be willing to share what the company did with others, and that he'd make that a constant project since he knew that taking your eye off the equity ball would get you right back to where you started.[20] Now that's courage personified and it's a genuine commitment to inclusion and equity.

And when it comes to making decisions about how to discipline those who engage in misconduct, be equally meticulous about sticking to your promise to be fair and equitable. Skip the short-sighted cost-benefit analysis: "It was a business decision" is a justification many companies who cover up for serial sexual harassers offer for their actions.

Every time a company makes a decision based on the "value" the harasser brings, they neglect to do simple math—by failing to subtract the cost of keeping him around. And that cost adds up to much more than just settlement amounts and legal fees. It's also high employee turnover, low productivity, dipping morale, and an incredibly negative effect on brand reputation—not to mention adding a hefty "crisis management" line item to your P&L.

In short, there is no good business reason for tolerating this behavior. And beyond the "traditional" business analysis of looking at profit and loss, a company that tolerates, enables, or encourages this behavior will send a strong message about its culture—and the message is one that fewer employees find tolerable. This then becomes an issue of brand management, talent acquisition, and retention.

You can't go wrong if you keep equity and inclusion at the center of your decisions.

Create a Culture of Continuous Learning

Develop a comprehensive plan to make sure everyone at your company knows that issues related to the health of your corporate culture is a journey, not just a one-time event to celebrate the launch of your new mission statement.

---

[20]Megan Dickey, "Salesforce Spent Another $2.7 Million to Adjust Pay Gaps Related to Race and Gender," Techcrunch.com, April 17, 2018. https://techcrunch.com/2018/04/17/salesforce-spent-another-2-7-million-to-adjust-pay-gaps-related-to-race-and-gender/.

Don't get me wrong, I want you to celebrate when you finish the hard work of updating your mission statement or your workplace policies. Just don't stop there.

Make sure you develop timelines for reviewing your work. If you implement new ways to deal with sexual harassment, understand that you will need to test and tweak those new systems. Make sure your employees understand that you're committed to this endeavor. That you don't see this as a one-and-done task, but rather as a long-standing and authentic commitment to creating a healthy workplace culture.

. . .

Implementing these five action steps is a great place to start on the road to identifying, preventing and addressing sexual harassment. By doing so, you'll reduce or maybe even eliminate workplace drama. And although I've said this a few times, it's worth repeating, especially when discussion is related to sexual harassment. Nothing in this chapter or in this book is meant to restrict employee fun. Respectful does not equate to boring. Professional need not be the same as robotic. Inclusive doesn't mean monotonous. Your workplace can (and should) be simultaneously committed to respect, civility, and inclusion *and* to playfulness, friendship, and lightheartedness.

3

Diversity, Inclusion, and Belonging . . . Not Just PC BS

The link between diverse organizations and financial performance has been studied extensively and the conclusion is clear: Diversity provides a competitive edge. This is especially true if the organization has a diverse leadership team.[1]

Given this reality, it's no wonder that companies in the United States spend hundreds of millions of dollars on diversity initiatives. And that spend increases every year. That begs the question: Are these initiatives working? Are companies getting a return on their multimillion-dollar investment?

Unfortunately, the answers are currently not so good. Despite the resources poured into initiatives to increase the number of women, minority, and other underrepresented groups, companies have seen little change and, most notably, almost no movement at the top leadership and board levels. As I'll discuss below, a key ingredient to a successful diversity program

---

[1] Vivian Hunt, Lareina Yee, Sara Prince, and Sundiatu Dixon-Fyle, "Delivering through Diversity," McKinsey & Company, 2018. https://www.mckinsey.com/business-functions/organization/our-insights/delivering-through-diversity.

is authenticity. Over the years I've seen organization after organization *say* they are committed to diversity, but really only giving lip service to an initiative. What these organizations don't realize is that being inauthentic not only means you'll see no results when it comes to diversity, but that you'll actually see negative repercussions for the insincere efforts.

But there is good news. There are companies who have successfully tackled issues of unconscious bias to improve hiring and retention of diverse talent. Hundreds of companies have designed and executed authentic and creative inclusion strategies that make all employees feel a deep sense of belonging, which leads to maximum engagement and loyalty. These companies remain steadfast in their commitment to diversity not only because it's the right thing to do, but also because it's the business-wise thing to do.

Unconscious Bias Explained

A foundational issue related to diversity and inclusion is the effect of unconscious bias on our decision-making at work. Although the study of unconscious bias isn't new, it's only recently become well known. But despite the increased awareness of the term, the influence it has on our decision-making is still not fully understood by most employees or company leaders.

Unconscious biases (also called *implicit biases*) are social stereotypes about certain groups of people that individuals form outside their own conscious awareness. In English, that means that all humans are wired to function on auto-pilot when necessary and, as a result, we sometimes have to make assumptions. Usually, these unconscious assumptions are harmless, but sometimes they can be damaging or even dangerous.

Despite our belief that our decisions are guided exclusively by logic and an objective interpretation of data, research proves otherwise. Our beliefs, and therefore our decision-making, are influenced by a number of factors including our upbringing, the news, social media posts, our past experiences, our personal or family values, and by what we see in popular culture (to name a few examples).

Based on these influences, we form judgments about certain people based on characteristics such as gender, race, ethnicity, religion, or sexual orientation.

We also base beliefs about people on issues such as level of education, whether we have things in common with them, physical attractiveness, socioeconomic status, where the person lives, and a host of other reasons.

This means we're making decisions at work that affect every aspect of employment—from interviewing to termination, and everything in between. In other words, we're making flawed decisions if they are based on unconscious influences that should have no bearing in the decision-making process.

Researchers have identified a number of categories of unconscious bias and have recognized that they have an impact on the workplace. Two of the most common types of unconscious bias are confirmation bias and affinity bias (sometimes called "like me" bias).

Affinity (or "Like Me") Bias

Affinity bias is defined as a positive response to people who are similar to us. It makes sense in the context of establishing relationships, whether friendships or deciding with whom we want to work. We all gravitate toward people with whom we can form connections. The problem is that if we only hire, promote, train, mentor, or value those who are "like us," we become organizations made up of clones rather than organizations made up of employees with innovative ideas, a cutting-edge approach to problem-solving, and with the gift of resourcefulness.

The blind orchestra auditions

Orchestra leaders, who considered themselves progressive and inclusive, noticed that professional orchestras were made up almost exclusively of men. In a well-known experiment, orchestras made an adjustment to the audition process: They had musicians audition from behind a screen, preventing the decision-makers from seeing the aspiring professional musicians. The results were immediate and dramatic—the number of women selected to play in orchestras increased. The researchers realized, however, that sometimes the decision-makers could identify whether the musician was a man or woman based on the sound of their shoes (since many female candidates wore high heels). Based on this, they made an additional adjustment. The musicians auditioned from behind a screen, but took their shoes off before walking over to the audition chair. The results were even more remarkable: This additional change increased the number of female musicians selected to an even greater degree.[2]

The dangers of affinity bias at work can be seen at any stage in the employee life cycle. One of the most significant is the hiring stage since the effects of biased decision-making during this critical phase contributes to the lack of diversity and inclusion, and also increases the probability of experiencing workplace drama.

Take the case of Fred. Fred needs to hire an accountant for the consulting company where he is a senior partner. He's rejected numerous candidates, many of them women and several men who are of a different ethnic background from Fred. He cites the same reason for rejecting each previous candidate—a lack of the specific work experience to help Fred in his specialized tax and accounting practice. Specifically, while Fred acknowledges that the rejected candidates have years of general accounting experience, they don't have experience helping global companies with complex tax issues. A few months into the hiring process, Fred interviews Jeremy, who not only lacks global tax experience, he's also only been in accounting for a few years. But Jeremy is friendly, eager, and enthusiastic and, Fred says, Jeremy reminds him of his younger self. Fred sends out an email advocating for Jeremy and says that while it's true Jeremy doesn't have experience, Jeremy promised he'd "give it 110%." Jeremy is hired.

The result? The workplace is now made up of one more person who both looks and thinks exactly like Fred. The organization lost the

---

[2]Claudia Goldin and Cecilia Rouse, "Orchestrating Impartiality: The Impact of 'Blind' Auditions on Female Musicians," Harvard Kennedy School, 2000. http://gap.hks.harvard .edu/orchestrating-impartiality-impact-%E2%80%9Cblind%E2%80%9D-auditions-female -musicians and *American Economic Review* 90, no. 4 (2000): 715–741. https://pubs.aeaweb .org/doi/pdfplus/10.1257/aer.90.4.715.

opportunity to hire candidates who might have been equally eager and committed, but who didn't remind Fred of what he was like years ago. And just as bad, all of these decisions are made in full view of current employees who are told that the company is committed to diversity and inclusion. So even if Fred's decision-making was not meant to purposely exclude certain groups, the result is exactly that.

What's a better way? How can we identify affinity bias so that it has less of an impact on our decision-making?

One approach is to build increased structure into the interview and hiring process. Companies have used this increased structure as a safeguard to prevent bias from affecting decision-making. Those companies do the following:

> Take a close look at the language used in job postings and job descriptions to eliminate words that might create subtle messages that attract one set of applicants and discourage another from applying for the job.
>
> Use low-tech or high-tech solutions to scrub resumes of information that does nothing to predict whether the candidate is qualified for the position. This includes information such as name (which could give away gender or ethnicity) or date of graduation (which might indicate age).
>
> Create a structured interview process that includes:
> - A preset list of relevant and insightful questions to ask each candidate so that every applicant gets an equal chance to talk about his/her experience, background, and ability to succeed in the position;
> - A hiring committee made up of diverse interviewers; and
> - A pre-set methodology to grade answers and give the candidate an overall rating.

Although creating a structure doesn't mean the process has no flexibility, taking steps like these reduces the likelihood that affinity bias (or other unconscious biases) will negatively affect decisions in hiring.

In fact, in the example with Fred, the company could have (and should have) taken one simple step to eliminate the drama. If the hiring process had included a decision *before* the interviews began about what was required to succeed in the position, the decision-making would have been based on those pre-established criteria, rather than the ad-hoc criteria set as the process moved along. If, for example, the decision-makers agreed that experience—general or specific—was an absolute job requirement, then Jeremy would not have even made it to the interview stage and they would have eventually hired a candidate with the requisite experience. If, by contrast, a decision was made that experience was only preferred but not necessary, then the candidates who interviewed for the job before Jeremy would have gotten a fair shake and been more likely to be evaluated for criteria other than their lack of experience.

Confirmation Bias

Confirmation bias is the tendency to notice evidence that supports our beliefs, preconceptions, and hypotheses, and to miss, ignore, or dismiss evidence that contradicts them. Instead of trying to falsify a hypothesis, we tend to try to confirm it.

English psychologist Peter Wason first coined the term "confirmation bias" as a result of an experiment designed to examine how people test hypotheses. Numerous studies have been conducted since that verify Wason's results and show that once our brain makes a judgment about something, we have a tendency to look for evidence that confirms that judgment, and we tend to dismiss or ignore evidence that refutes it.

Challenging preconceptions

In Wason's experiment, he gave participants a series of three numbers, 2–4–6, and asked them to try to identify the rule that described the sequence by offering other three-digit sequences. In response, almost all participants developed the hypothesis, based on the example given, that the rule was "three even numbers in increasing order of sequence" and therefore offered sequences such as 4–8–10, 6–8–12, and 20–22–24. The experiment leaders would respond to the participants with "yes" or "right" when a correct three-number pattern was stated, or "wrong" when a sequence was given that didn't follow the rule.

Since participants had already formed a belief that the rule was "three even numbers in increasing order of sequence" they continued to only offer sequences based on that rule and they continued to receive confirmation that strengthened their belief. If the participants had challenged their preconceived notion by offering a sequence that broke their rule, they might have discovered that the actual rule was quite simple: "three numbers in increasing order of sequence."[3]

As with affinity bias, the negative effects of confirmation bias in decision-making can be seen throughout the employee life cycle. One stage that receives too little attention but is critical for organizations that want to stay drama-free is confirmation bias when receiving, investigating, and resolving complaints of misconduct.

Here's how I witnessed it firsthand when doing work for a large employer:

Angelina complained that Brad had been harassing her for years. She complained to Jennifer, the head of HR and said she hadn't brought up her concerns before because she and Brad were coworkers, but now that Brad had been promoted to supervise her, she was concerned that the harassment could affect her success at work.

Jennifer dismissed Angelina's complaint, noting that she'd seen Angelina having lunch with Brad a number of times. During those interactions, she said, Angelina was clearly comfortable. Despite her assumption, Jennifer reluctantly agreed to conduct an investigation. Jennifer was convinced Angelina's "complaint" was most likely a way to excuse her declining performance.

Jennifer focused on interviewing witnesses who would provide information on what she thought were the two key issues: (1) that Angelina was a poor performer (she learned in an investigation training course to look for a motive to lie when determining credibility) and (2) that many coworkers knew that Angelina and Brad had a friendly and at times even playful working relationship. Jennifer didn't speak with the witnesses Angelina identified—colleagues she said she had spoken with over the years to recount her

[3]Fenna Poletiek, "Wason's Rule Discovery Task," in *Essays in Cognitive Psychology: Hypothesis-Testing Behaviour,* East Sussex: Psychology Press, 2001.

uncomfortable interactions with Brad. Jennifer decided that these witnesses would "take Angelina's side" and were therefore untrustworthy witnesses.

In short, Jennifer made a decision the minute Angelina finished expressing her concerns. Her conclusion was that Angelina was not exposed to inappropriate conduct and that she was most likely bringing up her concerns as a way to excuse poor performance. As a result of the judgment she made in the blink of an eye, she conducted an investigation to confirm that belief, focusing only on evidence that verified her belief, and ignoring information that may have contradicted her conclusion. This hardly qualified as an "unbiased" or "independent" workplace investigation.

The findings of her "independent" investigation were, not surprisingly, that Brad did nothing wrong. Because Jennifer made her entire investigation fit the narrative she'd developed at the outset, the company would never know whether her conclusions were an accurate depiction of what happened. The company therefore missed an opportunity to resolve the issues presented by Angelina. Even worse, it created an increased level of drama, since now Angelina viewed her company's HR department as an enemy of employees.

And unfortunately, as was true with the example of Fred at the accounting firm, other employees were keeping a close eye on how the organization approached Angelina's concerns. The chances of increasing gender diversity at a company that approaches allegations of sexual harassment in this manner are slim. So in addition to failing to resolve the specific issues related to Brad and Angelina, the company ended up sending a message that had the likelihood of making a significant percentage of employees feel as if they didn't belong and exponentially increasing the chance of more workplace drama.

So what are some practical ways to eliminate, or at least decrease, confirmation bias when we receive, investigate, and resolve conflict?

At the outset: Professionals in charge of receiving employee complaints must be meticulous about taking complaints seriously and refraining from making judgments about their validity before conducting a fair, thorough, unbiased, and good-faith investigation.

During the investigation: Investigators need to look at evidence that supports and contradicts the allegations and must reach conclusions that are not only reasonable and fair, but that also correspond with what the evidence says. Credibility determinations should be based on an analysis of all the evidence and findings should include a deep analysis, not just conclusory statements. One easy and effective way for investigators to test their analysis and conclusion is to play devil's advocate. When veering toward a decision, think about what advocates of the other side might say to make sure you haven't missed any important points.

After the investigation: Remedial measures should be equal to the misconduct found and should be structured to avoid a recurrence.

(Read more about how to conduct fair and thorough investigations and how to implement effective remedial measures in Chapter 11.)

D, I, & B . . . What's the Difference (and Why Does it Matter)?

Diversity programs have been around for decades. Initially, the focus was almost exclusively on numbers—in particular, getting "women and minorities" in the door. Although companies saw modest success with widening the recruiting net and including additional structure in the hiring, evaluation, and promotion process, the number of diverse candidates at all levels, and particularly in leadership, remained largely stagnant. It was clear that focusing only on numbers—getting people "in the door"—wasn't going to move the needle. One reason was a high level of attrition among diverse employees. Many candidates leaving companies explained that they found the work environment unfamiliar or even unwelcoming.

This chapter focuses primarily on diversity initiatives related to increased representation of woman and ethnic minorities. This isn't because other categories of diversity aren't important, but because most of the research and real-life examples involve these categories. Over time, more attention will be paid to other groups, but it's safe to assume that many if not all of the principles outlined here that are related to gender and ethnic diversity apply to other types of diverse characteristics. For example, there is every reason to believe that companies who value and highlight diversity based on factors such as disability, membership in the LGBTQ community, generational diversity, diversity in religion, veteran status, and other factors, would also lead to better business results.

The result? Companies began focusing not only on diversity (numbers) but also on inclusion. Organizations realized that while they might have had modest success getting candidates in the door, those same candidates left, often citing feelings of exclusion and discomfort as a reason for leaving.

This created a cycle: The already challenging task of recruiting diverse talent became more difficult since diverse candidates began asking about the company's demographics, and the failure to bring in new diverse hires only made the current employees feel less included, which increased the chances they'd leave the company, therefore making it harder to recruit new diverse employees. And so on and so on.

Companies kicked their efforts up a notch and in addition to having recruiting mechanisms to increase diversity, they began adding programs aimed at promoting, engaging, and retaining diverse talent. This included mentoring programs, affinity groups (groups to represent needs of and be a voice for diverse employees), diversity councils, and various other programs geared toward bringing diverse employees into the company fold.

More recently, companies have adopted the term "belonging" instead of "inclusion" or "fit." Belonging is the feeling of psychological safety that employees feel when they can be their authentic selves at work, without fear that they'll be judged. The theory is that by focusing on belonging, rather than making people "fit" a preconceived notion, there will be a greater sense of true unity and collaboration and that will not only translate into more success in a company's quest to achieve diversity, but will also translate into greater business success.

"Old School" Plans No Longer Work

There were a few other issues that came up along the road from "diversity" to "diversity, inclusion, and belonging." In fact, less-progressive companies are still somewhere on that path and might still be looking at diversity through the old-fashioned (and unsuccessful) lens of the 1970s and 1980s diversity plans.

When diversity was first introduced as an important workplace goal, it was often mixed in with compliance and legal issues. Many believed that achieving diversity was only a matter of complying with the law: enforcing antidiscrimination and antiharassment laws and implementing a legally compliant equal employment opportunity (EEO) policy. For those companies with federal contracts, they also complied with legal requirements related to affirmative action plans. Affirmative action plans require that federal contractors track their employee demographics, specifically focusing on issues of gender, race/ethnicity, and veteran status. The plans also require that companies set goals to increase employee percentages in those categories if they are lower than they should be.

Unfortunately, companies conflated these legal mandates with diversity programs. We therefore saw (and still see) companies who say their "diversity plan" is to prohibit illegal discrimination and harassment and to publish and enforce an EEO policy. While it's great that these companies are complying with minimum legal mandates, this is no diversity plan.

Why It Matters Now More Than Ever: Demographic Trends

For those of you who are on the fence about whether to start a diversity initiative (or strengthen an existing one), you should pay attention to two demographic trends that might influence your decision.

First, the United States is more racially and ethnically diverse and will be even more so in the coming years. In fact, by 2055, the United States will not have a single racial or ethnic group that makes up a majority of the population.[4]

Additionally, millennials—those born between 1981 and 1996—will surpass baby boomers as the country's largest adult generation.[5]

The combination of these two trends means that the millennial generation is the most racially diverse adult generation in U.S. history, with 43% indicating they are "non-white."[6]

Why are these trends important?

One recent survey provides an answer. It shows that millennials not only expect companies to be committed to diversity and inclusion for

[4]D'Vera Cohn and Andrea Caumont, "10 Demographic Trends That Are Shaping the U.S. and the World," Pew Research Center, 2016. http://www.pewresearch.org/fact-tank/2016/03/31/10-demographic-trends-that-are-shaping-the-u-s-and-the-world/.

[5]Ibid.

[6]Ibid.

business reasons, they see it as a moral imperative and have unique ideas about how to measure success—subjectively by measuring engagement and connection, rather than just through numbers. In fact, data from the survey indicates that more than half would take a pay cut to work for a company who shares their values and nearly half (47%) actively look to see if their prospective employer has a diversity and inclusion program before making a final decision about whether to join a company.[7]

This is not to say that companies should ignore the obvious and proven financial benefits that come from having a diverse workforce, including the competitive advantage of talent acquisition and retention, but it does mean that a modern initiative will incorporate subjective factors related to innovation, relationships, and a sense of belonging into their initiatives.

Best Practices and Emerging Trends for Creating, Executing, and Selling Your Initiative

So how do the concepts of diversity, inclusion, belonging, and unconscious bias work at work? What can companies do to successfully design and execute a diversity initiative?

Leading companies make inclusion part of their DNA—not just with employees, but with customers, suppliers, investors, and other stakeholders. Here are some specific ways they use their commitment to these issues as a key to stave off workplace drama.

Authenticity

I've talked about the importance of authenticity already, but it's worth repeating, especially in the context of diversity and inclusion. Too many companies *say* they're committed to an inclusive culture that welcomes diverse employees. They write about it at length on their website; their

---

[7]Anna Johansson, "The One Philosophical Difference That Sets Millennials Apart in Workplace Diversity," *Forbes*, November 13, 2017. https://www.forbes.com/sites/annajohansson/2017/11/13/the-one-philosophical-difference-that-sets-millennials-apart-in-workplace-diversity/#5e94285070c7.

recruiting and hiring managers know the "we love diversity" script by heart; and the company shows off the various diversity awards they've won over the years. There's only one problem—they don't really mean it.

When you dig a bit deeper with these companies, you realize they have a hard time recruiting and even more so retaining women, ethnically and racially diverse professionals, disabled individuals, members of the LGBTQ community, and those who are allies to members of those communities. But why? After all, these companies have affinity groups for all those employees, they have a diversity council and they have leaders who say they are fully committed. Yes, but . . .

The truth is that when push comes to shove, their decisions highly favor the status quo. There is rampant bias—women getting "low-balled" during salary negotiations, diverse employees asked to serve on diversity councils with no rewards for that work at compensation time, high-powered leaders allowed to get away with misconduct, and the list goes on.

Here's the truth about authenticity when it comes to diversity: A company is much better off being honest and saying it doesn't choose to emphasize diversity, instead of deceptively saying it is committed to it.

This point bears repeating: If your company isn't fully and genuinely committed to diversity (or is lukewarm in its commitment), it's better to be quiet about diversity than to promote it as a core value.

I guarantee that faking it will come back to haunt you. Saying you're committed to diversity to be PC, to improve your chances of getting investors to pay attention, to make it on a list of best places to work or simply to look good isn't enough, and employees will smell the bogus pledge from miles away.

Seeing through inauthenticity

Here's an example of a typical way in which a company with an inauthentic commitment to diversity fares.

A diverse employee joins the company believing the hype that the organization is a champion of diversity. Soon, that diverse employee discovers she is paid less than her male counterparts, she sees male leaders are allowed to get away with misconduct, she sees hiring and promotion policies being skirted for the boss's cronies, and she meets other employees who are equally dissatisfied with issues of fairness and equity.

This employee receives emails and attends events where the company brags about diversity awards and publishes its diversity newsletter touting the impact the company's diverse employees have in the industry.

Rather than having a positive effect, the company's disingenuous boasting about its commitment to diversity causes anger and backlash. "I mean, it's bad enough that the company isn't really committed to diversity," the employee thinks, "but what's worse is that the company leaders think I'm naive enough to believe they are, just because they publish glossy marketing material about it and brag about their substandard diversity numbers being only slightly better than the pathetic industry average."

All of the money, time, and effort this company has wasted on publicizing its commitment to hiring, promoting, and retaining top diverse talent is wasted and would be better spent on a corporate effort toward which the company has a true dedication.

Authenticity is a key ingredient to get your company to the top of the Healthy Workplace Culture Pyramid, but it's especially critical as it relates to a company's commitment to diversity and inclusion.

Trickle-Down Effect

Yes, a true commitment to diversity starts at the top, but that authentic commitment needs to flow down to other managers and supervisors.

As stated in McKinsey's leading report on inclusion and diversity:

Companies increasingly recognize that commitment to inclusion and diversity starts at the top, with many companies publicly committing to an I&D agenda. Leading companies go further, cascading this commitment throughout their organizations, particularly to middle management. They promote ownership by their core businesses, encourage role modeling, hold their executives and managers to account, and ensure efforts are sufficiently resourced and supported centrally.[8]

[8]Vivian Hunt, Lareina Yee, Sara Prince, and Sundiatu Dixon-Fyle, "Delivering through Diversity," McKinsey & Company, 2018. https://www.mckinsey.com/business-functions/organization/our-insights/delivering-through-diversity.

This means leading companies don't focus on old-fashioned metrics like setting numeric goals to evaluate manager performance (quota-setting); they develop fresh ways to teach managers how to create a sense of belonging. Leading companies teach managers innovative ways to discuss sensitive topics to help employees better understand each other, connect, and build empathy. Leading companies give managers clear information and guidance so they fully understand and are on board with the company's inclusion goals and can clearly communicate those goals to their own employees. And leading companies involve managers in decision-making about the initiative, so they feel a true sense ownership in the process.

Creative Communication and Branding

Words matter. While the terms "diversity" and "inclusion" should conjure up positive images, they have become politically charged words, often eliciting extreme reactions.

I'm not suggesting we ditch these words altogether, but I do suggest taking a careful look at your workplace to gauge whether or not such terminology will doom your efforts from the start. Try working with your company's marketing and branding experts to come up with a unique brand for your diversity efforts, including any training.

While there is no magic word or phrase, I've had success with slogans such as "We Are One," "Stronger Together," and "One Team." This and similar messaging that precisely defines the ultimate goal of your efforts—bringing together the entire mosaic of your talent—leads to a win–win for employees and companies alike.

Staying Current

Stay abreast of important terminology and what impact is has on your diversity and inclusion initiative. Your employees are probably hearing or reading about many of these cutting-edge terms on TV, podcasts, or on social media posts. A professional committed to inclusion must therefore keep up.

Belonging

Belonging isn't synonymous with "fitting in." Brené Brown, a professor at the University of Houston who studies vulnerability and belonging, explains the difference as: Fitting in and belonging are separate things. Fitting in involves people changing themselves in order to be accepted. Belonging allows people to be accepted as they are.[9]

Covering

New York University Professor Kenji Yoshino is a leading researcher on the topic of covering. Yoshino conducted research with his colleague Christie Smith based on a hypothesis that the pressure to "cover" sometimes prevents employees from bringing their authentic selves to work. He says, "under-represented groups pay a 'tax,' which we call 'covering,' in which they are asked to downplay their identity in order to fit into the mainstream." He asked study respondents whether they covered along four axes: appearance, affiliation, advocacy, and association.

In addition to collecting aggregate data, his survey also asked respondents to share stories. Two he notes are, "When I wore my natural hair it always seemed to be the subject of conversation as if that single feature defined who I am as a person" and "Even though I am of Chinese descent, I would never correct people if they make jokes or comments about Asian stereotypes."

Yoshino's research also found that straight white men often cover. He gives the example of Franklin D. Roosevelt, because the president was careful to hide his disability by sitting behind a desk for meetings and only being photographed or filmed from the waist up so people did not see him in a wheelchair.[10]

In fact, Christie has performed research that suggests that up to 45% of straight white men cover, for example, to downplay a mental health issue they might be experiencing.[11]

---

[9]Brené Brown, "Finding Our Way to True Belonging," Ideas.ted.com, September 11, 2017. https://ideas.ted.com/finding-our-way-to-true-belonging/.

[10]"Kenji Yoshino Explores the Costs of Conformity at Work," *NYU Law*, April 30, 2014. http://www.law.nyu.edu/news/kenji-yoshino-explores-the-cost-of-conformity-at-work.

[11]Dorie Clark and Christie Smith, "Help Your Employees Be Themselves at Work," *Harvard Business Review*, November 3, 2014. https://hbr.org/2014/11/help-your-employees-be-themselves-at-work.

The significance of this research is that it highlights the importance of creating a mechanism to make sure all employees at your organization feel safe and comfortable being authentic, without fear that showing who they are (within the bounds of professionalism and appropriateness) will result in exclusion.

Cultural Competency

With an increasingly diverse workforce that works with global colleagues and clients, it's essential that everyone at work becomes well-versed in customs, communication styles, and worldviews that are not recognized as stereotypically "American." While this doesn't mean we have to turn ourselves into pretzels or that we have to always be ultra-vigilant about political correctness, it does mean that if you're committed to being respectful and inclusive, and if you want to make everyone at work feel like they truly belong, then you will seek to not only become familiar with how others communicate, but will also be open to sharing information about your own preferences. This type of curiosity and mutual respect are hallmarks to a successful inclusion and diversity program.

Culture Fit

This term *culture fit* has received a bad rap, but for good reason. For too long, the term was used to weed out those who were considered "not like us" and that usually meant not of our race, ethnicity, religion, sexual orientation, or gender. The term itself has value, however. The key is to use the phrase precisely and to define it whenever it's used. It most often comes up during the hiring process when a hiring manager is choosing between candidates and wonders whether they will "fit" in their workplace culture.

If this term is used to exclude candidates based on a protected category, it's not only bad business, it's illegal. If, however, the term is being used to define the *work culture*—that is, the values, mission, and behaviors that make your company *your company*—then it's appropriate to use the phrase. But make sure everyone is on the same page. At an interview, tell the candidate, "At our company, we take our jobs seriously, but we don't take ourselves seriously. That means we are all committed to meeting our objective of working together and working hard to achieve our company goal to go public next year. We work long hours and everyone needs to wear five different hats in order to get the job done. But we're very casual . . . professional and respectful, but casual and fun. We're really like a family here. We've found that people who are on board with this type of corporate culture succeed here. Does that sound like the type of culture that you'd thrive in?"

One final word on culture fit: Hiring for fit shouldn't mean that you hire only those who will blindly follow what is currently being done. Hiring those who are a "culture add" is often an effective way to keep your ideas and actions innovative.

Equity

Leading companies focus on equality, sure, but they also focus on equity. The distinction is important—whether achieving equity in hiring, promotion, or pay, savvy inclusion professionals know the difference. In short, equality means treating everyone the same, assuming the same resources will lead to equal success. Equity means giving employees what they actually need in order to succeed. This means learning your employees' language of workplace motivation, being open to providing a different way of succeeding without judgment that it is different from "your way," and having honest conversations with employees about what tools they need to succeed. It might also mean changing systems to address possible systemic barriers to equity.

Insider/Outsider

There is no magic definition for these words. An "insider" is someone who feels like she belongs while an "outsider" feels like she's on the outside looking in. The importance of these terms isn't in their definition but in their application. If the goal of a sophisticated inclusion program is to make people feel authentic and as if they belong, then it's equally vital to recognize that there are a number of reasons why an employee might feel like an outsider. The trick is to develop mechanisms that recognize that some might feel excluded and then design plans to increase inclusion.

Intersectionality

Although still not widely recognized by the general public, *intersectionality* is a key term for anyone who wants to fully understand inclusion. The term was coined by legal scholar and law professor Kimberlé Crenshaw. She first used it in a 1989 essay that discussed how antidiscrimination law, feminist theory, and political movements aimed to eliminate racism all fail to address the experiences of black women because they only focus on a single factor—race *or* gender. Crenshaw says that because the intersectional experience is greater than the sum of racism and sexism, any analysis that does not take intersectionality into account can't fully explain the subordination black women are exposed to.[12]

Her research has been expanded to include other women of color as well as any other individual or employee who has intersecting characteristics. In fact, in the 2017 joint McKinsey/Lean In research study on women in the workplace, they found:

"The intersection of race and gender shapes women's experiences in meaningful ways. Women of color face more obstacles and a steeper path to leadership, from receiving less support from managers to getting promoted more slowly. This affects how they view the workplace and their opportunities for advancement. Overall, two patterns are clear: compared to white women, things are worse for women of color, and they are particularly difficult for Black women."[13]

Microaggressions

"Microaggressions are the everyday verbal, nonverbal, and environmental slights, snubs, or insults, whether intentional or unintentional, which communicate hostile, derogatory, or negative messages to target persons based solely upon their marginalized group membership."[14]

---

[12] Kimberlé Crenshaw, "Demarginalizing the Intersection of Race and Sex: A Black Feminist Critique of Antidiscrimination Doctrine, Feminist Theory and Antiracist Politics," University of Chicago Legal Forum, 1989. https://chicagounbound.uchicago.edu/cgi/viewcontent.cgi?referer=&httpsredir=1&article=1052&context=uclf.

[13] "Getting to Gender Equality Starts with Realizing How Far We Have to Go," McKinsey & Company, 2017. https://womenintheworkplace.com/.

[14] Derald Sue, "Microaggressions: More Than Just Race." *Psychology Today*, November 17, 2010. https://www.psychologytoday.com/us/blog/microaggressions-in-everyday-life/201011/microaggressions-more-just-race.

Although some might dismiss these microaggressions as meaningless because they tend to be minor slights, in the aggregate they not only cause psychological harm to the recipient, they decrease the sense of belonging and therefore can sabotage your diversity and inclusion efforts.

Privilege

According to author and professor Michael Kimmel, "privilege comes in a myriad of forms, including race, gender, wealth, physical fitness, safety, and educational attainment and indeed height. However, the people who have those things are usually unaware of their power and influence." He recommends that companies recognize and talk about the privilege and power that comes from having certain characteristics and use those to more evenly distribute power in workplace decision-making. Specifically, as it relates to gender relations at work, he recommends:

> Making gender visible and showing men why having these conversations and solving problems is just as important for men as it is for women.
> Tackling resistance to the idea of privilege in ways that increase understanding.
> Making a business case for gender equality at work.
> Making it personal by sharing stories about life at work and at home.[15]

. . .

Not every workplace will be ready to discuss some of these cutting-edge concepts in relation to their inclusion work, but for those of you who are ready to design and deploy a more advance, relevant, and elegant plan, understanding these terms, and helping your workforce understand them, is crucial.

Measure, Analyze, Adjust

A strategic plan related to diversity and inclusion goals must also include a way to measure a company's progress. First, determine your baseline—

---

[15]Fiona Smith, " 'Privilege Is Invisible to Those Who Have It': Engaging Men in Workplace Equality," *The Guardian*, June 7, 2016. https://www.theguardian.com/sustainable-business/ 2016/jun/08/workplace-gender-equality-invisible-privilege.

where are you now? These measurements might include demographic data related to your population and should also measure employees' sense of belonging, engagement, and statistics that track the employee life cycle to identify barriers. These barriers might be evidenced in promotion rates, disparate salaries, candidate statistics, and employment yield rates (how many diverse candidates are offered jobs; how many accept the position offered). Also look at data related to attrition rates and data related to complaints, investigation, and resolution of misconduct claims.

Once you've measured the information, analyze the data for possible blind spots or areas where additional intervention is necessary. And don't forget about the value of comments and stories. Combine those with the quantitative data to create a snapshot of where you are now, and create a plan for where you want to go (and how to get there).

Link to Your Business

Remain meticulous about linking efforts to drivers of business growth. Make the business case for diversity, but do so in a way that is customized for your organization.

Design Creative Training Programs

As I'll discuss in greater detail in Chapter 10, the key to workplace training is to focus on building skills, increasing understanding and empathy, and positively impacting behavior (as opposed to using fear-based, compliance-focused training, which companies have used for decades and which have done nothing to improve workplace culture).

One method I use in my "We Are One" sessions is to create meaningful connections. In an effort to promote genuine bonding and camaraderie, use training activities that highlight what employees have in common rather than focusing exclusively on differences.

Researchers from various universities banded together recently to explore this further. Specifically, they wanted to see if some creative diversity training techniques might be successful in creating greater understanding and connections.

First, the researchers used "perspective-taking" training, which "is essentially the process of mentally walking in someone else's shoes." They also used an activity involving goal setting, "asking training participants to set specific, measurable, and challenging (yet attainable) goals related to diversity in the workplace."

While the researchers recognize that their experiment involved a small-scale sample of undergraduate students, their findings are nonetheless instructive. They found that both these exercises (perspective-taking and goal setting) positively affected behavior. The participants displayed more support and engaged in less mistreatment toward marginalized minorities.

The researchers recognize that these activities might be better (or worse) suited depending on the employee. For example, the perspective-taking exercise might be especially effective for employees who lack empathy, and might not have the same effect on those who already have strong empathy skills (likely because empathetic employees essentially already do perspective-taking exercises on their own, even if they're unaware they're doing so).[16]

The value of this experiment is to both highlight the need for creativity in training and to shift the focus away from attitudinal outcomes (the bias felt toward a group) or cognitive outcomes (how well-informed a person is about stereotypes and biases), and instead focus on positively affecting understanding, empathy, and behavior.

Relinquish Control

A pioneer in the study of workplace diversity efforts, Harvard Professor Frank Dobbins correctly advocates for companies to give managers more control in the process of developing and executing an inclusion and diversity strategy. Professor Dobbins notes that tools used by companies that are not authentically committed to diversity instead use tools that are "designed to preempt lawsuits by policing managers." They are not meant to actually move the needle but instead are seen as an effective way to manage legal risk. But, Professor Dobbins notes, people often rebel against rules that are

---

[16] Alex Lindsey, Eden King, Ashley Membere, and Ho Kwan Cheung, "Two Types of Diversity Training That Really Work," *Harvard Business Review*, July 28, 2017. https://hbr.org/2017/07/two-types-of-diversity-training-that-really-work?autocomplete=true

meant to repress autonomy, and therefore these measures often do more harm than good ("Try to coerce me to do X, Y, or Z, and I'll do the opposite just to prove I'm my own person.").

Instead of trying to control managers, Professor Dobbins suggests we engage them in solving problems, increase their on-the-job contact with diverse employees, and promote social accountability (the desire to look fair-minded).[17]

Many companies have realized that paying attention to acquiring and retaining diverse talent, creating an environment of inclusion, and establishing ways to make all employees feel like they belong are key ways to prevent drama at work. The key is to study what leading companies are doing right and customize a plan in your organization to replicate those winning results.

---

[17] Frank Dobbin and Alexandra Kalev, "Why Diversity Programs Fail," *Harvard Business Review*, July–August 2016. https://hbr.org/2016/07/why-diversity-programs-fail# comment-section.

4

Ethics Lapses

They're More Common Than You Think

Live one day at a time emphasizing ethics rather than rules.

— Wayne Dyer

For most of us, hearing or reading about corporate scandals involving unethical decisions (think Enron) is not only alarming, but it's also outrageous. "Who would ever behave so unethically?" we ask ourselves. But the truth is that ethical people make unethical decisions all the time.

By definition, ethics draws a line in the sand between right and wrong. It's one part morality and one part codified principles and conduct that govern human behavior and decisions.

So, what's all the buzz with business ethics, and why are there still ethical lapses?

Where Ethics Lapses Begin

The average person's moral compass guides decision-making toward an ethical north. But decisions can quickly go south because they're influenced by external pressures that sometimes override internal points of reference.

While unethical behavior occasionally comes from egocentric tendencies, more often than not it occurs because of a fear of some consequence. Employees also adjust their behavior (and justifications for their behavior) based on their environment. For instance, some employees find they can't compete with the top performers who are cutting serious ethical corners and figure the only way to survive or beat them is to join in. They see that others aren't just getting away with devious behavior but are also rewarded for it. The message of "it's how things are done around here" becomes an accepted cultural norm.

The consequences of missing a deadline or benchmark are magnified at work. Employees are aware that their productivity is being scrutinized. If they fail to meet a goal, they risk missing out on raises, bonuses, and promotions. Under this lens, employees often zero in on the quickest means to reach the desired outcome, even if it's unethical. In the moment, it feels fair and justified. It's easy to lose long-term perspective when pursuing a series of short-term goals. Oftentimes employees become so focused in one direction, they forget to look east and west for alternative options. Instead, they follow an (often) well-trodden path that points south, making progressively bad judgement calls and defective decisions.

Unethical behavior goes beyond breaking laws and regulations. It doesn't have to involve a large-scale scandal to infect a culture or corrupt an entire value chain, as was the case with Enron.

While sexually charged misconduct and bias are further examples of unethical behavior, this chapter focuses on other types of unethical acts.

> Common types of ethical lapses include cutting corners on policy, misleading customers, corporate theft, bullying, accepting or giving gifts in exchange for a specified outcome, unethical accounting practices, and failure to comply with safety or environmental regulations.

Leading Causes and Warning Signs of Unethical Behavior at the Corporate Level

While all types of unethical acts are inexcusable, I'll focus on three of the most common in this chapter: cutting corners on policy, misleading customers, and corporate theft.

Cutting Corners on Policy

The most prominent but overlooked sources of unethical behavior involve unrealistic, incentivized, or fear-driven performance goals. Employees endure overwhelming levels of pressure to meet benchmarks. At times, they'll sacrifice their own morals to get ahead or even just to keep their heads above water. Other times, people engage in unethical conduct because they're simply following by example.

A sales employee at a large, multinational biotech company once told me: "The expectations were insane and we all ended up working 14- to 16-hour days just to try to keep up. Every day I saw fellow workers packing up their desks. People were getting fired left and right. My coworkers were cutting corners, making promises they knew the company couldn't keep, exaggerating about the efficacy of our products and fudging sales figures just so their sales numbers could 'look good' for this month or this quarter. But it was only a matter of time before it caught up with them. I was walking on eggshells thinking I could be next, especially since I knew that my boss didn't want to hear any excuses."

Dealing with their own pressures, leaders may be driving cultures that call on people to cut corners. In fact, a 2017 Ethics and Compliance Initiative (ECI) study revealed that nearly 20% "of employees experienced pressure to compromise standards."[1]

Employees under such duress are in the wrong state of mind to make rational decisions. The Wells Fargo scandal hits the top-10 list in terms of cutting corners on policy and setting people up for failure.

The banking giant baited its employees with handsome reward incentives to open new customer accounts. And between 2011 and 2016 that's exactly what they did, except many of the accounts were sham accounts. Wells Fargo's values and commitments, "Serving Customers and Helping Each Other," proved only half true, unless "Helping Each Other" involves scamming customers and firing 5,300 employees for failing to meet unfeasible account quotas.[2] Clearly, employees saw some inviting signals that they

---

[1] *The State of Ethics & Compliance in the Workplace.* Arlington, VA: Ethics & Compliance Initiative (ECI), 2018. http://www.boeingsuppliers.com/GBES2018-Final.pdf.

[2] "The Vision, Values & Goals of Wells Fargo." Wells Fargo – Banking, Credit Cards, Loans, Mortgages & More. Last modified September 4, 2018. https://www.wellsfargo.com/about/corporate/vision-and-values/.

could get away with this behavior—it was the norm for five years, after all. Wells Fargo's corrupt culture was more than an employee problem; it was a symptom of bad leadership and unrealistic performance goals.[3]

When it comes to cutting corners, leaders should watch out for some key warning signs. If noticed, these likely mean that employees are feeling pressure to perform:

- Increased or high rates of absenteeism due to stress
- Employees with extraordinary numbers in sales and accounts compared to others
- Employees working excessive hours or complaining of burnout
- Decrease in customer service ratings
- Angry customers, repeat repair tickets, or complaints that weren't effectively resolved the first time

Misleading the Public for Profit

Another surprisingly common practice among companies is deliberately misleading customers to benefit from the results. Whether leaders or employees take advantage by misrepresenting their product or promising outcomes that they're fully aware they cannot deliver, this is a behavior that typically begins close to the top and permeates an entire culture. It could be as simple as offering a satisfaction guarantee and then not honoring it when a customer tries to return a purchase, or as egregious as falsifying data about a product's functionality.

VW is perhaps the most notorious case of customer deception in recent decades. Full-scale investigations across multiple countries have revealed that the company purposely misled consumers to make a buck. Instead of playing by the rules when the Environmental Protection Agency mandated tighter regulations on automakers to reduce diesel emissions, VW installed "illegal cheat software"[4] that masked accurate readings of nitrogen oxide.

---

[3]Michael Corkery, "Wells Fargo Fined $185 Million for Fraudulently Opening Accounts," *New York Times*, September 8, 2016. https://www.nytimes.com/2016/09/09/business/dealbook/wells-fargo-fined-for-years-of-harm-to-customers.html.

[4]Leah M. Goodman, "Why Volkswagen Cheated." *Newsweek*, December 15, 2015. https://www.newsweek.com/2015/12/25/why-volkswagen-cheated-404891.html.

VW's autocratic and inauthentic leadership forged a culture of fear. Some employees reported the cheating to their superiors, but the powerful international automaker turned a blind eye. Most employees were afraid to speak up about the wrongdoings, feeling like they had no choice but to comply. If employees hesitated to act, management would resort to carrot-and-stick tactics and force them into submission.[5]

ECI's research indicates that culture is the number-one influence on employee conduct.[6] In the case of VW, the company's iron-fisted leadership and forced code of secrecy led to a stifled culture of employee apprehension, perpetuating a 10-year stint of conspiracy and deception.

A low number of recorded complaints is not always the sign of a virtuous culture, but could instead indicate fear, corruption, and retaliation in the workplace, warns ECI.[7] Emtrain's 2018 In the House Survey revealed that most employees (64%) didn't feel comfortable reporting claims of sexual harassment, indicating a "corporate culture that discourages acknowledgement of misconduct."[8] Whatever the type of misconduct, company culture often plays a central role in condoning and perpetuating such behavior.

When it comes to misleading customers and other stakeholders, leaders should watch out for some key warning signs.

- A majority or significant percentage of employees don't speak up (in meetings and in other settings).
- Former/current employees anonymously report online that managers don't care.

---

[5]Ibid.

[6]*The State of Ethics & Compliance in the Workplace.* Arlington, VA: Ethics & Compliance Initiative (ECI), 2018. http://www.boeingsuppliers.com/GBES2018-Final.pdf.

[7]Ibid.

[8]*Emtrain and In the House Survey: Sexual Harassment Prevention in the Age of The #MeToo Movement.* San Francisco, CA: Emtrain, 2018.

- Employees leaving the company report concerns at their exit interviews, saying they didn't feel comfortable making these reports without having secured another job first.
- Little to no internal reports of unethical conduct.
- High turnover rates under particular managers.
- Increase in leaders taking disciplinary action against employees, especially when the increase involves employees with previously good performance records.

If you notice a pattern of these behaviors, it might mean that employees have lost trust and that someone is trying to cover their tracks.

Unfair Treatment Leads to Theft and Unrest

Corporate America sees its fair share of theft, from embezzlement to expense account fraud to insider trading, among others. The Association of Certified Fraud Examiners' (ACFE) 2018 Global Study on Occupational Fraud and Abuse found that organizations worldwide lose an average of 5% of annual revenue to fraud, with the median loss for U.S. companies clocking in at $108,000.[9] Employee theft occurs for numerous reasons, and it can't all be blamed on the organization—there will always be some bad apples that take advantage of their position by skimming some money off the top or pocketing inventory. But an organization often isn't completely blameless either.

Following the same pattern that we've seen with other types of ethical issues explored in this book, employee theft frequently comes down to the example that company leadership sets and the culture that emerges as a result.

Walmart is an example of a workplace culture that employees perceive as greedy and therefore justify actions that might hurt the corporate giant. While its 38-page credo on values and beliefs includes "Respect for the Individual, Striving for Excellence, and Acting with Integrity,"[10] the

---

[9] *Report to the Nations: 2018 Global Study on Occupational Fraud and Abuse.* Austin, TX: Association of Certified Fraud Examiners (ACFE), 2018. https://s3-us-west-2.amazonaws.com/acfepublic/2018-report-to-the-nations.pdf

[10] *Global Statement of Ethics.* Walmart, n.d. https://www.walmartethics.com/uploadedFiles/Content/U.S.%20-%20English.pdf

big-box giant's culture is often portrayed, in the media and by current and former employees, as abusive and capable of looking the other way when it comes to legal requirements, thus creating a perception of corporate hypocrisy where employees can justify their own misconduct, including theft.

In one example, six Walmart workers conspired and stole almost $60,000 in merchandise between 2012 and 2013.[11] Many Walmart employees also steal money from registers, short-change customers, add cash-back charges to customer credit cards, siphon Walmart money onto prepaid gift cards, and steal money from self-checkout terminals.[12] These employees rationalize their behavior by citing the company's unethical business practices.

I've seen the effects of this reality in my own practice—employees justifying unethical behavior because of their toxic culture or a particularly toxic supervisor. For instance, I've worked with a number of companies who have had to deal with the consequence of time card or expense report fraud. In many of those cases, the employees confess to having added hours to their timesheets or charged the company for personal expenses for two reasons. First, they see their actions as a way of making the playing field even—"If the company behaves unethically, why shouldn't I do so as well," they ask. Second, these employees see their actions as the most effective way to "stick it to the man"—the "man" who they perceive as always taking advantage of them and who therefore deserves to lose a few bucks.

Leaders can watch for some key warning signs to be clued in on conditions that lead to employee theft and related unethical acts:

- High levels of conflict and accumulated grievances
- Secret meetings, union organizing, walkouts, and strikes
- Low morale, productivity, and job satisfaction
- Employees arriving late and leaving early
- Missing merchandise or unbalanced ledgers

[11]Pamela Sroka-Holzmann, "Wal-Mart Employee Jailed in Near-$60K Retail Theft Scheme," *Lehighvalleylive* (Easton), March 11, 2018. https://www.lehighvalleylive.com/bethlehem/index.ssf/2018/03/man_22.html.

[12]Tim Dees, "How Often Does Theft Occur at Walmart?" Quora – A Place to Share Knowledge and Better Understand the World. Last modified June 19, 2015. https://www.quora.com/How-often-does-theft-occur-at-Walmart.

If you notice these signs, they likely mean that staff is disgruntled and senses unfair treatment.

This chapter is by no means exhaustive in terms of corporate misdeeds. If we've learned anything from Wells Fargo, Volkswagen, and Walmart's examples, though, the underlying trend of unethical behavior within organizations is that you reap what you sow.

Best Prevention Techniques

See the ethics. Be the ethics.

The above examples illustrate what not to do. So, what *should* companies do to mitigate unethical conduct, keep employees satisfied, and get them to live by the espoused policy?

Constructive ideas for minimizing ethical missteps include:

- Adopt ethics as part of corporate conversation.
- Anchor values to expectations.
- Lead by example.
- Hire for values first, then skills.
- Link performance to soft skills associated with ethical leadership.
- Establish a system of checks and balances.

Adopt Ethics as Part of Corporate Conversation

Adopting ethics as a core corporate value that reaches beyond the Code of Conduct starts by integrating ethics into ongoing conversations. For example, Rockwell Collins, a global aerospace and defense enterprise, goes far beyond the letter of the law, treating its ethics-based values with the same prudence as compliance. Internal and external communications send consistent ethics messages centered on the values of trust and integrity within all aspects of work life.[13] And Rockwell's leadership articulates values throughout its

---

[13] "Ethics and Compliance, "Rockwell Collins – Building Trust Every Day." http://www .rockwellcollins.com/Our_Company/Ethics.aspx (accessed September 7, 2018).

employee and stakeholder value chain, even refusing to do business with vendors who don't agree to these standards. CEO Kelly Ortberg makes ethics part of his daily communication, actively fostering a culture where it's normal, accepted, and psychologically safe to talk about ethics. A decade-long trend of ethical behavior as reported by Ethisphere[14] and positive employee blog testimonials evince Rockwell's formal and informal ethical alignment.

Anchor Values to Expectations

Effective leaders of ethically strong organizations anchor ethics to expectations by communicating the company values, prescribed behaviors, and vision on an individual level. If the ideology is about trust, leaders should define trust and tie it to the employee's specific role. Next, they can pinpoint the ethical dilemmas an individual in a specific position might encounter and provide a decision-making process to help them critically think through the conundrum. This approach requires leaders across divisions to be on the same page, offering a similar level of concrete guidance to their teams when it comes to expectations of ethical, value-based behavior.

Lead by Example

You've heard the phrase, "Don't just talk the talk; walk the walk." But what does "walking the walk," or leading by example, actually look like when it comes to ethical behavior?

First and foremost, managers must be aware that they *are* the example. What managers say and do must match the company's mission, values, and practices. Any perceived incongruence smacks of disingenuousness, which elicits distrust. According to a 2017 Society for Human Resource Management survey, 61% of employees state that trust in senior management is extremely important for their job satisfaction.[15] Quite simply, employees

---

[14]Ethisphere, "Past Honorees." Ethisphere® Institute | Good. Smart. Business. Profit.® https://www.worldsmostethicalcompanies.com/past-honorees/ (accessed September 7, 2018).

[15]*2017 Employee Job Satisfaction and Engagement: The Doors of Opportunity Are Open.* Alexandria, VA: Society for Human Resource Management (SHRM, 2018). https://www.shrm .org/hr-today/trends-and-forecasting/research-and-surveys/Pages/2017-Job-Satisfaction-and-Engagement-Doors-of-Opportunity-Are-Open.aspx.

who stop believing in their manager will either leave or hop on the band-wagon and imitate the behaviors they see.

Even-handed enforcement is equally important. It's difficult for employees to believe that policy really matters when managers don't face the same consequences for violating policy or when they bend that policy for certain employees. Malleable values and uneven enforcement not only create a sense of unfairness that elicits bad attitudes, they blur the line between right and wrong, sending a signal that ethical conduct is merely window dressing. (See Chapter 11 for more on implementing fair and even-handed remedial measures when misconduct is found.)

I once investigated claims against a fundraising manager who doled out compensatory days to employees who worked overtime. His decisions were not based on policy but on personal discretion. The employees who didn't receive time off sensed unfairness and not only slacked in their efforts but also arrived late and left early. Perceived and practiced unfairness compromises ethics.

Hire for Values First, Then Skills

The old management style was centered on hard skills aimed solely at driving maximum performance, but that ship has sailed. Today's workplace demands leaders with ethics and people skills. People skills, otherwise known as soft skills, involve integrity, emotional intelligence, empathy, active listening, ethical stewardship, participative feedback, and goal setting. These competencies are the values at the forefront of this era of democratization of ideas and innovation.

The question is, how can we hire leaders who embrace ethics and possess soft skills?

First, redefine the criteria for the hiring process and prioritize innate soft skills over teachable hard skills. Second, train people on ethical conduct and soft skills. But how do you actually make it stick?

Link Performance to Soft Skills

You make it stick by holding *all* employees accountable for soft skills in their performance reviews. This requires redesigning performance appraisal systems. For some reason, companies can't see the forest for the trees. How on earth can they profit when tying hard-skill performance goals to rewards leads to unethical behavior, which ultimately costs more in personnel turn-over, lawsuits, and legal penalties?

Instead, performance metrics should be based on 360-degree assess-ments that measure soft skills such as ethics, respectability, approachability, and reliability. Imagine leaders who actually think before they act. Now imagine employees who emulate them.

Companies that fail to hire people with soft skills (and who fail to provide effective education to keep these skills sharp) and tie those skills to performance goals also fail to heighten ethical awareness and ethics-based decision-making.

Establish a System of Checks and Balances

Research shows that when employees are invited into decision-making processes and their ideas are valued and acted upon, they'll feel like they have a stake in the outcomes and thus take ownership of the goal.

So how do we bring this to fruition?

We can form committees of leaders and employees that tackle the root causes of employees' ethical lapses. These committees can also create and endorse new policy or table old policy initiatives through a series of approv-als that serve as a system of checks and balances.

While we'll explore some of these solutions in fuller detail later in this book, I'll leave you with this: Leaders aren't just the curious eyes and ears of the company; they represent the touch of company values. Leaders directly influence employee experiences, perceptions, attitudes, and behaviors. If that influence isn't ethical, employees will likely abandon ethics, too.

PART II

"Hiking" to the Top of the Healthy Workplace Culture Pyramid

5

Reaching the Top of the Healthy Workplace Culture Pyramid

The Three Fs

Now that you've learned more about harassment, bias, diversity, and ethics, it's time to identify a path that is equal parts ambition and realism to achieve a drama-free workplace. In fact, in my view, making your way to the top of the Healthy Workplace Culture Pyramid is much like taking an actual hike up a mountain.

As anyone who has gone on a hike knows, before embarking on your journey, you need to check conditions (weather) and location (where is your starting point and where are you headed, at least generally), and you need to have an understanding of possible hazards.

Similarly, before implementing a plan to prevent workplace drama and "hiking" to the top of the Healthy Workplace Culture Pyramid, you need to:

- Check conditions. (How much of an appetite for change is there at the employee and leadership level?)
- Establish your current and desired locations. (Are you in a toxic workplace where you need to start from the bottom, or are you already at a company with a good culture?)

- Identify possible hazards or roadblocks and develop a plan to avoid or deal with them. (What are the realistic challenges that lie ahead and how can you both predict and prepare for them?)

Getting Started

Before starting your journey, you need to assess and prepare. Here are some questions you should consider:

- Are there threats you need to anticipate? If so, how can you courageously distinguish between reasonable and unreasonable fears, and how can you prepare to tackle hazards you might encounter?
- What is the workplace "terrain" like—do employees already feel valued and fairly treated, or do you need to work on actual and perceived fairness? The answer to this question will determine the type of metaphoric "footwear" you'll need for the journey. If, for instance, your culture is toxic (the equivalent of hiking on a path filled with boulders and fallen trees) then you'll need the best hiking boots money can buy. If, on the other hand, you're further up the Healthy Workplace Culture Pyramid, expecting only to hit some pebbles and streams along the way, you might be able to take your hike in a pair of sturdy hiking sandals.
- How will you make sure that your fellow hikers understand that, while there are necessary guardrails you'll install to keep them safe during the journey, your goal isn't to impose barriers to inhibit their freedom or their ability to enjoy the hike to the top of the pyramid?

The next few chapters will serve as your guide to the top of that pyramid. To begin our journey, we'll need to explore what I call the 3 Fs that are essential to any healthy workplace culture. They are: fearlessness, fairness, and freedom.

Fearlessness

Sir Winston Churchill wisely stated, "Fear is a reaction. Courage is a decision." Organizational courage is an essential component of every healthy workplace culture, but many corporations respond to controversy and challenge from a place of fear because it's easier than exploring what causes that fear and analyzing whether the fear if reasonable.

In Chapter 1, I introduced the topic of corporate cultures that have been ruled by fear—in particular, the fear of legal claims. Since this is such an ever-present fear, and since my own experience tells me that it's the number-one reason organizations resist doing things to improve their cultures, let's start by looking at some hard-to-dispute figures.

What Are the Odds of a Company Being Sued for Sexual Harassment?

- According to the United States Department of Labor, the number of women over the age of 16 in the U.S. workforce fluctuated between 75 and 76 million from August 2017 to August 2018. For the purposes of my calculations, I'll use 75 million.[1]

- Numerous studies show that anywhere between 25% and 85% of women say they experience sexual harassment at work. For purposes of my calculation, I'll use the figures found in the latest Pew Research study. According to Pew, 6 in 10 women say they have "received unwanted sexual advances or experienced sexual harassment." Given the number of women in the workplace, that means that there might be as many as 45 million incidents that women would describe as sexual harassment.[2]

- In 2017, the EEOC received a total of 84,254 charges for all protected categories. Of these, *6,696 were charges alleging sexual harassment.*[3]

---

[1] "Table A-1. Employment Status of the Civilian Population by Sex and Age." United States Department of Labor, Bureau of Labor Statistics, October 5, 2018. https://www.bls.gov/news.release/empsit.t01.htm.

[2] "About six-in-ten women say they have been sexually harassed." Pew Research Center, 2018. http://www.pewsocialtrends.org/2018/04/04/sexual-harassment-at-work-in-the-era-of-metoo/.

[3] Chai Feldblum and Victoria Lipnic, "Select Task Force on Sexual Harassment in the Workplace." U.S. Equal Employment Opportunity Commission, 2016. https://www.eeoc.gov/eeoc/newsroom/release/1-25-18.cfm.

Using the admittedly simple but impactful figures highlighted above, we glean the following:

> *The odds of an incident of sexually charged misconduct at work becoming an EEOC claim are 1 in 6,720. Put differently, there is a .000149% chance that an incident of sexually charged misconduct will become an EEOC claim (only 6,696 sexual harassment charges filed out of 45 million incidents). Put differently, there is a 99.999851% chance that a single incident will NOT become an EEOC charge.*

Let's put this figure in perspective. Let's use the popular "what are the odds of getting struck by lightning" question as a comparison. The odds of becoming a lightning victim in the United States in your lifetime is 1 in 3,000.[4]

Let that sink in. You're twice as likely to be struck by lightning at some point in your lifetime than you are to be part of an organization where a single incident of harassment becomes an EEOC charge.[5]

And yet, every day of every week of every month of every year, companies make decisions about their employees based on this faulty risk assessment—an assessment based on the probability of becoming embroiled in an employment-related lawsuit.

Even worse, by focusing on this fear, too many companies fail to put their energy and focus into taking steps that are *actually proven* to reduce

---

[4] "Flash facts about lightning," *National Geographic*, 2005. https://news.nationalgeographic.com/news/2004/06/flash-facts-about-lightning/.

[5] There are also charges filed with state agencies, but those numbers are also smaller than most assume. For instance, in its latest annual report, the California Department of Fair Employment and Housing, the nation's largest state enforcement agency, indicates that it received 683 complaints alleging sexual harassment in 2017 (https://www.dfeh.ca.gov/wp-content/uploads/sites/32/2018/08/August302018AnnualReportFinal.pdf). While I recognize that the number I use for claims (EEOC filings) might underestimate state claims as well as claims that are settled prior to the filing of an EEOC (or analogous state) charge, taking these into account would not likely have a statistically significant impact on this simple but powerful analysis. Additionally, while I don't add up every claim made, I also base my analysis on EEOC charges brought. Making an EEOC charge does not always result in a lawsuit being filed, so the number of actual lawsuits is actually much smaller than the numbers I use (EEOC charges claiming sexual harassment).

the likelihood of an employee bringing a claim (see the "Fairness" section below). By engaging in unfeeling, compliance-driven decision making, they actually make it *more likely* that they will be sued.

I know this sounds counterintuitive given everything you've ever been told about fearing lawsuits, but stay with me here.

Why Are We Persuaded by Fear, Even If It Means We Act Irrationally?

In their groundbreaking book, *Sway: The Irresistible Pull of Irrational Behavior,* brothers Ori and Rom Brafman answer this very question (and make an argument for readers to avoid succumbing to this seemingly irresistible pull!).

Drawing on cutting-edge research from various fields, the Brafman brothers reveal hidden psychological forces that influence every aspect of our lives. Their findings on loss aversion (our tendency to go to great lengths to avoid perceived losses) are especially relevant for our discussion of overcoming the fears that keep us from making the well-worth-it-trek to the top of the Healthy Workplace Culture Pyramid.

In one of many fascinating sections of the book, the authors assert:

> The word *loss* alone, in fact, elicits a surprisingly powerful reaction in us. Companies like Avis and Hertz, facing the challenge of selling a product that is both useless and overpriced, have capitalized on this powerful effect. When we rent cars, our credit cards—not to mention our own car insurance—automatically cover us should anything go wrong with the vehicle. But the rental companies push additional coverage that not only is redundant but would cost a whopping $5,000 on an annual basis. Normally, we'd scoff at such a waste of money. But then, as the sales rep behind the counter is about to hand over the keys to that newish Ford Taurus, he asks whether we'd like to buy the *loss damage* waiver. When we hear those words, our minds begin to whir: What if I have bad luck and end up in a wreck? What if, for some reason, my credit card won't cover me after all? Normally, we'd never dream of taking out an extra policy at an astronomical rate just to be doubly safe, but the threat of a loss makes us reconsider.[6]

---

[6]Ori Brafman and Rom Brafman, *Sway: The Irresistible Pull of Irrational Behavior.* Broadway Books, 2009.

The most interesting aspect of this theory when it comes to the workplace is that this loss-aversion approach ("be careful with the employment decisions you make, since every step is a landmine that might get you embroiled in an ugly lawsuit"), is not only irrational, it's also counterproductive.

It's what I call the *litigation-avoidance paradox*. Using scare tactics—don't do this or that because you *might* get sued, don't take that action because it will be used against you later—is not only irrational (and ineffective if your goal is to affect behavior), the paradox is that it is *exactly* this mentality— we don't care about culture, we only care about compliance—that vastly increases the likelihood that a lawsuit will be filed.

In short, the more steps you take to avoid an employment-related lawsuit, paradoxically, the more likely you are to have one filed against you.

In fact, let's extend the hiking metaphor and talk about the fear of getting attacked by a mountain lion. Despite the reality that mountain lions often roam, well, in the mountains, this doesn't stop brave hikers from going out to enjoy a hike.

Does this mean that the wise and careful hiker goes out after he's read about numerous sightings of mountain lions in a certain area? Of course not. These are the types of issues a hiker will take into account when preparing to go out to enjoy nature.

A question asked and answered in a useful guide about mountain lions is:

Q: "Are mountain lions dangerous?"

A: "To deer, yes! To people, not so much. Human encounters with mountain lions are rare and the risk of an attack is infinitely small. You are more likely to drown in your bathtub, be killed by a pet dog, or hit by lightning. If lions had any natural urge to hunt people, there would be attacks every single day. Instead, they avoid us."[7]

Similarly, am I suggesting that you throw caution to the wind and embark on your journey to the top of the Healthy Workplace Culture Pyramid with no fears whatsoever? Hardly. What I'm saying instead is that

---

[7]"Frequently Asked Questions." Mountain Lion Foundation. http://mountainlion.org/ FAQfrequentlyaskedquestions.asp.

rational fear, fear that corresponds to the actual dangers, should be your guide. And if the irrational fear of encountering the mountain lions of the workplace—lawsuits—is keeping you from making the trek up the pyramid, then you're missing out on one heck of a journey.

How Do We Resist That Tempting Pull to Behave Irrationally?

The informational website about mountain lions goes on:

> [I]f you live, work, or play in cat country, **be alert!** Avoid walking alone between dusk and dawn when lions are most active. Keep your children and pets close to you. Never approach or corner a mountain lion (or any wild animal). If you do encounter a mountain lion, **STOP. DO NOT RUN**. Unlike safety advice for encountering bears, do not act timid or play dead in front of a cat. Instead: Maintain eye contact. Stand tall. Look bigger by opening your coat or raising your arms. Slowly wave your arms and speak firmly. Throw items at the lion if necessary. Give the cat room and time to move on. In the rare event of an attack, fight back. Most people succeed in driving the mountain lion away.[8]

It's good advice that can be applied to conquer fears you might have as you make your way to the top of the pyramid. Here's how:

- Be alert! I'm not suggesting that you ignore compliance. Of course you should comply with legal mandates. What I am advising you is to stay alert so you don't fall into the trap of decision-making that is ruled exclusively by an *irrational* fear of being sued.
- If you encounter a hazard, don't let your fear sway you back to the "they're out to get me so I should do things to avoid a lawsuit or defend myself" mentality. It'll backfire every time. Instead, take a deep breath, remember that the chances of an incident becoming a legal claim are miniscule, and proceed with best practices that you know will improve your culture; do not just minimally comply with the law.

---

[8] Ibid.

- Keep in mind the paradox at play when your culture is one that seeks only to treat employees as individuals waiting for a gotcha moment they'll use to sue you—by taking this approach, you will actually increase the chance of having a claim filed against you (more on this in the "Fairness" section below).

At the end of this chapter, I'll discuss what thousands of project managers already know about prudent corporate decision-making: The analysis must take into account both risks *and* opportunities. While conducting an assessment of reasonable risk is important, you're only doing half the job if you stop there.

Think of the opportunities nature lovers would miss if they based their decision about whether to go on a hike on the risk associated with encountering an unlikely danger like a mountain lion, without taking into account the fabulous opportunities that come from taking a journey up a beautiful mountain. This metaphor should help you stay on track with making it to the top of this workplace mountain—and once you're there, you'll see the view is spectacular and the trip well worth the effort.

Fairness

I've spent a substantial percentage of my career focusing on the issue of fairness—actual and perceived. My guess is that you probably have, too. Whether you're a C-suite executive, a mid-level manager, an HR professional, or new to your career, you've surely heard people talk about being victims of unfairness at work. While some individuals may instinctively reach for the cliché response, "Life's not fair," this dismissive answer won't reduce your workplace drama. This response will also do nothing to help you make your way up the pyramid that ultimately gets you to a healthy, inclusive, and drama-free workplace.

Actual Fairness

Actual fairness involves facts. Was it fair that your supervisor criticized your performance? If your performance description was accurate, then probably so. Was it fair if others were making the same mistakes as you, but he singled you out for criticism? No, selective fairness isn't fairness. Was it fair that you were chosen for the layoff? If the company established criteria based on their best business judgment and followed that criteria in a consistent and objective way, then yes, it was fair. But, is it fair if you were passed over for a well-deserved promotion and the position was instead given to the boss's unqualified son? No—this not only sounds like nepotism, it also sounds like a terrible business decision.

That said, fairness doesn't mean treating everyone in the exact same way. In the employment context, factors that influence actual fairness involve consistency and transparency. Of course, attitudes toward fairness vary, but there are definitely instances in which unfair decisions are made, no matter what your definition of fairness.

Perceived Fairness

Actual fairness is not the end of the story when we talk about justice at work. Equally important is the *perception* of fairness.

There's an entire branch of organizational psychology dedicated to the study of "organizational justice," or the perception of workplace fairness. Specifically, it focuses on employee perceptions of their organization's behavior, decisions, and actions and how these influence the employee's own attitudes and behavior at work. Numerous studies have focused on different types of organizational justice and how they influence employee attitudes regarding trust and productivity, as well as the likelihood of an employee quitting, engaging in counterproductive behavior, or suing after a termination.

Social scientists have identified three types of organizational justice:

1. *Procedural justice:* Whether the organization has established a procedure to handle a variety of workplace issues and whether the established procedure is consistently followed. Employees perceive fairness when:
   - There is an established procedure, and that procedure is made clear up front.
   - No person or group is singled out during the resolution process.
   - Decisions are based on the collection of accurate and full information.

- Companies make important decisions only after receiving input from all stakeholders.
- The company establishes a process to appeal decisions.
- The company follows generally accepted norms of professional conduct.

2. *Distributive justice:* Whether rewards and punishments are distributed in an even-handed way. Employees have a perception of fairness if:
   - They work at an organization that rewards employees based on their contributions, thus fostering a sense of equity.
   - Their organization makes decisions about compensation and other benefits based on objective criteria, avoiding large variances in salary within similar positions.

3. *Interactional justice:* Whether employees are treated respectfully and professionally by immediate managers and other leaders. This involves two interrelated components:
   1. Interpersonal justice; and
   2. Informational justice (whether relevant information is shared with employees).

Researchers have studied whether recently terminated employees are more likely to file a legal claim if they perceived procedural, distributive, and/or interactional unfairness.[9] The study analyzed other issues, but in terms of the connection between filing a legal claim and the perception of organizational unfairness, they found that *employees are less likely to pursue legal action when they perceive that the company followed fair procedures for their termination (high procedural justice) and/or when the employees feel that the company handled the termination with respect and sensitivity (high interactional justice).* The study concluded that managers could "use fair procedures or considerate treatment to mitigate the harshness of layoffs . . . on workers." *Put differently, perceived fairness can go a long way in avoiding legal issues with employees.*

---

[9]B. M. Goldman, "The Application of Referent Cognitions Theory to Legal-Claiming by Terminated Workers: The Role of Organizational Justice and Anger," *Journal of Management*, 29, no. 5 (2003): 705–728. https://doi.org/10.1016/S0149-2063_03_00032-1.

I've seen the importance of perceived fairness throughout my career and have studied it extensively because it plays such an important role in both the creation and resolution of workplace drama. Anyone who has conducted multiple workplace investigations has likely developed the ability to identify the moment when an issue went from being merely bothersome to truly reportable—thus requiring a formal investigation (more on this in Chapter 6). In a significant percentage of cases, those tipping points involved the *perception* of unfairness—perhaps a company leader took a procedural shortcut, the supervisor was dismissive or rude, or an employee failed to get a promotion, which she saw as the last straw in a much longer chain of unfair events.

Goldman's findings—that perceived injustice is a vital component in an employee's decision to sue her employer—are an important final link to explain the *litigation-avoidance paradox*. As discussed above, the paradox begins with the pull employers feel to follow the irrational argument that creating a compliance-focused environment is the best way to manage legal risk. Goldman's research helps to define why this is not only irrational, but paradoxical. You see, the research is clear; when deciding whether to file a lawsuit against their employer, employees very often care less about *what* was done, and more about *how* it was done. Inconsistency in following an established procedure, a lack of an even-handed distribution of rewards and punishments, and disrespectful treatment increase the likelihood that an employee will be motivated to sue. So the advice to approach employment decisions in a cold, unfeeling, compliance-only manner actually increases the probability that an employee will perceive injustice and sue.

Stated in a positive way: An employee who disagrees with an employment decision but perceives the decision was made via a fair procedure, and feels the decision was communicated respectfully, is not likely to become a plaintiff.

This statement is not only supported by research and my own experience. I've heard the same thing from plaintiffs, counsel for plaintiffs, and mediators who oversee employment-related disputes. In speaking to them, I've heard hundreds of similar stories: the employee would have been willing to "let go" an unfair decision if only their employer had treated them humanely, with respect, empathy, authenticity, and transparency.

What Corporate Decision Has the Greatest Impact on the Perception of Fairness?

In my experience, there is no example that is more powerful when it comes to perceived unfairness than the uneven distribution of "punishments" (discipline) after someone is found to have engaged in misconduct. This type of skewed decision-making creates endless workplace drama (and contributes to a higher probability of becoming embroiled in a legal claim).

It's impossible to maintain a healthy, inclusive culture—regardless of compensation, benefits, and engagement—if the corporate message is that rules, or consequences for violating those rules, apply only to certain employees.

This issue is particularly prevalent in sexual misconduct cases. While media, entertainment, and tech sectors have dominated the news cycle when it comes to stories of turning a blind eye to allegations of sexual harassment, there are a number of industries dealing with this issue behind the scenes—especially those where certain employees are perceived as highly valuable. Rainmakers and top producers are too often allowed to get away with behavior that's unacceptable according to company policy and values statements because they're considered indispensable.

Only enforcing policies among employees deemed replaceable is a guaranteed way to create a toxic environment of perceived, and actual, unfairness.

I've conducted hundreds of investigations that involved high-producing sales employees, law firm partners perceived as big rainmakers, and financial services executives whose client list was seen as simply too big to lose to a competitor. Employees watch these situations very closely and too often they don't like what they see. We're all familiar with these common stories: a law firm partner who is repeatedly accused of sexual harassment but whose accusers are fired or convinced to settle in exchange for their silence; a harasser who is allowed to continue his behavior and is even emboldened to intensify his inappropriate actions; a VP of sales who is having a thinly veiled affair with a subordinate but whose leaders look the other way, because an "affair" is none of their business.

This—the effect of uneven discipline based primarily on the perceived value of the person engaging in misconduct—is an actual hazard but, interestingly, one that rarely receives the same type of litigation-risk analysis as do other, more innocuous workplace decisions. Instead, while companies do conduct a risk-analysis in these scenarios, the analysis is based almost exclusively on the potential loss the company will suffer (in terms of revenue, notoriety, or some other benefit the "high value" employee brings) if they lose the person who engaged in the misconduct.

The problem with this analysis is two-fold. First, as I discussed in Chapter 2, this analysis involves flawed math since the company uses a formula that includes addition (revenue in), but neglects subtraction (expenses out as a result of legal fees, settlement, lower productivity, brand reputation, turnover, etc.).

But there is another problem with this analysis: It fails to take into account the effect it has on the employees who might hear "we want to have a healthy and fair workplace" but see "when we say 'fair' we recognize that some employees are more equal than others."

Ignoring the negative impact perceived (or actual) unfairness has on your ability to make it to the top of the pyramid is dangerous and will likely make your path steeper and more treacherous than it needs to be.

Conversely, analyzing the opportunities and benefits that come from having a workplace that is both actually fair and is perceived as such will go a long way toward reaching the pinnacle: a drama-free workplace.

What would your employees say if you asked them whether rewards and punishments were evenly distributed at your company? Would they immediately reply that your organization has a fair and transparent process for handling allegations of misconduct, and that if misconduct is found leaders impose even-handed, fair discipline?

Unless your answer is a resounding "yes," you have a problem with the perception of fairness at your organization. That perceived unfairness is a key ingredient that can incite workplace drama.

Freedom

James Madison said this of the Constitution: "It will be of little avail to the people that the laws are made by men of their own choice if the laws be so voluminous that they cannot be read, or so incoherent that they cannot be understood." Even in the 18th century, it was recognized that overregulation and tedious, exhaustive rulebooks aren't the best way to manage large groups of people—be they countries or companies.

Given the focus on compliance, however, having fewer rules might sound counterintuitive to many managers and HR leaders. It might even sound irresponsible. But, companies who treat their employees like responsible adults are more likely to hire and retain responsible employees and experience less workplace drama. In fact, the more rules an organization has, the more likely it is to lose highly intelligent, capable employees due to the sheer tedium of silly, unnecessary rules that limit their creativity and success.

Since we are comparing our journey to an invigorating, even if somewhat strenuous, hike up a metaphorical mountain, imagine the difference between going up a mountain that has necessary guardrails—security measures that will, for example, keep you from falling—but does not have barriers that keep you from exploring the natural beauty that drove you to the mountain in the first place, and even allows you the freedom to forge a new path.

> Organizations need structure, which typically comes in the form of rules. Some rules are essential—health and safety rules, for example—and some are legally mandated. But, we're often guilty of taking rules too far, turning them into restrictive handcuffs rather than necessary guidelines for appropriate, professional, and safe behavior.

In a healthy workplace culture—one in which employees have been vetted not only for knowledge, skills, and abilities (KSAs), but also for emotional maturity and commitment to success—leaders don't use rules as a means to exert more and more control over their employees. In fact, rules in such thriving workplace cultures don't restrict employee freedom—they enhance it.

But what does this kind of freedom look like? Wouldn't it be utter chaos? How can we let go of our detailed, structured rulebooks that delineate every nuance of what's allowed and what's not and begin to structure rules that enhance employee freedom?

Step 1: Reinvent Rule-Making

First, we must rethink the way we design and enforce rules. Often, the issue isn't with the rules themselves, but rather with the failure to design and enforce truly useful rules. Company policies and guidelines are filled with unnecessary, poorly thought-out rules that serve little to no purpose. Before addressing a workplace issue by instituting yet another rule, ask yourself these two questions:

1. Does the rule really solve a problem or address a question?
2. Are you actually prepared to enforce that rule? If so, how?

Without asking *and* answering these questions, it's easy to create count-less new rules that employees will see as arbitrary and restrictive—which translates into illogical and unnecessary. This creates a strong incentive for employees to work around these perceived unnecessary rules.

Take the rules about tending to personal work during work hours that companies sometimes develop but either don't enforce or do so sporadi-cally. Does your rule about prohibiting work email to be used for personal purposes apply when the company VP uses the email system to let everyone know his daughter is selling Girl Scout cookies and that the order forms are in the kitchen? Or is the issue that you trust your employees will use their good judgment when they use work email and when they solicit their colleagues? Will you really enforce your rule banning employees from using the internet to do online shopping or to check their Facebook status? Or is the real issue that you're concerned about people either wasting time online (instead of doing their work)? Or perhaps you have an employee who gets all her work done quickly and needs more of a challenge. The point is not to encourage your employees to ignore rules by creating unnecessary or overly controlling policies that serve no real purpose.

Too many companies think it's better to have a rule for everything. They spend an inordinate amount of time crafting carefully worded rules without stopping to ask and answer the two critical questions above. This often comes back to haunt them in a variety of ways, including:

- *Frequent violation of certain rules* that employees don't understand or that make their jobs more difficult. Make sure that necessary rules are clearly explained in order to encourage compliance.

- *Employees feel overly controlled and mistrusted* due to unnecessary or arbitrary rules, leading them to distrust leadership and negatively impacting team productivity. Ensure that every rule is well thought out and all ramifications are considered before putting it into place.
- *People develop an inflexible, rules-based mindset* that can quickly become counterproductive. Picture a conference security guard requiring that a baby have a badge to enter the event because of a rule stating that everyone must have a badge (a true story from a conference I recently attended). That type of rigid mindset isn't helping anyone!
- *A hasty new policy creates three more problems* as a result. Avoid quickly developing a new rule to deal with a single, specific issue without first doing your research and talking it through with your team.

Step 2: Give Employees Freedom by Treating Them Like Adults

Second, let's start treating employees like responsible grown-ups. It's time for company leaders to act less like middle-school hall monitors and more like the middle-school teacher who encouraged you to explore and be curious. Yes, there will be people who need more detailed guidance than the official rules provide, but that's exactly what your senior leaders and middle managers are there to do—provide specific guidance and leadership to their teams when needed.

Not convinced that this type of slimmed-down rulebook can actually work? Let's take a look at the dress code policy at General Motors (GM).[10] When she became CEO of GM, Mary Barra dramatically changed the dress code policy at the company from a bloated, 10-page policy to two words: "Dress appropriately." This guideline certainly doesn't mean the same thing to every employee at GM—appropriate dress for a GM factory worker will be totally different from that of a GM business executive. But, instead of mandating exactly what every type of employee should and shouldn't be wearing, Barra left it up to the individual leaders and managers to determine appropriate work attire with their employees.

---

[10]Leah Fessler, "GM's Dress Code Is Only Two Words," *Quartz at Work*, April 3, 2018. https://qz.com/work/1242801/gms-dress-code-is-only-two-words/.

Barra made this change in policy to help improve workplace culture and cut out ridiculous regulations, but it wasn't an easy change for the company to make. From HR to senior leaders, Barra faced negative feedback and complaints about the nonspecificity of the policy. She had to encourage leaders of individual teams and sections of the company to discuss with their employees the most appropriate dress for their specific jobs. Ultimately, though, the change paid off. Not only did it limit the burdensome dress code, it empowered employees and management to responsibly decide their own needs and exercise a measure of independence and leadership.

The GM dress code is just one dramatic example of how companies can create far too many rules that serve little to no purpose. Instead of focusing on creating a rule for every possible scenario, companies should focus on creating commonsense policies that their senior and middle managers can address in more detail as needed with their teams and employees.

Creating thoughtful rules and policies that protect your employees and company, without overburdening or overregulating them, takes thought, time, and effort. It's easy to just address every little issue that arises with a new, specific rule that everyone has to follow until one day you have your own 10-page dress code that no one reads and everyone resents just a tad. That route leads to lots of silly, unnecessary rules that most employees won't take the time to learn, let alone follow.

Give your employees—and the managers enforcing the rules—back a little of their freedom by remembering that they're responsible adults that you hired for a reason. Resist the urge to create more red tape and you'll encourage your employees to take an interest in the rules and regulations that *are* in place for everyone's safety and the benefit of the entire workplace. By emphasizing fewer rules and more adulting, you'll be well on your way to keeping your workplace drama free, and you'll clear a path that will make it that much easier to reach the top of the Healthy Workplace Culture Pyramid.

Why Your Hike Requires Measuring Risk *and* Opportunity

Now that you've started your brisk but invigorating walk to reach the pinnacle—a drama-free workplace—you need to put fearlessness, fairness, and freedom into action. One important way to do that is to study risk and opportunity management.

Although this concept is familiar to project managers, it might not be familiar to everyone. After a time during which project managers only looked at risk management, the decision-making model evolved and a new approach was introduced—one that continues to measure risk, but also recognizes that every decision along the way might also present an opportunity.

"Risk and opportunity management" provides a method to identify, assess, and reduce uncertainty in a structured way. The uncertainties inherent in the development of any project can have a negative impact (risks) or a positive impact (opportunities). It is therefore just as important to look at the opportunities created by taking a particular route as it is to measure and prepare for the risks associated with that decision.

Since the question of risk management is one that most decision-makers have been grappling with for years (focusing on the legal risk of making a particular employment decision), the important missing piece is what opportunity management looks like when embarking on your quest to make it to the top of the Healthy Workplace Culture Pyramid.

Does this mean doing away with legal risk management? No. But it does mean that companies would be wise to add an additional step when implementing a large-scale program to improve their workplace culture. This step should highlight the endless opportunities and benefits that come from having an employee base that is loyal, engaged, feels as though they truly belong, and will be active participants on your journey to the top of the Healthy Workplace Culture Pyramid.

This could be as simple as calculating the savings because of an expected decrease in turnover or the increase in revenue and profit because of the expected increased engagement and productivity. You could also look at the cost of conflict in the workplace and look at the opportunities presented by a steep reduction in conflict. Or you might track something even more tangible, like the decrease in the number of sick days that employees take as a result of their own health improving right along with the health of your organization.

By looking at the opportunities created by being fearless, providing fairness, and giving your employees freedom, you'll be able to ease your path as you develop a workplace free of drama.

6

Anticipating and Preparing for Drama-Causing Events

Assuming you're able to resist the pull of irrational fear when deciding whether to make the trek to the top of the Healthy Workplace Culture Pyramid, you might astutely recognize the need to identify hazards that you might encounter along the way. And you might equally recognize the need to identify ways to avoid or prepare for these potential threats.

Anticipating Workplace Drama

Too few companies identify critical turning points, moments in time that inevitably give rise to workplace drama. Although my experience as an investigator brought me to the workplace when a crisis was already unfolding, I was able to identify the point in time when a conflict turned into full-blown drama. I could write a timeline that spotted the moment a decision was made, an action was taken (or not taken) or a word was spoken (or not spoken) that turned run-of-the-mill workplace strife into full-blown drama.

101

I began to see patterns and categorized the triggers that helped to predict drama and also identified steps companies could and should take to head drama off at the pass.

Many drama triggers are behavior-based and are outlined in detail in the chapters about sexual harassment (Chapter 2), bias and diversity (Chapter 3), and ethics lapses (Chapter 4). But what I've seen over and over in the workplace is drama triggered not only by the way in which someone was treated (disrespectful interaction), but also because of:

- A perception of unfair decision-making related to a process (either the company has no process in place, making it impossible for the employee to feel the decision was fair, or there is a process but it is applied unevenly).
- A perception that rewards and punishments are unevenly distributed.

This chapter focuses on the triggers related to these perceptions of unfairness and provides practical ways to eliminate these triggers, therefore eliminating the drama that would usually follow them.

Leading Drama Producer: Corporate Change

Charles Darwin said, "It's not the strongest or most intelligent who will survive, but those who can best manage change."

We all know people are afraid of change. But despite knowing this, we seem to forget this axiom when we're going through a corporate transformation. There are a number of organizational changes that, if handled poorly, are a guaranteed entry into the world of workplace drama.

Corporate Reorganizations

Dawn was an employee at a global company who felt left out of the decision-making process during a departmental reorganization. Even worse, she said, under the new structure she no longer had any direct reports. She therefore considered her new position a demotion, even though she retained the same pay and title. She was embarrassed by what she perceived as a position downgrade.

To add insult to injury, her colleagues kept asking her about her new role, with the knowing implication, she felt, that her contribution was clearly not valued since her voice meant nothing during the decision-making process.

She was also upset at the way her leaders rolled out the new plan. Although she knew department leaders were working on some kind of reorganization, she didn't know when it would be implemented and was taken aback when she received an email about her new role, with no explanation or ability to ask questions. She eventually met with HR to tell them she felt unfairly treated.

After conducting many investigations with similar facts and allegations, I saw a few common themes emerge—themes that created a sense of unfairness and gave rise to drama.

Decision Turning Points: Triggers and Resolution

Drama Trigger: Working in a silo.

In every one of my investigations triggered by reorganizations, the team in charge of making decisions about organizational changes was committed, eager, and approached its work in good faith. When I reviewed their work, I saw agendas, timelines, memos, draft documents with notes, several versions of presentations, notes on the committee's weighing of pros and cons of taking one path over another, and cost analysis. But in every instance there was another pattern— little or (usually) no employee participation, and little participation from middle managers who would be tasked with executing the details of the reorganization.

When the team rolled out the plan to the employees who would be affected by the change, those employees had not been a part of the planning process and were therefore unfamiliar with both the plan itself and the reason for the change. The result? Resistance to the proposed changes, at least by those who believed the new structure hurt them personally. They perceived the plan to be directly detrimental to their professional growth.

Solution: Collaborate and include.

☑ Involve line managers and employees in decision-making. They have their finger on the pulse of how the change will affect them.

☑ Develop a way for employees and middle managers to provide that input. Make sure it doesn't interfere with the timeline to complete your work, but provides them with a forum to be heard.

☑ Since those directly affected will take the changes personally, consider having private meetings with those whose role will change (duties and/or reporting structure) to go through their own implementation plan.

☑ For those with new reporting structures, anticipate questions/concerns about what might be perceived as a demotion or a lack of appreciation for the value they bring.

☑ For those with new job duties, seek their input as you develop a new job description and consider providing additional training if they will be expected to perform new or different tasks.

Involve those who will be affected by the decisions. This doesn't necessarily mean the process will come down to a democratic vote, or that employees have to participate in every phase, but it does mean that they are provided with some forum to make suggestions, point out possible flaws, or offer alternatives.

Doing this improves the process in two ways. First, it improves the decision making itself since input for all will allow the decision-making team to sidestep avoidable errors. Second, inviting and welcoming participation from those who will be most affected by the changes will increase the likelihood that they will fully understand the reasons for the change, will accept the changes, and will become champions for advocating for the value of the changes.

And, of course, doing this diminishes the likelihood that those affected will view the changes as unfair and therefore reduces the incidence of workplace drama.

Drama Trigger: Poor execution.

Too often, all effort is put into designing the plan, with little or no effort put into implementation and execution. All the beautiful presentation slides and graphics will do nothing to help explain how this will affect the individuals who hold the positions in the organizational charts. I've seen this play out in the following ways:

- Poor communication in rollout. Sending out a surprise email with final decisions is always a recipe for dissatisfaction. What's worse is a plan rollout that fails to explain the big picture. You need more than explaining that a change is being made, you also need to explain why the change is necessary and will be better for all in the long run.

- Tone deafness in rollout. In addition to failing to explain the reasons for the change and highlighting how the changes are aligned with the company's mission and values, too often organizations fail to recognize the good work done by the team so far and only focus on how much better things will be under this new structure. The implication, from the viewpoint of many employees, is that the "old" way of doing things was bad.

- Ignoring the challenges ahead. Organizations often also fail to recognize that change is hard. In their zeal to present their plan in a positive way (which is a good place to start), the message becomes, "anyone who reacts negatively to our proposed changes is just a Debbie Downer." While maintaining a positive and can-do approach is great, it's okay to authentically admit that you understand that change is hard and that there will be bumps in the road as you execute the new plan.

Solution: Thoughtful implementation.

- ☑ Help employees understand the big picture since doing so will provide an additional way to connect employees to the company's overall mission, and gets everyone on board with where the company is headed.
- ☑ Be specific about why the changes are being made, how the changes are expected to positively impact the company/department, and provide a step-by-step plan about how the changes will be implemented.
- ☑ Recognize achievements under the previous structure and explain the business need for the change.
- ☑ Do not refer to the "old" system or the "old" way of doing things.
- ☑ Be honest about potential challenges and offer support throughout the implementation process.
- ☑ Explain how long it will take to implement the changes and identify what you know might make implementation more challenging.

Helping guide employees through the inevitable angst associated with change greatly reduces the chance that you'll have to deal with unnecessary workplace drama. Taking these practical steps will help.

Drama Trigger: No why and how.

Too often those who are given the task of implementing the plan are left flat-footed. They are given few if any resources to answer questions—high-level ones about the purpose of the changes, as well as specific ones about the step-by-step implementation plan. Without these resources, these key managers either provide inaccurate information or, even worse, admit that they don't understand the need for change and blame "management" for making unnecessary changes. This is a recipe for disastrous drama.

Solution: Provide thoughtful resources.

☑ In addition to meeting with the managers who will communicate the plan, develop scripts for them to help them precisely and persuasively communicate the why and the how (see Chapter 8 for more on communicating precisely and persuasively).

☑ Develop a comprehensive but easy-to-understand FAQ document to proactively address inevitable questions.

Leadership Changes

Since any type of change is a leading trigger for drama, it's no surprise that a change in leadership, whether at the department or organization level, is yet another cause for drama. But you can implement safeguards to prevent that drama.

1. **Bringing in an "outsider"**

   Karim applied for the department supervisor position. He felt fully qualified; he not only had the technical skills to do the job, he was also well-liked by his peers, all of whom assumed he was a shoo-in for the promotion.

   Alma, the department VP, had a different idea though. She thought it was important to bring in a lateral candidate with more industry experience to help her implement a plan to modernize the entire business unit. Although Alma interviewed Karim and gave him positive feedback, she ultimately hired an outside candidate from a competing company.

Karim was disappointed and his coworkers promised him they'd never accept the new supervisor and would make her life difficult.

2. Promoting an "insider"

Meanwhile, at another company, Alicia did get the internal promotion she wanted. She'd worked hard to showcase her technical expertise and now she finally is getting her chance to lead her department. There's only one problem: She's not quite sure how to transition from peer to manager. She hasn't received any guidance on how to make that tricky transformation. Without guidance, all she can do is continue to treat the employees as friends and colleagues, hoping that's enough to motivate them.

3. Leadership change at the top

And at yet another company, the board of directors decided, after lots of handwringing, that their CEO had to go. He hadn't been meeting goals and was accused of misconduct to boot. They placed an interim CEO but last month they finally found and placed a new CEO, George, who promised to ring in a new era of corporate success. Industry leaders praised the decision and the company employees were excited.

Unfortunately, that excitement quickly wore off when, within 30 days of joining the company, George made two huge changes. First, he changed numerous processes, claiming he knew a better way to do business. He also "let go" some top-level employees. The replacement employees who made up his "new team" were all former colleagues of his.

From the employee standpoint, every message George sent was "Your 'old' way of doing things was clearly a failure. There's a new sheriff in town with bigger and better ideas. I'll revolutionize this place and I only have use for team members who are fully on board with my ideas."

The surprising issue in each of these examples is how unsurprising the results were. Failing to implement change methodically and thoughtfully predictably leads to drama. But there are things you can do to prevent it.

Decision Turning Points: Triggers and Resolution

Drama Trigger: An "outsider" in our midst.

In the first scenario, the company failed to anticipate how loyal the department employees (including the one who was passed over) would feel and how much they would resist the new department leader. This common scenario presents three different drama traps. First, if handled badly, the internal candidate will wreak havoc because of the disappointment and embarrassment for not being selected for the position. Second, the other department employees might choose to make the new lateral employee's life difficult, thus greatly diminishing the likelihood of a successful transition. And third, the new candidate will feel ambushed if you don't properly prepare her.

Solution: Pave a smooth road.

- ☑ Give the new manager information about the internal candidate's application and identify any possible challenges ahead (without saying anything negative about the internal candidate).
- ☑ Get the internal applicant on board by fully and respectfully explaining why you decided to go with the outside candidate.
- ☑ Give the internal candidate a path for success and recruit him to be an advocate for the new manager.
- ☑ Talk to the department employees, individually or together depending on what's most appropriate, to gain their confidence and assurance that they will give the new manager a fair shot at success.
- ☑ Work with the new manager to develop a transition plan.

Hiring managers often feel trapped in these situations. Should they just tell the new manager everything, they ask themselves, or will that sound like unnecessary gossip? Isn't it better, they often conclude, to provide little information? While it's true that engaging in gossip is wrong (and a big contributor to drama), leaving the new manager in the dark is equally dangerous. Hiring managers should develop a way to speak with the new manager to prepare her for the challenges that come from being the new kid on the block.

Drama Trigger: Transition from peer to boss.

In the second example, Alicia is promoted for her technical ability, but left stranded on how to be a manager. This scenario is bad enough in a situation where Alicia joins a new department, but it's particularly treacherous if she also needs to navigate the dangerous colleague-to-boss transition waters. How is she supposed to evaluate, motivate, coach, and maybe even discipline or fire her friends and former colleagues?

Solution: Pave a smooth road.

- ☑ Develop a robust new manager training course that covers general management skills as well as manager issues unique to your company and culture.
- ☑ Start with the most pressing issues, especially the skills needed to transition from nonmanager to manager, particularly if you are supervising former peers.
- ☑ Develop a training course that covers other management skills, but offer the training at intervals, because you don't want to overwhelm the new manager.
- ☑ Consider assigning a mentor or an ambassador, another employee-to-manager veteran to whom the new manager can turn with questions or concerns.
- ☑ Do not place unrealistic expectations on the new manager.
- ☑ Do not expect the new manager to address serious performance concerns with someone who was the manager's peer just a few weeks or months earlier. Assign someone else to initially handle performance issues that need to be addressed immediately.

When I interview nonmanagers, a large percentage of them tell me that their goal is to "get into management." This is an admirable goal and when an employee finally achieves this milestone there is initial happiness. Keep those positive vibes going by implementing a transition plan to help the new manager understand that while technical ability got them the job, management skills will be key to succeeding in the job.

*One important note that applies to newly hired department managers (whether hired laterally or from within) is the new boss who sets performance expectations that are completely different from his predecessor's. Employees will see new expectations as unfair if their performance was previously judged as acceptable but now, under a new boss, is deemed to be below expectations. If there are concerns, be careful not to be the "zero-to-60" boss who decides it's his job to fix long-standing but previously unaddressed performance issues ASAP.

Drama Trigger: Quick-triggered leader.

In the final scenario, the board and the search committee for a new CEO made a huge assumption—that a leader experienced enough to take the highest position at their organization would be savvy enough to move slowly and deliberately. This seems obvious, but it's startling how often even experienced high-level leaders fall into the trap of "too much too fast."

Solution: Set expectations.

☑ Know ahead of time whether the new leader plans to bring in his own team and help him develop a timeline and a plan to do that.

☑ Remind the new leader to take an observe-and-learn approach before making any major changes.

☑ Develop a timeline for the "watch and learn" period before you expect the new leader will make any substantive organizational changes (a 90-day time period is typical).

☑ Anticipate and be prepared to answer questions about whether there will be a change in the corporate culture as a result of the new leader's style.

☑ Encourage the leader to bring in innovative ideas to improve the business, but know ahead of time if there will be a seismic shift in how business will be conducted.

While a board doesn't want to tell a new leader how to do his job, some parameters can and should be set. A vital parameter is to remind the executive of the dangers of creating the wrong perception when he moves too quickly, and when he brings in a new team and gives the message that the company had been doing everything wrong prior to his arrival.

The bottom line is that change is hard. On everyone. Accept that and plan for some level of resistance and the difficulties associated with corporate change will become infinitely easier to manage.

Leading Drama Producer: Faulty Processes that Lead to Poor Decision-Making

The failure to implement procedural safeguards often leads to bad decisions. These bad decisions lead to feelings of unfairness. Those feelings cause workplace drama.

There are numerous points in the employee life cycle that require clear procedures, but three that seem to cause a significant percentage of workplace drama occur during the hiring process, when reintegrating returning employees and when communicating about performance.

Bad Hiring Practices Lead to Bad Hiring Decisions

Recruiting and hiring are difficult tasks. They require subject matter expertise, constant learning to stay abreast of emerging trends, and organizational skills to develop a structure that is equal parts uniform and flexible. It's no wonder that top-notch talent acquisition and talent management professionals are sought after.

Unfortunately though, not all companies have the luxury of having folks dedicating all their time and talent to recruiting and hiring. In those cases, the organization has no plan or implements poor plans to recruit, interview, and hire. This, of course, leads to drama.

Consider this real-life scenario: Angela is a high-energy recent college graduate. She graduated with a degree in supply chain management and worked as an intern at a large, established defense contractor one summer. She is thrilled when she gets an interview with a company that is working on various exciting and cutting-edge projects. The company has funding but is still in the start-up phase.

The department manager, Jose, meets Angela at a college recruiting fair and is impressed. She's smart, articulate, well credentialed, and excited about the work they're doing. It seems like a natural fit.

A few months into her work at the company, Jose is utterly disappointed. Angela is a high-maintenance diva who doesn't understand that at startups, everyone is expected to wear multiple hats and get in the trenches. Angela is equally disappointed and believes the company is teetering on the edge of committing ethics violations because they are understaffed, overworked, and have no processes in place.

What became clear to me very quickly was that the critical moment in time occurred at the interview stage. Two ships (Angela and Jose) crossed in the night, both thinking they understood perfectly what was to come, but each was speaking to the other in a foreign language.

What also became clear was that this moment in time was allowed to occur because the company had done no work to prepare a smooth path for the hiring managers to select qualified, vetted, and knowledgeable candidates. What was missing?

- A process to identify the essential knowledge, skills, and abilities that a candidate needed to succeed
- Training on how to ask behavior-based questions during interviews so hiring managers didn't have to rely solely on a "gut reaction"
- Training to make sure that candidates understood the unique nature of working at a start-up company
- An objective method by which to grade or rank candidates

Angela thought her job at this exciting but new company would be exactly like the internship she'd had at the established but boring defense contractor. But due to a failure to use the right tools, this mistake led not only to an unhappy candidate and manager, but also to a claim by Angela that she was being treated unfairly.

Decision Turning Points: Triggers and Resolution

Drama Trigger: No process or training on interviewing and hiring.

The company failed to design and execute a process through which candidates could be fairly assessed for their relevant knowledge skills and abilities.

Solution: Implement a straightforward process and conduct necessary training.

- ☑ For effective recruitment and hiring, do the following:
  - ○ Make sure job postings accurately reflect not only the position's essential duties, but also address issues related to the company, industry, or culture.

○ Use tools like job descriptions and performance evaluations (assuming they are current) as reference points to craft your job posting.

○ Develop an interview process that gives all applicants a fair shot, with questions that focus on these same issues (job duties, corporate environment, industry nuances).

○ Train managers on how to reach a diverse pool of candidates.

○ Train managers on how to follow the established hiring protocol and on effective interview techniques.

○ Train managers on the dangers of unconscious bias that could negatively impact their decision-making.

By taking these steps, you are much more likely to make better decisions during the recruiting and hiring process and avoid unnecessary drama.

Reintegrating Returning Employees

All of us have either attended or been invited to attend a session on the intersection of laws related to leaves of absence. This area of law is complicated, often involving overlapping legal obligations and detailed record-keeping requirements. While these sessions are helpful to provide guidance on legal mandates, they usually don't cover the topic that I find causes workplace drama—how to reintegrate employees who are returning from pregnancy, worker's compensation, medical, or some other leave of absence.

Here are the two scenarios I've encountered most often:

1. During the leave:
   ○ An employee is out on leave (for whatever reason) and feels disconnected. In more drastic cases, they feel ignored or shunned. While they understand that their colleagues are continuing to do their work despite their absence, they wonder why no one is calling to ask how they're doing or to fill them in on news.
   ○ In the meantime, the company firmly believes that an unspoken "rule" when it comes to leave is that the employee who is out of work should be left alone (to recuperate, to bond with their child, etc.). They are busy and only pay attention to the issues related to the employees on leave once they return, or maybe a few days before they come back to work.

2. Once the employee returns:
   ○ The employee feels thrown back into the workplace, often returning to a different environment, perhaps with new structures, new employees, or changes in policies or practices. In the worst cases, they feel unfairly punished for having taken the leave—citing the fact that before they went on leave everything was fine, but now that they've returned things aren't the same.
   ○ The company assumes that returning employees will be able to become reintegrated easily and therefore usually puts in minimal effort to ease the transition back to work.

Decision Turning Points: Triggers and Resolution

Drama Trigger: Focus on paperwork before leave, no contact during leave.

Because leaves of absence involve documentation-heavy work, most of the focus is understandably on proper notice, proper tracking, and proper distribution of documents. While these are necessary steps, too often companies forget the human side of leaving work for an extended period of time and fail to set expectations about what will happen while the employee is gone. This leads to assumptions about what to expect and ultimately to drama.

Solution: Set expectations and parameters about contact during leave.

☑ Supplement your current leave protocol to make sure it includes talking about realistic expectations. Empathy and compassion are your friends during this process.
☑ Set clear expectations about contact while on leave:
   ○ If the employee is going out on a medical leave, for example, either set parameters about when (or if) that employee will be available or decide that there will be no contact to allow the employee to recuperate.
   ○ If the employee is in a job that requires some contact while on leave, set parameters for that as well.
☑ There is no hard-and-fast rule about checking in, sending a card, or taking some other action to show the employee they haven't been forgotten. Use your best judgment.

*Drama Trigger: **Failure to establish a reintegration protocol or a specific plan for each returning employee.***

Making assumptions is risky. It's especially risky when people make different assumptions (the company assumes reintegration will be easy; the employee assumes the company will have a reintegration plan in place). In the case of returning employees, companies who fail to plan to reintegrate returning employees do so at their own peril and can expect drama.

*Solution: **Establish a reintegration protocol.***

- ☑ Develop a packet of resources, from a checklist to an FAQ document with information and links to resources to help both employees who will be going out on leave and managers who have to handle the business issues that arise as a result of having an employee out on leave.
- ☑ Consider a "ramp down" and "ramp up" period for a short period of time before an employee goes out on leave and when they return.[1]

Evaluating Performance

When it comes to performance evaluations, giving feedback that is continuous, honest, and precise is your best bet. It's important to be candid and respectful, to provide both coaching and the necessary resources to succeed and to know when to make a determination that someone simply isn't well-suited for the position he or she holds. You do employees no favors by pretending they can do the job long after its obvious that's not the case.

And yet despite these obvious points related to providing performance feedback, too many supervisors fail to heed this advice. Instead, they fall into one of three traps. They might fail to provide any feedback, often waiting to drop a bomb on the employee when the annual evaluation is provided. Or they provide only criticism but fail to give the employee instructions

---

[1] Noodles & Company has provided this, as well as additional benefits associated with adoption, childbirth, and baby bonding. Stephen Miller, "Phased Maternity Leave Enhances Parental Benefits." Society for Human Resource Management (SHRM) online, September 26, 2018. https://www.shrm.org/ResourcesAndTools/hr-topics/benefits/Pages/phased-parental-leave.aspx?_ga=2.251657606.1032395813.1537973806-2052757120.1532623197.

on how to improve—and fail to provide the resources necessary to succeed. Or, based on advice they get about the "need to document," they check all the boxes about providing feedback, but do so in an inauthentic way that everyone knows is really just the perfunctory steps necessary to "justify" eventually terminating someone's employment.

I remember an investigation early in my career involving an HR manager who had worked for a small but growing city for over a decade. Over that time, despite mediocre performance, she'd been given stellar annual evaluations. When I interviewed her previous bosses, they cited the same reason for lying to her: They didn't want to hurt her feelings, especially since she tended to become overly emotional whenever they gave her any criticism.

Eventually, a new city manager decided it was time to tell her the truth about her performance deficiencies. Given that she'd never been criticized before, the HR manager assumed the criticism was actually gender bias. Although the evidence was clear that gender bias (or bias of any type) played no part in the evaluation of her performance, it was equally clear that her organization had done her a serious disservice. They'd lied to her. In their quest to be "nice," they'd failed to provide her with a great gift—a gift of truth and a promise to help her become a world-class HR director. (For more on being a "compassionate sharpshooter," see Chapter 8.)

Instead, she floundered. When I interviewed her and asked her to share with me her short- and long-term plans for dealing with the realities of a fast-growing city, she gave me a deer-in-headlights look and continued to tout her successes as a great HR administrator. She was very proud of the fact that the leave paperwork she filled out was in order and that no one had sued the city for any issues related to leave management. While this was certainly something to be proud of, she was the head of HR for a growing organization who still saw herself as a paper pusher. But having received no feedback or opportunities to develop and sharpen her leadership skills, she had no other accomplishments to hang her hat on.

Decision Turning Points: Triggers and Resolution

Drama Trigger: Failure to establish an authentic way to provide performance feedback.

Too many companies are filled with leaders and employees who dread the evaluation process because in many instances it has lost its true purpose.

There are a number of reasons to develop a system to continuously evaluate performance, including: to help an employee achieve peak performance; to help the company identify employees who need more time in a position versus those who are ready to move up; and to provide a two-way, mutually beneficial method to determine whether the employee is progressing. Instead, it is viewed by most as yet another example of an HR process that is mandatory but not very useful.

Solution: Establish an authentic process and communicate the goals of the process with managers and employees.

- ☑ Emphasize that performance feedback should be continuous, honest, and precise.
- ☑ Emphasize the fact that the company's goal is to evaluate, provide honest and respectful feedback, and use the evaluation process as yet another tool to improve the overall workplace culture.
- ☑ Design a system and provide effective training to teach people the skills to understand your company's commitment to providing honest and helpful feedback—for the good of the individual employee and the organization.
- ☑ When it comes time to give formal feedback (the annual review, for example):
  - ○ Make sure your forms and instructions are up-to-date and that they accurately reflect expectations. (You should compare the evaluation criteria to the job duties listed in the job description.)
  - ○ Provide helpful guidelines and training to managers—both on completing evaluation paperwork and meeting with employees.
  - ○ Provide a process to review written evaluations to ensure accuracy and consistency, and to serve as a resource for nervous managers.
  - ○ If you know the evaluation meeting will be difficult, offer the manager additional resources and even consider doing a practice evaluation meeting to address the emotion/reaction that is likely to arise during the meeting.
- ☑ Stay current on emerging trends about how to best manage issues related to performance.

Leading Drama Producer: Failure to Observe, Analyze, and Course-Correct

Bart was a rising star at a global organization. He was energetic, smart, and charming. He learned the business quickly and as a result was rewarded—financially and with several promotions—in only a few years. The only problem was that during that same time period, Bart also racked up a series of allegations related to his flirtatious personality, his tendency to hire and promote women who had a "certain look," and his growing reputation as a hard-partying bro who often interacted with "the boys" on his team (and male clients) as if he were still at his fraternity house.

Over a period of a few years, he had nine allegations of inappropriate and sexually charged conduct lodged against him. The only problem was that because this was a global company and because each investigation arose out of events in different parts of the country, they were all conducted by different internal investigators and the company's system was not integrated to show the series of allegations. The other problem was that in each and every investigation, the investigators reached a "finding" of "inconclusive" based solely on his denials (more on why this isn't enough evidence to reach a finding in Chapter 11).

As a result of this failure to coordinate, his immediate bosses (the decision-makers on raises and promotions) had no idea that Bart had been repeatedly accused of misconduct. And since he'd always been "cleared," Bart figured the allegations and the investigations that followed were simply a cost of doing business and of being a successful manager.

My investigation report included more than just a summary of evidence and my analysis; it also included a detailed timeline showing, in one column, his meteoric ascent into a high-level management position, and in another column, the allegations made about his conduct. In many instances, a raise or promotion came immediately after a claim of misconduct (though the person who approved the raise or promotion had no idea about the allegations).

In short, the organization failed to use tools, resources, and technology to track trends. In this case there was a serious failure to use tools to make decisions about one employee, but it was clear that their lack of reliable and comprehensive systems to track even basic information was having an organization-wide impact.

Decision Turning Points: Triggers and Resolution

Drama Trigger: Failure to implement systems to track trends and course-correct.

In very small organizations, everyone knows everything. But as organizations grow, it becomes harder to operate without the implementation of sophisticated systems to track trends, to identify what your company is doing well and where it can improve, and to course-correct if necessary. In the case of Bart's employer, the failure to have a centralized system to track important information critical for decision-makers to see before making employment decisions caused several unforced errors. It also deprived the company and Bart of an opportunity to course correct. It's impossible to know for sure, but there is a strong probability that with better systems in place, Bart might have understood the impact his behavior was having and would have changed it, thus decreasing the chance he'd be accused of misconduct again. More important, the company would have avoided the unintended consequence of giving him raises and promotions after allegations of misconduct, which sent him the message that his behavior was acceptable.

Solution: Harness the power of HR tools and cutting-edge technology and data analytics to improve your decision-making.

- ☑ Use your company's IT talent (or hire talented vendors) to create systems to track trends, collect data, and have the ability to easily generate reports that allow companies to make better decisions.
- ☑ Collect and analyze turnover data, not just the numbers but information that might point to higher (or lower) turnover in certain departments, locations, divisions, and so on to allow the company to identify hot spots.
- ☑ Collect and analyze data for departments—who is leaving, who is being promoted, who is receiving raises/high evaluation scores—to track trends that might show evidence of unconscious bias.
- ☑ Collect and analyze compensation figures to ensure pay equity.
  - ○ Make sure there is no significant difference in pay among men and women and among employees of different races and ethnicities.

○ Use the information as a tool to determine how compensation is determined (then incorporate that information into job descriptions and evaluations).

☑ Exit interviews are your friend. In addition to collecting data about departing employees, look at whether important issues are raised during this process that might help you make the workplace better for employees who stay.

Although this is only a partial list of the issues that give rise to workplace drama, they provide a solid foundation to learn ways to identify and correct it, making it infinitely easier for you to achieve the goal of getting to the top of the Healthy Workplace Culture pyramid.

7

Make Your Journey Easier

Choose the Less Treacherous Path

Organizations struggle with creating and maintaining a drama-free, healthy culture, but the truth is that their failure is sometimes due to making the process harder than it needs to be. One way to make it easier is to look at the success stories in other corporate arenas.

As you embark on your quest to become a healthy and inclusive workplace, you're likely to encounter forks in the road. Sometimes you'll have to choose between a path that's rocky and uncharted, and one that's already been explored and is therefore less treacherous. Although taking the uncharted course might make you a trailblazer, often the already-paved path will help you achieve a drama-free workplace more quickly and easily.

One good place to start is taking a look at corporate safety programs. They provide us with a great roadmap that we can easily tweak to use in the workplace drama arena.

What We Can Learn from Companies That Embrace a Safety Culture

Employers first addressed workplace safety issues because they were forced to. Laws and regulations came about because of the alarming number of on-the-job injuries and deaths. In addition to the new laws, the government established a new enforcement agency, the Occupational Safety and Health Administration (OSHA). OSHA imposed what seemed like drastic mandates aimed at reducing workplace accidents, injuries, and deaths, and employers were initially resistant to being forced to change their ways. But then something significant happened: Companies saw the value in having a safe workplace and fully embraced creating cultures of safety instead of only caring about compliance with safety laws.

Today, any company worth its salt embraces and celebrates a culture where safety is an absolute core value and the thought that companies once did this only because they were legally obligated to seems odd. Organizations with a true safety culture have successfully infused a sense of mutual trust and responsibility, creating a feeling that each person is accountable not only for her own safety, but also for the safety of her coworkers, customers, and anyone else who comes into the work space.

This begs the question: How did organizations achieve this great feat? And, it also begs a follow-up question: How can we replicate this success to help us reach the coveted top of the pyramid and achieve a drama-free culture?

Safety Programs: The Road to Success

Talk to someone who was in the workforce in the 1960s (and before then), especially those who worked in factory or industrial jobs, and they most likely have distressing stories about the state of workplace safety back then. In fact, OSHA (established in 1971) estimates that approximately 14,000 workers were killed in on-the-job accidents in 1970. Fast-forward to 2009 and we see a startling difference—a workplace fatality rate of 4,340.[1] While even one death is too many, the steep decline is something to be celebrated—and replicated.

---

[1]"Timeline of OSHA's 40 Year History." U.S. Department of Labor, Occupational Safety and Health Administration. https://www.osha.gov/osha40/timeline.html.

Without a doubt, the enactment of strict safety laws and the establishment of OSHA were two critical components that contributed to this decline. But there is something else that has greatly contributed not only to a steep reduction in work-related deaths, but also in workplace accidents: *corporate America's full embrace of workplace cultures that value and place a high premium on physical safety.*

What began as a legal mandate morphed into a true desire to make the workplace safe for everyone.

The Road from Legal Mandate to Cultural Mantra

Successful safety programs maintain a laser focus on safety culture. This means protecting employees from injuries is not just window dressing; it's a core value, central to the organization, at all levels and at all times. In these cultures, safety isn't just discussed at safety meetings and after accidents occur. In true safety cultures, people are looking for ways to make the workplace safer at all times. Employees in these organizations not only discuss (and track) accidents, they discuss accidents that didn't occur to learn from near-misses. They also learn from a job well done.

Rather than focusing on the burden of having to comply with a legally mandated program, or doing the sheer minimum, these organizations embrace the opportunities created by putting safety first. (See Chapter 5 for a discussion of the importance of managing risks and opportunities.)

Safety cultures have the following characteristics:

- *They have a "we are all in" mentality.* Great safety cultures are characterized by good working relationships at all levels. These relationships enable open and honest conversations about what is and isn't working, mistakes that have happened and what needs to change. Safety cultures start at the top, but don't stop there. They take a top-down AND a bottom-up approach. And they don't ignore the critical middle manager who is often in the best position to implement and monitor safety protocols. Taking this approach increases trust since everyone participates and everyone has a stake in creating a safe environment.

- *They reinvent corporate attitudes about reports of possible hazards.* In a safety culture, companies make it crystal clear that they want to know about *every* accident, *every* injury, and even *every* near miss. No exceptions. Employees feel they are a critical piece of the safety puzzle and they embrace the mantra of "report, report, report," trusting that doing so will come with no negative consequence. Everything about the culture screams, "We want to know, otherwise we can't get better."

- *Their investigations don't focus on blame; they learn from mistakes.* Safety cultures understand that mistakes present a great opportunity to learn. Investigations seek to get to root causes; they are not only conducted to assign blame. Since employees have full faith and trust that they won't be penalized if they speak openly, honestly, and fully with management, they help to create a virtuous cycle of report-investigate-fix.

- *They are not just about lip service.* A safety culture is deeply authentic. In these organizations, there is a true commitment to providing a safe workplace, not just a commitment to comply with the law.

- *They don't take their eye off the ball.* Safety cultures stay vigilant. These organizations understand that safety is an ongoing program that requires absolute commitment. Leaders at these organizations share their vision of safety since it's understood that everyone needs to be on the same page when establishing and meeting safety goals.

Translating Safety Accomplishments to Achieve a Healthy Workplace Culture

Although safety protocols haven't completely eliminated accidents and work-related deaths, their success is undeniable. Not only have the number of accidents and deaths been dramatically reduced, the implementation of these systems has caused a seismic shift in how people view safety at work: not through the lens of blame, fear, and compliance, but instead through the lens of proactive hazard identification and control, and a sense of shared responsibilities and rewards.

This same approach can and should be taken as companies grapple with issues related to the reduction of workplace drama. Two points that contribute to world-class safety cultures are particularly applicable to our goal to reduce or eliminate workplace drama.

1. Foster a deep and authentic commitment to safety—physical and emotional/psychological—where:
   a. Workplace "hazards" are proactively identified, rather than identified in the midst of crisis.
   b. Reports are seen as opportunities that allow issues to be identified and fixed.
2. Implement a system of forward-looking accountability and train investigators to include "learning lessons" in their work.

Deep Commitment to Employee Safety and Well-Being

In his book *Dying for a Paycheck*, Jeffrey Pfeffer, a professor at Stanford's Graduate School of Business, summarizes his work involving the physical and psychological toll workplace stress takes on employees. He makes the case for treating psychological injuries just as seriously as physical injuries: "Meanwhile, stress at work, not subject to OSHA reporting or intervention, and seemingly invisible and accepted as an inevitable part of contemporary workplaces, just keeps getting worse for almost all jobs, resulting in an even-higher physical and psychological toll."[2]

He's right. While everyone agrees that some level of stress is indeed normal at work, it is undeniable that employees working in companies with toxic cultures are exposed to an unreasonable and unnecessarily high level of stress. And studies, including those cited by Pfeffer, make it clear that in their most serious forms, they are no less dangerous than physical injuries.

Pfeffer goes on to identify 10 management decisions that affect employee health. Four are particularly applicable to our discussion about workplace drama and a healthy workplace culture:

- Having relatively low control over one's job and job environment, including having relatively little freedom and decision discretion at work.

---

[2] Jeffrey Pfeffer, *Dying for a Paycheck: How Modern Management Harms Employee Health and Company Performance—and What We Can Do About It.* New York, NY: HarperCollins, 2018.

- Facing high job demands such as pressure to work fast.
- Being in a work environment that offers low levels of social support (for instance, not having close relationships with coworkers that provide social support to mitigate the effects of work stress).
- Working in a setting in which job- and employment-related decisions seem unfair.[3]

Any of these, or a combination of these, Pfeffer says, will have a negative impact on your employee's physical well-being.

Translating the deep commitment organizations have to physical safety to the world of workplace culture will require two things:

1. To adopt a mind-set similar to what is embraced in safety cultures one where compliance is almost an afterthought, complying with the law is not viewed as burdensome, and the focus is singularly on creating a sense of shared responsibility for well-being.
2. I'll talk about this more in my chapter on communication (Chapter 8), but the second step is to teach employees and managers to speak a language that no longer focuses exclusively on legal principles. "We are committed to complying with the law and promise you that we won't harass, discriminate, or retaliate" doesn't cut it anymore. Your organization needs to stop reaching for the bottom of the barrel and instead reach for the healthy culture pinnacle.

Proactive Hazard Identification and Control

A hallmark of a true safety culture involves identifying hazards prior to the hazard turning into an accident or causing an injury. Sometimes, workplace misconduct might be more difficult to identify than, say, a wet floor, but it is not impossible to identify and certainly not impossible to control and eliminate. Just like mopping up a wet floor to prevent you or a valued colleague from slipping and falling, so too can we all identify and control workplace drama.

---

[3]Ibid.

So what are the "hazards" present in the workplace that we need to identify and control? I uncovered some of these hazards already:

- The predictors of sexual harassment include corporate tolerance, a shortage of female leaders, and compliance blinders. Other "hazards" related to workplace sexual harassment include: powerful employees who abuse their power and feel they do not need to be accountable; complaint mechanisms that discourage reports; a lack of connection among employees making it less likely that witnesses will intervene if they see or hear misconduct; and a corporate attitude of "we don't really take these issues seriously" making it less likely that targets or witnesses of harassment will intervene or report. (See Chapter 2 for a more in-depth discussion.)
- I also outlined some of the predictors for workplace drama in Chapter 1. Those include, among others, a lack of authenticity, confusion about behavior that is unfair versus illegal, a lack of transparency, a culture of complicity, and a refusal to admit wrongdoing.

Reports Are Welcomed and Encouraged

As I've previously cited, the data and research are clear: incidents of workplace misconduct, including sexual harassment, are vastly underreported. There are a number of factors that contribute to this reality, but without a doubt a failure to create an environment that truly welcomes reports is a key one.

In a survey of corporate counsel, Emtrain and In The House found that even in-house attorneys acknowledge that too few employees feel comfortable coming forward with complaints of misconduct—whether they are the targets of the misconduct or witnesses to it. In that survey, only 36% of respondents "believed that their employees were comfortable reporting harassment they experienced and only 33% believed their employees were comfortable reporting harassment directed at others." In fact, one person responding to the survey said, "Secondhand stories indicate that employees tend to avoid reporting incidents since they do not trust the process to be fair."[4]

---

[4] *Emtrain and In the House Survey: Sexual Harassment Prevention in the Age of The #MeToo Movement.* San Francisco, CA: Emtrain, 2018.

We must do better. As noted in the Emtrain/In the House survey, "Complaints are an opportunity to improve the workplace. Remember, you can't fix what you don't know. Judging your company solely on low numbers of reported misconduct complaints can be very misleading because this is often an indicator of insufficient reporting, not a lack of misconduct."[5]

2. Forward-Looking Accountability

Too often, the word "accountability" is synonymous with blame and negative consequences. In successful safety cultures, accountability focuses on looking forward more so than looking backwards. Backward-looking accountability is only about placing blame—identifying who made the mistake and figuring out an appropriate punishment. Sometimes this is right and necessary, but that's not enough to actually create a safer work environment.

By contrast, forward-looking accountability recognizes mistakes made and harm caused by those mistakes. But the bulk of the work involving accountability is in looking forward in time—identifying learning lessons, making necessary changes, and developing systems to build safe habits. All of this is aimed primarily at preventing a recurrence, rather than only focusing on how to punish the person who made the mistake.

So how do we use the idea of "forward-looking accountability" in the world of workplace drama?

To begin, it's critical to acknowledge that when it comes to workplace conduct, there is an absolute need to determine whether the reported behavior rose to the level of misconduct. If it did, then the person who engaged in the misconduct must obviously face the consequence of his actions. In Chapter 11, I'll talk in detail about not only investigating claims of misconduct, but also incorporating a practical methodology to impose appropriate discipline for that wrongdoing.

Implementing forward-looking accountability does not mean that we eliminate looking backward to assess the severity of the misconduct and select an appropriate remedy, it means that we add a second step to fixing the problem. That second step focuses on identifying environmental factors that might have played a part in allowing the misconduct to occur in the first place, and implementing ways to eliminate those environmental hazards to make sure it doesn't happen again.

---

[5]Ibid.

As usual, the best way to make my point is to use a real-life example.

I've conducted more investigations than I can count involving allegations of workplace extramarital affairs, but one that is particularly applicable here involves two people I'll call Jack and Diane. Jack was the CEO of a mid-sized business. Diane was a director-level organizational leader. I was tasked with investigating a claim by the VP of HR, Meg, who objected to Jack's recent decision to create a new EVP position for Diane. Meg and several other VPs were bothered by the fact that they would now have a dotted-line reporting relationship to Diane.

Although the primary questions I needed to answer included: (1) whether there was enough proof to show that Jack and Diane were romantically linked (they were), and (2) whether an inappropriate management decision about Diane's employment was influenced by that relationship (it was). It was also critical that I identify "hazards" that might have contributed to an environment where this misbehavior was allowed to occur.

For example, in the course of my investigation it became clear that Jack and Diane were blatant about their affair, but no one said anything since they felt it was "none of their business" (until, of course, she was promoted to be their boss). It was also clear that the organization's board of directors had given Jack too much autonomy and allowed him to run amok, creating a perception that he was accountable to no one.

At the end of my investigation, I reached findings about the underlying conduct and about Jack's decision-making. The board decided on and implemented corrective measures related to the misconduct Jack engaged in. More important, I provided the board with a list of additional "hot spots" that I had identified as part of my work and gave them recommendations on how to improve their overall business practices and decision-making processes, and also provided them with feedback on how to make sure that, in the future, employees felt comfortable raising concerns before they became too big to fix. And of course, we also talked about ways in which the members of the board could work with a CEO in a way that didn't overly restrict his freedom or autonomy, but provided some level of safeguard to make sure an issue like this didn't happen again.

Workplace investigators are taught to look at events only in hindsight. They are tasked with finding out only whether the events, occurred as relayed, and, if there was some misconduct, to identify who was at fault.

That's a good and necessary first step, but savvy investigators go one step further to not only assign blame and decide on appropriate discipline, but also to identify learning lessons and make recommendations about ways to improve the overall culture. Incorporating a backward- *and* forward-looking approach will require a paradigm shift—from focusing only on cause, to also focusing on how and why the drama occurred and to candidly talk about ways to prevent it. But the work will be well worth the effort since, in the end, it will get you closer to the top of the Healthy Workplace Culture Pyramid.

Accident/Injury Reduction versus Drama Reduction: A Side-by-Side Comparison

Another way to translate successes in the world of physical safety into the world of psychological safety is to do a side-by-side comparison that shows just how differently these two issues are approached. There are dozens of reference points to do this, but I'll focus on three:

1. The tone set in policy language related to safety versus policies related to drama (focusing on policies prohibiting harassment)
2. The approach taken to prevent workplace injuries
3. How reports of injuries are addressed

In looking at these areas, we'll see themes emerge that will make it easier to translate safety successes into our quest to achieve a drama-free workplace.

Tone and Content of Policies

The tone of safety policies is almost always positive and focuses on a deep commitment to keeping employees out of harm's way. The policies mention legal obligations but don't obsess over compliance. By contrast, harassment prevention policies are almost all legalese and focus on keeping the company out of legal hot water. (For more on how to draft clear and helpful policies, see Chapter 9.)

Sample Policy Language: Safety

OSHA declares: "The main goal of injury and illness prevention programs is to prevent workplace injuries, illnesses, and deaths, the suffering these events cause workers, and the financial hardship they cause both workers and employers."[6]

A quick review of model policy language related to safety reiterates this general point. Policies focus on expressing the company's commitment to making physical safety a vital workplace goal. Sample language includes:

- "[We] consider injury and illness prevention equally important as operations, customer service and administration . . . The prevention of injuries . . . is an objective for all employees in the organization. Each manager/supervisor shall make the safety of employees an integral part of his or her regular management function . . ."[7]
- "An injury and illness prevention program is a proactive process to help employers find and fix workplace hazards before workers are hurt."[8]

Note that the policies do not say, "Workplace injuries might get us into legal trouble, so please don't get injured." The sense created by safety policies isn't "We need to keep you safe and injury-free because it's the law," but rather "Your safety is of paramount concern to us."

Sample Policy Language: Workplace Conduct

By contrast, policy language related to workplace harassment, discrimination and retaliation, has a completely different tone. Most start with a preamble that says something like, "Sexual harassment is offensive, is a violation

---

[6]U.S. Department of Labor, Occupational Safety and Healthy Administration, "Injury and Illness Prevention Programs White Paper," 2012. https://www.osha.gov/dsg/InjuryIllnessPreventionProgramsWhitePaper.html.

[7]Preferred Employers Insurance Company, "Model Injury and Illness Prevention Program," 2012. http://www.preferredworkcomp.com/active/WebDoc.asp?s=1040245120&P=974250368.

[8]U.S. Department of Labor, Occupational Safety and Health Administration, "Injury and Illness Prevention Programs White Paper," 2012.

of our policies, is unlawful, and may subject our company to liability for harm to targets of sexual harassment." This language hardly provides comfort to employees who want to be protected from the harm that someone's misconduct might bring.

Here are snippets from various policies covering the topic of harassment and discrimination:

- Harassers may also be individually subject to liability.
- Employees of every level who engage in sexual harassment, including managers and supervisors who engage in sexual harassment or who allow such behavior to continue, will be penalized for such misconduct.
- Our company is committed to achieving and promoting compliance with the laws, rules, and regulations . . . . Any employee who believes they have been subjected to conduct they believe to be discriminatory, retaliatory, fraudulent, illegal, or unethical must submit a report.
- Actions of harassment directed at an individual based on a legally protected category are deemed unacceptable.
- Sexual harassment will not be tolerated.

In sharp contrast to the tone in safety policies, these policies sound scary, punitive, and focus exclusively on the dangers (to the company) of legal liability.

Translation

How can we take a page out of the safety book of policies and translate them into the world of workplace conduct? Here is one suggestion:

Our company prides itself on instilling our mission and values into everything we do. We know we can't live up to our mission statement, or serve our customer base without providing you, our most important resource, with a safe, comfortable, positive, and productive work environment.

To that end, our leadership gives you our word that we are committed to providing a healthy work environment where you can effectively perform your job and where you can thrive—as an individual and as valuable member of a supportive team. Whereas some companies promise a "harassment-free workplace," our goals are much loftier than that. This isn't simply a guarantee that we won't violate the law. Our word to you is that we will not only do our part to prevent and resolve unlawful harassment, but that we are committed to creating and maintaining a diverse, inclusive, and professional environment.

Of course, as I've reiterated throughout this book, these promises are only words on paper if they aren't supported by an authentic commitment to generate this type of culture, and to take actions to back up those words.

Looking to other influencers

In addition to employers making changes to the way they approach prevention and resolution of workplace misconduct, we need other influencers to do their part.

For example, many state legislatures have passed sweeping legislative mandates in response to the #MeToo movement. Government's commitment to help employers eliminate workplace harassment is admirable. Unfortunately, too many of these new laws are the same old same old—emphasizing legal liability, providing only one avenue (a lawsuit) for employee redress, and only giving lip service to the much more important issue of creating a workplace culture that is respectful, inclusive, and professional.

In addition to needing better legislation, enforcement agencies can also do their part to implement guidance that will help employers achieve this type of culture. OSHA makes it mandatory for employers of a certain size to implement an injury and illness prevention program and it also encourages employers who are more ambitious and forward-looking to adopt a voluntary prevention program. This sends a strong message to employers that, while complying with legal mandates is the floor, it is not the ceiling. Federal and state enforcement agencies who are tasked with enforcing employment laws should examine this approach to help companies set the right tone and stop focusing exclusively on legal compliance.

Finally, the insurance industry could and should do its part to have an impact in this arena. In fact, it is in the insurance industry's interest to decrease claims so there is a strong business incentive to require companies to set up effective ways to prevent misconduct and to help employers set up mechanisms for early intervention.

To give you an idea of how far we have to go, here is a snippet from the website of a large insurance agency that provides employer practices liability insurance (EPLI) to guard against claims of discrimination and harassment:

> You're at risk of an employment claim from the moment you interview a prospective employee. For example, if you choose not to hire the interviewee, that individual could allege some sort of discrimination. Or, if you hire that person and later fire them due to poor attendance, that discharged employee could claim wrongful termination.[9]

It will take a comprehensive, all-hands-on-deck approach to solve the issue of toxic workplace cultures, but our employees are well worth that effort.

Prevention Techniques

Safety policies are laser-focused on preventing accidents and injuries. They don't talk about preventing only major accidents or serious injuries, they talk about preventing *all* accidents and injuries. Unfortunately, most harassment prevention policies only focus on preventing unlawful behavior and send the wrong message about the company's commitment to a respectful and inclusive workplace culture.

Sample Language: Safety

Read any company's policy about their commitment to safety and you'll see that central to this commitment is their focus on preventing accidents

---

[9]Nationwide, "Protect against Employee Lawsuits with Employment Practices Liability Insurance (EPLI)." https://www.nationwide.com/business/insurance/employment-practices-liability/.

from occurring in the first place. These companies are obsessed with identifying hazards, fixing them quickly, and learning lessons at every stage. They also create an environment where this commitment permeates throughout the company, which creates an incomparable openness to identifying and reporting any possible hazards.

From OSHA:

Most successful injury and illness prevention programs include a similar set of commonsense elements that focus on finding all hazards in the workplace and developing a plan for preventing and controlling those hazards. Management leadership and active worker participation are essential to ensuring that all hazards are identified and addressed.[10]

One model policy defines manager and supervisor responsibility as follows:

- Set the proper example for safe behavior and never act unsafely or violate a safety rule or an established safe work practice.
- Be continuously vigilant of unsafe conditions that could contribute to an injury and take corrective action to eliminate or control unsafe conditions or work practices immediately.[11] (In other words, establish a "find and fix" approach to safety.)

The message is clear: "We really, really, really want to know about anything that might make our workplace unsafe because we don't want anyone to have an accident or get injured, especially if we could have prevented the accident. So please help identify any dangers so we can all be healthy and safe."

Sample Language: Workplace Conduct

In sharp contrast to the "we really want to know about anything that could pose a danger" language found in the world of safety, when it comes to expected workplace conduct, the message is, "Don't come to us with minor issues . . . we want to know only about problems once they're serious enough to constitute a policy violation or if it could get us into legal hot water."

---

[10]Ibid.

[11]Preferred Employers Insurance Company, "Model Injury and Illness Prevention Program," 2012.

Typical policies related to reporting and preventing workplace misconduct say:

- All employees are encouraged to report any harassment or behaviors *that violate this policy.*
- Managers and supervisors are required to report any complaint that they receive, *or any harassment* that they observe or become aware of.

The failure to address issues early — which includes the failure to provide employees the tools necessary to resolve issues on their own — means that any promise to identify and prevent hazardous workplace conduct is disingenuous. (See Chapter 9 for more on drafting effective harassment prevention policies.)

Translation

Taking a cue from safety, a better way to send a message of wanting to identify issues early is to say:

It is our goal to provide an environment where employees treat each other respectfully and professionally. While we understand that we all have bad days and might occasionally let our frustrations or stress get the best of us, we expect everyone to do their best to listen, be patient, allow everyone's voice to be heard, and create an environment where all our employees feel they belong.

If you experience or observe behavior that you think falls below this expectation, you should feel free to address it yourself if you're comfortable doing so, or feel free to enlist the assistance of your manager, HR, or anyone else who you can partner with to resolve the problem.

We know that this is easier said than done, but we are deeply committed to fulfilling our obligation to provide you with a world-class workplace culture. This means we all have to do our part and one of many promises we make is that we will not only help you build technical skills, we will also teach all our employees skills in communication, conflict resolution, and empathy so that with each conversation, each meeting, and, yes, each bump in the road, we get better and better at becoming partners in culture.

Now that would send a strong message that the company is truly committed to preventing misconduct long before it reaches the point of unlawful harassment.

Addressing Injuries

Safety cultures seek to prevent injuries, no matter how big or small. They seek to become aware of all injuries, no matter how big or small. They seek to treat all injuries, no matter how big or small. The same can't be said for the majority of corporate policies or practices in the world of preventing harassment or other misconduct in the workplace.

Sample Language: Safety

Closely related to the commitment to identify hazards is dealing with reports of injuries. The safety message is short and sweet: Make certain all injuries, no matter how minor, are treated immediately.

Sample Language: Workplace Conduct

As outlined above, almost all policies and practices related to workplace conduct give a very different instruction. Instead of asking employees to report issues early, employees are instructed to make reports once they are serious and possibly unlawful.

Imagine if safety protocols followed a similar path. Rather than saying, "All injuries need to be treated immediately," the instruction might say: "Only major injuries should be immediately treated. Major injuries include partial or total loss of limb, obvious bone fractures, and serious head wounds."

The imaginary response sounds absurdly callous, but too often this is essentially what employees who complain about rude, belittling, demeaning, disrespectful conduct that has caused emotional or psychological harm are told when they report an "injury" that seems minor (compared to unlawful behavior, which would be considered either severe or pervasive).

Translation

How about this instead:

We understand that creating a culture that aligns with our core values requires many moving parts. One critical part is helping our employees resolve issues early. While we (management) can't intervene in every single instance of workplace conflict, we are committed to doing two things: (1) to provide you with the tools and resources necessary to resolve conflict on your own when appropriate and (2) to become your partner in resolving conflict early so that it doesn't escalate.

We have a variety of ways to help you sharpen your communication and conflict-resolution skills so that we can all lower the temperature when necessary. But if doing this on your own isn't feasible, we want to help. That means that we don't want you to wait until the conflict becomes unbearable to approach us for help.

Over time, as all of you become experts in using emotional intelligence to communicate persuasively, you will need our intervention less and less, but please know that we are here to help whenever you need a partner in doing your part to make ours a topnotch workplace culture!

It's in everyone's interest that we change our approach to addressing misconduct early so that it never reaches the point of full-blown drama.

It's time for all professionals in charge of eliminating drama from our workplaces, especially those in top leadership positions, make a better promise to employees about workplace conduct—one that isn't only rooted in legal compliance. As one CEO stated when asked to give his company's safety philosophy:

Establishing safety as a value rather than a priority tells our employees and our customers that safety is built into our culture, not something we do to merely comply with regulations.[12]

Those of us tasked with creating a culture free of workplace drama would be wise to listen to this CEO.

---

[12]U.S. Department of Labor, Occupational Safety and Health Administration, "Injury and Illness Prevention Programs White Paper," 2012.

8 | Reduce Drama Through Precise and Persuasive Communication

The single biggest problem in communication is the illusion that it has taken place.

– George Bernard Shaw

Learning to communicate effectively and persuasively, and teaching your employees to do the same, is essential to reach the top of the Healthy Workplace Culture Pyramid. Issues related to poor communication at work involve both one-on-one conversations and corporate communication. A breakdown in either arena could be fatal in your attempts to keep drama away from your organization.

The Most Common Communication Failures That Lead to Drama

A breakdown in communication which leads to workplace drama tends to fall into one of two categories:

1. Saying nothing, usually for fear of saying the wrong thing.
2. Saying the wrong thing.

There are countless examples in both categories, but I'll focus on the ones that I've found to cause the most drama at work.

- Employees let emotions get the best of them, causing drama and making it more difficult to stop the drama once it starts.
  - Often this means viewing issues only through a narrow personal lens, never considering the other person's point of view.
  - When emotions are high, logic often fails us. We forget our end goal and instead focus on being right. Our communication sometimes spirals into personal attacks, which increases the temperature of the situation.
- Many of us aren't taught skills of persuasion. Without those skills, we often behave in ways that hurt more than help, which leads to unnecessary conflict.
  - We fail to adapt our communication styles to make it more likely that we are heard.
  - We communicate imprecisely. Words are extremely powerful and a lack of clarity leads to confusion, assumptions, and, of course, drama.
- In the workplace context, one way that these deficiencies culminate is through the improper use of legally charged terms, or personal allegations that someone is an "ist"—a racist, sexist, ageist, and so on. This problem stems from our failure to teach a language that isn't rooted in legal terminology. We become trapped in the vicious cycle of: She complained about harassment so now I have to put my compliance hat on . . . she's putting her compliance hat on so I better start protecting myself . . . there she goes protecting herself, which means she's out to get us . . . she thinks I'm out to get the company so . . ."

I've seen every one of these issues play out in the workplace and each time I realize that teaching people to communicate more clearly, more precisely, and more persuasively would have a tremendous ROI in terms of reducing the cost—monetary and otherwise—of workplace drama.

Improve Your Emotional Intelligence to Communicate More Precisely

Chances are, if you're reading this book you've heard about and maybe even studied the importance of emotional intelligence (also referred to as EQ which is short for an individual's emotional quotient). But just in case you need a refresher, EQ is your ability to recognize and understand emotions in yourself and others, and your ability to use this awareness to manage your behavior and relationships.

In their book *Emotional Intelligence 2.0*, authors Travis Bradberry and Jean Greaves identify four emotional intelligence skills that pair up under two primary competencies: personal competence and social competence.

1. Personal competence: Your ability to stay aware of your emotions and manage your behavior and tendencies. Here, the focus is on you, rather than on interactions with others. This includes:
   o Your self-awareness, which is your ability to accurately perceive your own emotions in the moment and understand your tendencies across situations.[1]
   o Your self-management skills: Your ability to use your awareness of your emotions to remain flexible and direct your behavior in a positive direction.[2]

2. Social competence: Your ability to understand other people's moods, behavior, and motives in order to improve the quality of your relationships. The focus here is on how you are with other people. This includes:
   o Your social awareness, which is your ability to accurately pick up on emotions in other people and understand what is really going on with them. This often means perceiving what other people are thinking and feeling, even if you don't feel the same way. Two of the most important elements of social awareness are listening and observing.[3]

---

[1] Travis Bradberry and Jean Greaves, *Emotional Intelligence 2.0*. Enhanced new edition. San Diego, CA: TalentSmart, 2009.

[2] Ibid.

[3] Ibid.

o Your relationship management, which is your ability to use your awareness of your own emotions and those of others to successfully manage interactions.[4]

So does our emotional intelligence really play a significant role in our ability to communicate effectively and persuasively? Are we really less likely to experience workplace drama if we sharpen our emotional intelligence skills? Absolutely. I've seen story after investigation story that centers around people accused of creating drama because of their lack of emotional intelligence. Here are a few.

Stories from the Trenches

The Socially Unaware Dude

His name was Jim. He managed the warehouse for a large company. Everyone knew Jim was old school. He made it clear that he didn't understand the company's obsession with diversity.

Because his position required it, he sat on the supplier diversity planning committee. Jim made it known that he thought the committee's mission—to create and implement strategies to increase the number of qualified woman- and minority-owned service suppliers—was garbage. He'd take every opportunity to be un-PC at meetings. No one phrase was egregious on its own, but put together his comments were enough to create a strong and reasonable impression that he wasn't fond of working with people who weren't like him. Eventually (and inevitably), a woman with biracial children filed a complaint saying Jim was keeping her from a sought-after promotion.

The evidence supported her claim that Jim was impolite and clearly had no filter, but it did not support her claim that his behavior affected any promotion decision (in fact, he wasn't even in a position to have a direct impact on her work).

Regardless, it was clear that Jim was lacking two critical skills, and this deficiency created an understandable perception that Jim was biased. First, he was almost completely lacking in social awareness. He was what

---

[4]Ibid.

I call a bad workplace meteorologist, unable to read the temperature and adjust his words and conduct accordingly. Jim was also lacking strong empathy skills and therefore was not very self-aware. He was unable to understand why his comments created a perception that his "anti-diversity" stance would make diverse employees uncomfortable (other supporters of diversity were equally dismayed by Jim's actions). He was unable to see it from their point of view and thought they were being overly sensitive.

The Cheating Salesman

The complaint actually came from the subordinate's husband. "My wife's boss, the VP of sales, is sexually harassing her. I've seen the texts he sends her and they're inappropriate. She's too scared to complain so I'm doing it for her." The unfortunate spoiler alert is that while it was true the boss was sending the texts (and emails, and IMs, and videos), this was, sadly for the husband, very much a consensual affair (I won't go into the gory details but suffice it to say, the evidence to prove this was overwhelming).

Although no employee had complained, the company was now aware of a serious allegation so they asked me to investigate.

The VP was one of the most hostile people I've ever interviewed for an investigation. He spent part of the interview trying to convince me that there should be no investigation since no one from within the company complained. He then switched gears to give me a series of farfetched explanations to "prove" to me that there was no affair (for the record, I found out a few months later that the VP and the employee left their spouses to be with each other). He spent the rest of the time trying to convince me that there was nothing suspicious about the subordinate receiving the department's highest raises and bonuses. He was evasive and dismissive, not remembering that as the decision-maker, my judgment would have an impact on his job. Also, for the record, his unacceptable behavior did not affect my independence—I based my conclusions on the evidence.

Despite the fact that he was an extremely valuable member of the executive sales team, his company fired the VP. They based their decision only partially on the fact that he'd exhibited poor judgment by having an affair with his subordinate (though that would certainly warrant termination, given the evidence I found). Instead, the company's decision was primarily driven by the fact that he'd been combative and dishonest during the investigation process (not just with me).

This VP forgot that his goal *should have been* to keep his job and to do his part to repair the loss of trust that resulted from his behavior. Instead, he wanted to be right. This is a person whom I would guess would score quite low in the self-management category of an EQ test.

The Lovable but Tone-Deaf Nurse

Laura had all the characteristics of a great critical care nurse. She was compassionate and kind, especially when it came to patient care. She was also known by her coworkers as a fun-loving person who was always ready to praise, congratulate, and celebrate.

Nina was an administrative assistant in the department. She had been very open about her religious beliefs and explained to everyone that she strictly adhered to the teachings of her faith, including the fact that her religion prohibited her from celebrating birthdays or other celebrations.

Laura, who was of a different faith, thought celebrating birthdays was a must. She told Nina her beliefs were silly and that no harm could come from celebrating birthdays—especially your own. Nina stayed away from all other office celebrations but when her birthday rolled around, Laura came to Nina's desk with a cake and balloons. She sang "Happy Birthday" to Nina and when Nina began to object, Laura told her not to be such a stick in the mud and to stop stressing about getting older. Laura told Nina she should enjoy and appreciate the gesture. Nina was dismayed and coworkers who were watching said it was as if it was happening in slow motion. They were horrified by what they saw and heard. The rest of the team could see that Laura's social awareness and social management skills needed some sharpening, but this was lost on Laura.

Each of the characters in these real-life investigations could have kept drama away (and could have kept their jobs) if they had honed their emotional intelligence skills. Sure, some of the characters inspire more sympathy than others, but these are three typical stories of the type of workplace drama that unfolds every day because of a failure to manage individual emotions and an inability to look around to gauge how others react.

Using Emotional Intelligence to Keep Drama Away

If the failure to use emotional intelligence in communication is such a common precursor to workplace drama, what strategies can companies implement to help employees communicate clearly and transparently?

Some suggestions follow.

You Are What You Say, So Be Meticulous with Your Words

Words matter, so be impeccable with your word. This is the first of the Four Agreements proposed by Don Miguel Ruiz. Ruiz's theories are rooted in Toltec wisdom. That sounds mysterious and otherworldly, but the truth is that his simple advice to be impeccable with our language really is about emotional intelligence.[5]

For example, calling diversity efforts stupid creates a reasonable and expected belief that you are antidiversity. If that's the image Jim wants to have, then he's done a good job being impeccable with his choice of words. But here's the rub: *If that's what Jim believes, then he must face the reasonable and expected consequences of his choice to say these things.*

If, on the other hand, Jim seeks to be viewed as someone whose opinions do not affect his decision-making at work, then he must be more precise and less emotional when he speaks about these topics. In fact, in real life, Jim was shocked to hear that people viewed him as antidiversity or biased in any way. Jim might have benefited from learning to look at his behavior from another person's point of view. Instead, his choice to let his emotions dictate made him someone that few wanted to work with.

Does this mean that the Jims of the world—those who think we've gone too far with being "PC"—have to stifle their opinions? No, but they do have to accept the fact that their words are very likely to cause drama. And when an organization has a Jim in its midst, it has to decide whether failing to take steps to avoid and resolve drama is in line with its culture. If Jim's words and actions fall short of your commitment to create a culture of respect and inclusion, then this type of behavior must be deemed unacceptable.

---

[5]Don Miguel Ruiz, *The Four Agreements: A Practical Guide to Personal Freedom (A Toltec Wisdom Book)*. San Rafael, CA: Amber-Allen Publishing, 1997.

Pivot from Defensiveness to Genuine Curiosity: Being Right Isn't Always Right

You can't sow confrontation and expect to harvest peace. That's not how things work in life, and it certainly isn't how they work at work.

In the case of the cheating VP, his ego—his need to be right—was his Achilles heel. I don't know what his organization would have done if he'd simply admitted that he used extremely poor judgment and asked for a second chance. But instead, he dug in.

I certainly understood his reluctance to admit to an extramarital affair since doing so would have dire consequences at work and at home. The problem was that the evidence was overwhelming; he and the subordinate were clearly having an intimate affair. And worse, this otherwise highly intelligent man behaved illogically by focusing on meaningless minutiae like, "Well, since no one from inside the company is complaining, then there should be no investigation."

The one and only issue that made him listen was when I asked him if he could imagine that because people believed they were having an affair, others on his team would think they were at a distinct disadvantage when it came time to evaluate performance and give raises. He was willing to briefly see things from the perspective of his other employees and understood that his behavior eroded trust and created a strong sense of unfairness. Unfortunately, this brief glimpse of emotional intelligence quickly vanished and he pivoted back to defensiveness and wanting to prove me wrong.

If you have employees or leaders at your organization who get trapped by their own fixation to be right and react defensively, perhaps providing lessons in improving empathy skills, as well as relationship management skills will help you salvage that person's career at your company before they cause irreparable drama. Doing this will also help your company plant seeds of ethical decision-making and integrity, and that will most certainly reap a worthwhile harvest.

Use Helpful Communication Tools

Provide employees with tangible and easy-to-use tools to strip communication of personal attacks or needless emotion. This doesn't mean you create a robotic workplace, but it does mean that you give employees options to communicate in more precise ways.

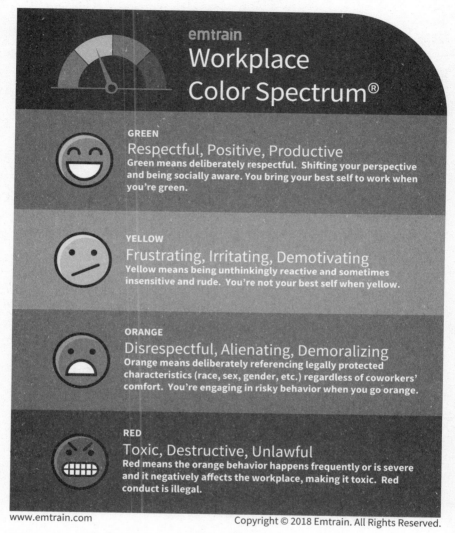

Figure 8.1   Emtrain's Workplace Color Spectrum

Emtrain uses the Workplace Color Spectrum®[6] for this purpose (see Figure 8.1). This simple communication tool categorizes behavior by color, ranging from green, for respectful and positive behavior, to red, for illegal and toxic conduct. This tool serves numerous purposes. The first is that it creates an easy and

---

[6]Reprinted with the permission of Emtrain. For a full-color copy of the Workplace Color Spectrum®, log on to www.Emtrain.com.

safe way to call out objectionable behavior. And it does so in a way that makes it about the conduct and not about the person. So, "Laura, your insistence that I celebrate birthdays is annoying and discriminatory, you're being a real jerk," becomes, "Laura, I know you like celebrating birthdays, but I've told you I don't and I can't. Your behavior is orange at best and bordering on red. Please stop."

This example also shows the tool's second purpose. As I've stated numerous times throughout this book, a huge driver of workplace drama is relying exclusively on legal language to express dissatisfaction. Too often, employees use "harassment," "discrimination," and "retaliation" inaccurately and end up escalating the drama by doing so. This tool provides employees an option to speak to each other in English instead of in legal-speak.

The other way employees use this tool is to increase empathy and understanding. Emtrain has found that in using the tool, employees sometimes differ in how they rate certain words or behavior. Sometimes women rate a situation as orange while men see it as green or yellow. Sometimes subordinate employees see the actions of a supervisor as orange while the supervisor herself thinks she's being respectful and therefore green. As a result of seeing that we all view behavior through our own lenses, we're able to help others understand our point of view.

Since the tool gives words to prompt further discussion (words like positive, demotivating, alienating), the tool is most effective when used as a starting point for a longer, honest and respectful discussion about workplace conduct. This decreases needless emotional reactions and increases understanding. Together, this translates into a steep decline in workplace drama.

Seek to Be Understood: Not Everyone Will Agree with You, and That's Okay

Do your part to fix drama quickly when you can, but your goal should be to clearly and precisely state your point, knowing that people might disagree. Don't let this reality kill your spirit or your commitment to continue to communicate in a respectful and clear way with all your colleagues.

Of course, this advice is easier to give than it is to follow. But it is possible and the reward—decreased drama at work—is well worth the effort.

Let's go back to Ruiz's Four Agreements to explore this concept further. Ruiz's second agreement is "Don't take anything personally," and the third agreement is "Don't make assumptions."

Providing further context to "Don't take things personally," Ruiz says: "Nothing others do is because of you. What others say and do is a projection of their own reality." Explaining "Don't make assumptions," Ruiz advises: "Find the courage to ask questions and to express what you really want. Communicate with others as clearly as you can to avoid misunderstandings, sadness, and drama."[7]

Helping your employees understand that people often say or do things because of their own reality, not to purposely hurt or anger the listener, helps lessen the sting.

For example, when the VP expressed his anger in my direction, it would have been easy for me to take it personally and lash out with my own anger. But that wouldn't have helped me get to the bottom of the issue. I understood that his anger, directed at me at that moment, was really a projection of his fear and frustration. After all, he'd just been caught red-handed doing something he knew was wrong. That doesn't excuse his behavior, but looking at it from the "this isn't personal" lens allowed me to step back and focus on doing my work, rather than focus on getting angry right back. And clearing my mind of any assumption or judgment allowed me to focus on being objective. After all, I wasn't there to pass judgment on an affair, I was there to gather information about whether his behavior had a negative impact on the workplace.

Teach your employees these concepts so that they can erase the emotional blinders that come from taking things personally or making assumptions. You'll see an immediate improvement in communication and understanding. Doing this will go a long way toward achieving your goal of creating a respectful workplace where drama is a thing of the past.

. . .

Consider supplementing any current training you offer with training on how to increase emotional intelligence so that your employees are well-versed on using these types of techniques to increase empathy, cooperation, and collaboration. It's not a magic pill, but understanding your own emotions and improving your ability to understand others are critical skills to help reduce workplace drama.

---

[7]Reprinted with the permission of Emtrain. For a full-color copy of the Workplace Color Spectrum®, log on to https://www.emtrain.com/workplace-color-spectrum/.

The Cassandra Curse: How Not to Be Persuasive

Although there are varying details to the legend of Cassandra, in a nutshell it goes like this:

God Apollo fell in love with Cassandra and granted her the gift of prophecy. When Cassandra denied Apollo's advances, he placed a curse on her, so that no one would believe her words or her predictions.[8]

In short, Cassandra's gift – the power of prophesy – was completely eliminated by her curse – the *inability to persuade* anyone to believe her visions and act accordingly. So while Cassandra was always at least one step ahead of everyone around her, this gift of prophesy didn't help her since people did not heed her warnings. Drama.

There are three primary reasons why people ignored Cassandra's cautionary pleas:

1. Cassandra spoke in oblique riddles, making her message unclear at best and impossible to understand at worst.
2. Cassandra wasn't in a position to be taken seriously. Her lack of power and voice diminished her ability to be heard and her warnings were therefore disregarded.
3. She asked for too much. Too often, she wanted those around her to see the future as she saw it, rather than meeting them where they were so that she could provide solutions that were doable. This part of the curse also meant that she was asking others to completely dismiss their own beliefs and embrace hers instead.[9]

You're probably thinking, Greek mythology . . . what does that have to do with the workplace and with achieving a drama-free environment? It's all about being persuasive. Without the ability to communicate precisely and persuasively—at the individual and organizational level—getting to the top of the Healthy Workplace Culture Pyramid is impossible.

---

[8]"The Myth of Cassandra," *Greek Myths & Greek Mythology.* https://www.greekmyths-greekmythology.com/the-myth-of-cassandra/.

[9]Shankar Vedantam, host and narrator, "The Cassandra Curse: Why We Heed Some Warnings and Ignore Others," *Hidden Brain*, NPR, September 17, 2018. https://www.npr.org/templates/transcript/transcript.php?storyId=648781756.

The Cassandra Curse: Workplace Edition

The Case of the Oblique Messenger

Nigel supervises employees in the menswear department of a famous design company. Andi and Emily are designers on Nigel's team and while Nigel is mostly pleased with Emily's work, he is not happy with Andi's. He's noticed that, in addition to presenting tired ideas for next year's fashion line, Andi has less enthusiasm for the job and pays less attention to details—two characteristics he views as nonnegotiable for designers on his team. Nigel heard rumors that Andi and her husband recently bought a coffee shop and he believes that Andi might be spending time on that endeavor with the ultimate goal of leaving the company and dedicating herself to being a full-time small business owner.

Unfortunately, rather than sitting down with Andi and speaking with her candidly and clearly about his concerns, he gave her cryptic messages—a mistake made by too many managers. Sometimes he attempted humor— "Okay, Andi, these designs aren't going to create themselves." Other times he was even more passive aggressive—"it must be nice to be able to roll into the office at 9:30 every day." The one thing he didn't do was talk to her to express his concerns and to try to find a solution.

Over time, Andi interpreted Nigel's comments as sexist since she felt they were only directed toward her. Although this claim was hard to prove for several reasons, not the least of which was that Nigel did not make similar comments to Andi's female coworkers, Nigel's oblique messages created a reasonable and expected perception in Andi's mind and this failure resulted in unnecessary drama.

The Case of the Wrong Messenger

Ruth was a successful attorney who was generally liked by her colleagues, but she rubbed a few people the wrong way. Some disliked her for legitimate reasons, while others viewed her negatively out of pettiness and mean-spiritedness. Unfortunately, Ruth didn't do herself any favors by giving those who disliked her, including numerous top leaders, more reasons to think of her as pushy and overly aggressive (we'll set aside for now whether a male attorney with her personality characteristics would have been similarly regarded). She also lost support and sympathy when, in her frustration, she began to complain about everything that didn't go her way.

Eventually, Ruth complained about something very legitimate—a fellow attorney who was a master at creating workplace drama. Others agreed to support Ruth and even signed their name to her complaint. Unfortunately, since Ruth was viewed as "the ring leader" and had a long-standing reputation with leadership as "a complainer," her statements fell on deaf ears.

It eventually became clear that Ruth's complaints were spot-on, but it was too late. Ruth's predictions about the drama king came true; not only was he emboldened to continue his bad behavior, but it actually got worse. The company ignored her complaints because they viewed her as the wrong messenger. And while this had a negative effect on Ruth, it had an even more devastating and long-lasting effect on the company. The increased drama caused others, including many women, to leave the company. The company also saw a steep decline in the morale and productivity of the employees who opted to stay.

The Case of the Impractical Corporate Message

In their quest to improve their workplace culture, a large organization implemented two big ideas: (1) it would try to keep up with tech company perks that many of their employees talked about—free food, a pool table, and more organized social events—and (2) they introduced an app-based "suggestion box," through which employees were encouraged to provide ideas, no matter how zany.

Unfortunately, what started out as a plan to increase employee engagement and loyalty ended up having the opposite effect.

First, the company didn't take into account the foundation of the Healthy Workplace Culture Pyramid. At a minimum, employees must feel fairly compensated before a company can make its way up the pyramid. In this case, employees universally hated each new perk since, in their eyes, "That money could and should have gone toward long overdue raises." The company was asking too much of the employees—to ignore the obvious pain point of feeling underpaid and instead focus on how much fun it would be to play pool with their colleagues.

Second, the company expected too much of the employees with their free-for-all suggestion box. They received hundreds of comments, many complaints and a good percentage of pie-in-the-sky ideas that could never work. As a result, none of the ideas came to fruition. The employees, especially those who submitted suggestions, were upset. And the finance department, who saw this as a waste of money, was equally upset.

By failing to meet the employees where they were—starting with salary reviews and giving more guidance on the type of suggestions that were doable—this company's great ideas turned into drama in the form of increased employee anger and frustration.

At the root of Cassandra's suffering was her complete inability to persuade those around her to believe what she knew would be the truth, whether it was her failure to communicate clearly, her failure to understand that she wasn't always the right messenger, or her failure to explain her prophesies in a way that could be accepted. Ultimately, her curse was that she was unable to communicate convincingly. Although Cassandra was doomed, there are a number of lessons based on her plight that you can leverage to make your workplace healthier.

Breaking the Curse: How to Be More Persuasive

Not all of us were gifted with the power of prophesy, but luckily neither were we cursed with the misfortune of always being ignored. It turns out that Cassandra's three downfalls provide great lessons for the workplace and serve as a roadmap to help employees communicate more precisely and persuasively. Goodbye, drama.

Lesson 1.   *Become a Master Persuader by Using the "P2 Filter"*

Run your conversations through the P2 filter to make your communication more *p*recise and *p*ersuasive. That means using your best emotional intelligence skills and your persuasion skills to wordsmith messages to ensure that you say what you mean, and mean what you say.

In the case of Nigel and Andi, Nigel might have avoided workplace drama if he'd been more precise in his conversations with Andi, eliminating any ambiguity or confusion. Like most managers, Nigel found it difficult to deliver performance concerns. He let this fear, along with his own increasing frustration with Andi's declining performance, dictate his actions. By using imprecise language, he made things worse.

What if he'd said this instead:

Andi, over the past few months I've noticed changes in your performance and in your level of enthusiasm about your work. I know it's tough to hear feedback that's less than stellar, but I want to assure you that my goal is to have an open and candid dialogue so we can work through this together.

By starting out in this way, Nigel is not only being transparent, he's also stating the purpose of the conversation and his goal right away. Too many managers launch right into performance criticism, often putting the employee in a defensive mode. By stating his intention at the beginning, Andi knows that Nigel's goal is to make things better.

He might have continued with:

The last batch of designs you gave me missed the mark. They actually looked a lot like last year's designs. I know in the past you've done background research to study the latest trends, and even come up with trendsetting styles, but these designs didn't have your signature creativity. Let's talk about what's going on so that I can be sure to provide you what you need to get back on track.

Here, Nigel has wordsmithed his message to do a few things:

- He was direct (he didn't sugarcoat the fact that her work missed the mark).
- He praised her for past work, recognizing that she has the talent to do better.
- He made it clear that his goal was to do his part—he was willing to provide her the resources necessary to get back on track.

I call this being the *compassionate sharpshooter*: communicating in ways that are equal parts direct and caring.

Nigel could have continued with:

I've also noticed that you're not as enthusiastic about your work lately. I completely understand that each of us has good days and bad days, but given the nature of our work, enthusiasm and passion are crucial. Do you agree?

Here, Nigel is again being a compassionate sharpshooter, but he's doing one other thing: He's seeking Andi's buy-in and opening the door for Andi to talk about the reasons for her lowered level of excitement. Andi might have confirmed the rumors that she was planning to leave the company, in which case they might have negotiated a mutually beneficial exit plan. Or it might turn out that those rumors were false and Andi might have acknowledged her loss of interest in her job, which would give rise to a healthy discussion about next steps to help her improve.

One additional way to make conversations like these easier is to practice. If you're in HR, offer this as a resource. Give your managers the opportunity to rehearse how they will give feedback. Ask the manager how he anticipates the employee will react and play the part of the employee. If the manager thinks the employee is going to get angry, sad, or defensive, then play that part and let the manager work through the kinks. And if you're a manager working at a company that doesn't already do this, encourage HR to offer this resource. This will allow managers to come up with the best language to give their message, and it also helps them anticipate what might get them off track. Doing this always results in performance evaluation meetings that are more focused and productive.

These are not easy conversations to have, but they are necessary if you want to reduce workplace drama. Nigel would have saved himself, Andi, and the company a lot of time, stress, and energy if he'd run his conversations through the P2 filter.

Lesson 2.   *Become a Master Persuader by Learning What Makes People Tick*

Understanding what might motivate or persuade your audience is a key way to keep drama away.

In the case of Ruth, she mistakenly thought that the answer was to enlist support and to write a lengthy complaint letter, detailing every misstep the drama-producer had ever committed. But she'd become the workplace "girl who cried wolf" since she'd complained too often already (often about insignificant issues). She'd also lost credibility by rubbing people the wrong way. Fair or not, she should have known that a message, even one that was true, might be ignored if it came from her. To make matters worse, instead of focusing on the three or four examples of egregious behavior she and others suffered at the hands of the abusive colleague, she threw in every slight, every insult, every example of poor judgment. She watered down her message to the point of completely diminishing its value.

Help employees understand the power of knowing what motivates others to make them master persuaders. Don't mistake this advice for being manipulative or dishonest. As I've said over and over, none of the advice I offer works if it's implemented in a disingenuous or inauthentic way. But if your goal is truly to make yourself heard, then use the right language to make that more likely.

In Ruth's case, if her goal was to alert the company to a real issue so the company leaders could take proper action, she should have done one of two things. She should have either taken herself out of the equation altogether, knowing that management would diminish the importance of the concerns if her name was associated with them, or she should have done a better job expressing her concerns by focusing on the three or four issues that mattered most, rather than writing a short novel detailing every mistake ever made. In other words, Ruth should have figured out what was most likely to motivate leadership to take the complaints seriously and to act.

Teaching employees to identify how they are motivated and how others are motivated will increase the chance that communication will become persuasive. Once people understand each other better, a drama-free workplace is just around the corner.

Lesson 3.   Become a Master Persuader by Being Collaborative and Practical

When the company in the last example implemented their ideas, they forgot to first take the collective organizational pulse. If they'd done so, they could have easily predicted that taking these two steps would end in drama. With that information, they might have changed course and invested their time and money into areas that not only eliminated the possibility of drama, but would also have had the desired effect of increasing employee engagement.

For example, a quick review of the company's employee surveys would have uncovered ample data showing extreme dissatisfaction with salary and raises (or the lack of raises). The comments in those surveys also would have eliminated the need to spend money on a suggestion box app since the concerns raised in the surveys needed to be resolved before moving into the more sophisticated arena of seeking employee input for more innovative ideas.

It was impractical to think the company could skip over basic steps to fix the employee engagement problems with these cosmetic fixes.

A final point is about pivoting. If your organization falters, learn from the setback and try again. Here, the company would have been best served by sending a company-wide email acknowledging their misstep and promising to do better.

. . .

Whether it's individuals who miscommunicate or don't communicate at all—or organizations that fail to deliver clear and understandable messages to their workforce—a failure to communicate precisely and persuasively will undermine your organization's quest to achieve a drama-free workplace. Learn to be precise and persuasive, and teach others in your organization those skills, and you'll see a dramatic reduction in workplace drama.

A DIY Roadmap for Creating and Maintaining a Drama-Free Culture

9 | Policies, Schmolicies ...How to Write and Enforce the Right Rules

The last three chapters of this book focus on implementation and execution. This do-it-yourself part is divided into two sections:

1. Things you can do to prevent drama from happening in the first place (write policies your employees will actually read and follow, and provide training that will positively impact understanding and behavior).
2. Innovative but time-tested methods to resolve drama if it does occur (receiving, investigating, and resolving claims of misconduct).

We'll start with policies. Though policies are universally recognized as useful tools to prevent misconduct, too many organizations pay little attention to writing and enforcing policies that will have that desired effect. Let's be honest, no one really reads the employee handbook. More precisely, no one reads the typical handbook. (I do know of a few companies who've written clear, precise, transparent, and entertaining policies, but they are, unfortunately, the exception rather the rule.)

161

So how can you take a fresh new approach to writing policies? How can you write policies that become an integral component of your journey to becoming a drama-free workplace?

- First, as I discussed in detail in the "Freedom" section in Chapter 5, policies that restrict freedom do more harm than good. So write policies that set expectations and communicate your commitment to a healthy workplace.
- Second, policies have become nothing more than yet another legal CYA tool—an additional element in the company's quest to "protect" itself from lawsuits, rather than a truly helpful guide. Be bold. Chuck the legalese and instead write policies that employees want to read, with guidelines they understand.

I'll end the chapter by focusing on sexual harassment policies, summarizing the top 10 mistakes I've seen in those policies and providing a roadmap, including sample language, to avoid those pitfalls.

Taken together, these sections will help you authentically state your expectations as you make your journey to the top of the Healthy Workplace Culture Pyramid.

Policies Should Set Expectations, Not Restrict Freedom

Should policies be written to give employees the right to do something, or should they be written to encourage employees to do the right thing? If you've been paying attention, you know that I believe the best way to prevent workplace drama is to encourage employees, to promote greater connection and empathy, and to give them a sense of fairness.

So why do so many workplace policies seem to do the opposite? The primary reason is that most companies see their handbook, or individual policies, through the tiny lens of legal compliance. The handbook has become a way to "protect" organizations from employees who are always lurking just around the corner to find a way to bring a claim against you.

But policies have also been rendered all but useless for other reasons.

First, there's the canned language. Go look at your handbook to see how many times it says "up to and including termination ..." I'll bet it says that a lot. Some of my other favorites are: "Discrimination or harassment on the basis of any protected category is prohibited" and "We will not tolerate retaliation." These are great promises, but they lose their oomph when 10,000 other companies cut-and-paste the exact same language.

Second, too many policies are written to address the misconduct of one employee. Essentially the policy seeks to punish everyone for one person's mistake or poor judgment. Someone wore clothes you find distasteful, unprofessional, or distracting? Let's add that to the dress code. Someone is logging onto social media or doing their online shopping at work? Let's write a policy naming the specific sites that are off limits. What do these situations have in common? The people in charge of enforcing behavioral expectations are failing to do their job. Rather than taking the direct route —sitting down and talking to the person behaving badly—they take a passive-aggressive approach. Before you know it, you have a 100-plus-page handbook that's been band-aided over the years. This isn't helpful to anyone.

Policies also often contain punitive language with no real teeth. Are you really going to enforce your policy that says that someone who eats their lunch at their cubicle will be disciplined? Do you mean it when you say that you'll fire someone if they fail to report the fact that they went out on a date with a coworker last week? These policies almost always have one of two results. The first is that employees don't believe what you're saying. The policies become nothing more than a source for employee ridicule since they are not enforced (or they're enforced inconsistently). The other option is that your employees do believe you and start wondering if this scary workplace is one they want to be a part of.

Finally, too many policies fail to explain the "why" related to the policy, making them sound like nothing more than language taken from an ancient law book.

Here are some examples and ways you can improve your policies:

- Timekeeping policies shouldn't just be a way to keep tabs on employees. Let employees know that in addition to legal requirements, you have timekeeping mandates because you are committed to making sure everyone gets paid for all the work they do.
- Also in the world of timekeeping, rather than just telling employees that they "must" take rest and meal breaks and that failure to do so could result in discipline ("up to and including termination"), tell

them that the intent of this policy is to make sure employees don't get burned out. A well-written policy tells your employees that you value their physical and mental health and want them to work hard when they're working, but to take time to decompress, too.

- Disability policies should cover more than legal obligations. Yes, your organization is required to provide an accommodation request if, after a good faith interactive process, you find an accommodation that is reasonable and will be effective in allowing the employee to do her job. But a great employer does more than comply with this requirement. Stating the "why" gives you a chance to tell employees that your goal is to make the process a win–win proposition. Explain that while it's not always possible to find an accommodation that works, you're committed to approaching the process with a can-do mindset. This reminds employees that yours is a company that complies not only with the letter of the law, but also with the spirit of the law.

- Bullying policies are often vague and fail to define what is meant by "respectful" or "professional." Does this mean that saying one curse word after stubbing your toe is wrong? Or does it mean that a boss who throws things at employees is behaving acceptably because he's "high spirited?" (I've investigated both these claims.) First, if you think it's necessary to have a policy on abusive or demeaning behavior, give specific examples and be realistic. Follow up by discussing this more during training. And finally, if you opt to have a policy emphasizing your commitment to a respectful workplace, enforce it. Consistently. Too often I see companies who say "we want a respectful workplace" on paper but the reality is that bullies run rampant and people are too scared to do anything, especially if the bully is in a position of power.

- Policies about evaluations and salary reviews could help create a more seamless process, but unfortunately many policies make the process more bureaucratic. Inauthentic, canned language sends the message that you only see the evaluation process as a necessary evil and don't really do much analysis when deciding about salary increases. Add language that sets expectations for managers and employees. This might include your organization's commitment to continuous feedback (along with training on what that means), helpful supplements with answers to FAQs, and an offer to help if someone is struggling with how to give feedback. For employees, you can provide similar resources to let them know that the evaluation process isn't something you do because your lawyers force you to; it's a process you view as a vital employee development tool.

Take a look at your current handbook with these suggestions in mind to start the process of setting expectations that will help free your organization of needless drama.

And one final note: Be creative and innovative. Speak to your employees in the format and language that will most resonate with them. Here are a few ideas:

- *Videotape some of your policies.* That doesn't mean you don't put them in writing, but having a short introduction or a series of videos to present your expectations might help your employees pay attention.
- *Host periodic town hall meetings.* Make sure top-level leaders are there to speak and to answer questions. Make it fun and engaging and make sure what you cover corresponds with the other efforts you're taking to create a healthy culture. Make it into a game show to see who can talk about your policies most accurately and enthusiastically.
- *Share success stories.* HR is often viewed as the equivalent of the vice principal's office in high school—it's where you are sent when you're in trouble. Change the narrative and make the HR department (or whatever you call your department) a place that is actually human, and provides resources. If someone successfully used your leave policy and expressed appreciation for the guidance you provided during that difficult and emotional process, celebrate that. Ask the employee to tell his/her story—again, perhaps via video or some other engaging avenue (without disclosing any personal information, and assuming the employee is comfortable doing so).
- *And if you're really bold and playful, do something that's completely outside the box.* Develop a contest related to your handbook. Include stories that help illustrate your points. One company slipped in nonsensical policies to see if anyone actually read the handbook. And the HR director awarded prizes to employees who spotted the fakes. One of the pretend policies said, "If you quit within three months of hire,

you have to wash the HR director's car for six months after your departure."[1] This type of playfulness may not work with all companies, but if you think it won't fly at your workplace, maybe the answer is that you need to inject more fun into your organization!

Top 10 Mistakes in a Typical Sexual Harassment Prevention Policy

An employee handbook contains dozens of policies, but in today's post-#MeToo world, many organizations are focusing most of their attention on their harassment prevention policy. I've reviewed thousands of policies in my work as an attorney, investigator, and expert witness. I can probably recite your policy without ever having seen it because there is very little difference between policies, regardless of company or industry.

Here are the top 10 mistakes I've seen in the typical harassment prevention policy. These aren't listed in the order of importance but are instead listed in the order that most policies follow:

Overall Tone

1. *The focus is singularly on the law.* If the emphasis is exclusively on the law, the message is that all you care about is minimal compliance.
   a. It may seem like minutiae, but words are powerful. Does the title of your policy make it clear that you expect respect, collaboration, and inclusion, or does it sound like a scary legal document?
   b. Is your harassment prevention policy 10 pages long? If so, that's too long. There is no magic formula, but if your policy is that long then my guess is that you've put little thought into it. (The one exception is for employers in the State of New York, who must use the language in the state's long "model" policy.)
   c. Make sure the definitions you provide are precise. Be meticulous with language. That means you make a distinction between

---

[1] Rebecca Mazin, "Does Anyone *Really* Read the Employee Handbook?" *allBusiness.* https://www.allbusiness.com/does-anyone-emreallyem-read-the-employee-handbook-15747840-1.html.

lawful and unlawful behavior. I often use "Harassment" (with a capital "H") and "harassment" to make that distinction. Or you can use the phrase "unlawful harassment" or "illegal harassment" versus behavior that is inappropriate, bothersome, demeaning, demoralizing, exclusionary, or belittling.

    d. Make sure your definition of "unlawful harassment" is precise and complete. Some policies provide a definition that is under-inclusive. For example, leaving out a necessary element and giving the misimpression that certain behavior is unlawful when it isn't. Other policies are overinclusive and provide more information about both the definition of Harassment and the examples of unlawful behavior.

    e. Now that you've got the legal issues out of the way, add language that makes it clear that your goals are much loftier than only legal compliance. (See sample language below.)

2. *Vague zero-tolerance language.* While the use of the term *zero tolerance* started with good intentions, the term has lost its purpose and effectiveness. If you feel the need to use the term, then define it precisely. What exactly will you "not tolerate?" If the answer is "we won't tolerate unlawful harassment," then that implies you will tolerate really bad behavior, so long as it doesn't rise to the level of illegality. If you don't specifically define what you will or won't tolerate, then the implication is that anything that is perceived as inappropriate, unprofessional, or bothersome will be "dealt with swiftly." But that's not true since in many instances this type of behavior is technically "tolerated," meaning it's not cause for firing someone. I'd encourage you to stop using this language and use language that better defines expectations and corresponding consequences.

3. *Harsh language regarding supervisor responsibility.* Supervisors, especially middle managers, are your company's lifeline. They straddle that difficult space of dual responsibility—they have bosses to answer to, but they're in daily contact with employees. Often they're in contact with unhappy or dissatisfied employees. They're in the best position to observe behavior—good and bad—and to be your organization's eyes and ears to address smoke before it becomes fire. Supervisors are also expected to lead by example. This is a lot to ask, but it's what comes with the territory. Make your supervisor's jobs easier, not

harder. Provide them with a roadmap to help them understand the critical role they play in making yours a fantastic workplace culture. Sure, they have to know legal parameters, but more important, they need to understand how they can contribute to a drama-free workplace. This means enough with the punitive language—"you must report all harassment . . . failure to do so will result in discipline" ("up to and including termination"). Of course you need to make it clear that you're relying on them to observe behavior and to either resolve or report bad conduct. But rather than focusing on their legal obligation (or, at the very least, in addition to stating this legal obligation), tell them what you expect. (See sample language below.)

Reporting Misconduct

4. *The policy says "tell us if you've been harassed."* If you're telling your employees to wait until the conduct is this severe, you're missing the boat. From a legal standpoint, courts have repeatedly stated that an organization can defend itself against a harassment lawsuit if it can show that it took reasonable steps to prevent harassment. (See Chapter 1 for a discussion on using legal requirements to shield you from legal liability.) You can only prevent behavior from escalating to the point of illegal conduct if you set up a reliable and effective way to address conduct when it's mild, so that it will never reach the crisis point of illegality. But this brings us to the point that is much more important than legal obligations or legal defenses to harassment lawsuits: It is impossible to achieve a drama-free workplace if your message is, "We will leave you unprotected up until the very last minute, when the behavior is persistent and intolerable."

Organizations must do better than this. Here's a better approach.

- First, make it clear that you want to address unacceptable behavior early. That means teaching employees and managers how to intervene in the moment if appropriate. It also means providing safe and open spaces for complaints to be heard and taken seriously (in the event employees are not comfortable intervening, or if the intervention doesn't stop the objectionable conduct).

- Next, once employees know that you welcome complaints since you see them as opportunities rather than burdens, teach them *how* to report. Rather than giving them instructions to tell you about the "harassing conduct," ask them to tell you: (1) what happened; (2) how the behavior affected them; and (3) how you can work together to find solutions and move forward.

- In many instances, you'll have to then conduct a formal investigation. However, by using this language you eliminate the need to open a formal inquiry into every report made, since often a complaint requires action rather than an investigation. If, however, you do determine that you need to launch an impartial workplace investigation, you're starting out ahead of the game by having a clear understanding about the nature of the complaint. And you're sending a strong and important message to your employees about your commitment to staying drama free.

5. *The policy makes reporting difficult or scary.* Many employers write and distribute policies that essentially state "Take care of this on your own" or "We can't be bothered with your complaints." In many instances, this message is inadvertent. In their zeal to "comply," many organizations turned to language that has been used forever without realizing the damage that language might have. This includes:

   a. If your policy says employees are "required" to report (or worse, required to submit a form or otherwise put their complaint in writing), the unintended consequence is that employees feel like they have to jump through procedural hurdles before they'll be heard (much less believed). What you really mean is that you can't fix what you don't know. Your policy should therefore emphasize your true commitment to creating an environment in which employees feel comfortable expressing concerns. And preferably that's done before the conduct is severe, so that you can partner with the employee to resolve issues early. But by using words like "require" and "in writing" that overall message gets lost.

   b. Although not as common, some policies "require" that the employee confront the person engaging in misconduct. Again, while we want to educate and encourage employees to use their voices—whether they are the targets or witnesses to bad behavior—this sends a message that the responsibility for bad behavior falls on the recipient, rather than on the person who is *actually* engaging in misconduct.

c. Also beware of providing insufficient avenues to raise concerns. If an employee only has the option to go to their immediate supervisor and maybe one person in HR, they may opt not to say anything. The number and types of complaint mechanisms will vary depending on your company size (and resources) but make sure you provide options so that employees understand that you're serious when you say you want to hear their concerns.

6. *The policy creates a chilling effect by referring to "malicious" or "frivolous" claims.* Another mistake I see regarding reports of misconduct is this stark warning: "If we find that you've lodged a frivolous complaint, there will be consequences." Talk about creating a chilling effect! This implies that if a person's claims are not fully substantiated (which happens often), then they might be subject to some disciplinary action. What most employers mean to say is that they expect all their employees to act in good faith and with integrity, and that includes lodging complaints. Either use more precise and less punitive language like "good faith" to achieve your intended result, or scrap this language altogether. If you've written other policies well, and if you have a workplace that is rooted in integrity and values, this is implied. And, in my experience, this is another example of a policy with no teeth. Unless you can conclusively prove that the complainant lied and did so with malicious intent (a high bar), are you really going to discipline or fire that person? (See more on the investigation and resolution of claims of misconduct in Chapter 11.)

Investigations of Misconduct

7. *The policy only promises to investigate claims of "harassment."* See the discussion above related to only allowing employees to complain about harassing conduct (mistake #4). The legal obligation, and the smart decision, if you want to have a healthy workplace, is to look into claims of misconduct. You can certainly further define what you

will and won't investigate, but replacing "harassment" with "misconduct" (or a similar word/phrase) is a good place to start.

8. *You make promises about investigations that you can't keep.* The investigation process is detailed. While you can and should include general information about investigations, there is no need to go into great detail. And don't overpromise.

   a. Promise "limited confidentiality" rather than a promise that you'll conduct a "confidential investigation." In fact, you might consider replacing "confidential" with a word like "discreet" so that the message is clear: "We will do everything in our power to keep private information private, but a promise of complete secrecy means we can't conduct a fair and thorough investigation."

   b. Also look out for promises related to communicating with the parties after the investigation, or promises that you'll share your entire investigation file with them. While you want to have a transparent process and you should absolutely report back with the main parties when you're done investigating, this doesn't mean you share everything. (See Chapter 11 for more on this topic.)

Fixing Problems

9. *The policy says you'll take action* only *if the behavior is unlawful or violates the policy.* If after your investigation you find any level of misconduct, you need to take action. Period. The severity of the consequence will depend on numerous factors, but if you find misconduct and do nothing, then you are emboldening the bad actor to continue with the objectionable behavior. You're also sending a message that rules apply only to certain people. That's a recipe for disaster for any organization that wants to remain drama free. (For more on the topic of instituting appropriate remedial measures, see Chapter 11.)

10. *You use canned language related to discipline.* While there is nothing wrong with having a progressive discipline policy, it's not necessary. Most employees understand that actions have consequences. They

also understand that different actions have different consequences. Go back and look at your language on discipline to make sure it's achieving its desired effect and not causing confusion or setting unrealistic expectations ("it says in the policy that a first violation would only get me a written warning . . .").

This is a long list, I know. But unfortunately most organizations have spent years, maybe even decades, writing and distributing the same old same old. It's time to pay close attention to the true purpose of policies and handbooks. Although they've too often morphed into yet another compliance tool, taking a fresh approach and seeing policies as a key to achieving no drama at work will put you at the top of the Healthy Workplace Culture Pyramid in no time!

Say Goodbye to Legal Jargon and Hello to Clarity and Positivity

Some policy language is legally required, but that doesn't mean you have to stop there. Ideally, policies should focus more on the promise of a healthy, productive, and respectful workplace culture.

My suggestion? Reinvent the workplace policy. Take the opportunity to craft policies that showcase your company's commitment to making respectful treatment a mutual responsibility, a two-way street where respect and inclusion are core values that the organization expects everyone to adhere to.

Here is some sample language. Feel free to use this language, or, better yet, use this and other parts of this book as inspiration to draft your own language.

1. Instead of "We promise a harassment-free workplace," consider stating:

   We've covered the legal issues separately but we want to take this opportunity to address something that is more important to us than legal compliance. Don't misunderstand, we are deeply and genuinely committed to a workplace with no unlawful sexual harassment. But we want to make a much bolder promise than "We vow to comply with our minimum legal requirements." The promise we make is that rather than focusing exclusively on compliance, we will do all we can to create, maintain, and promote a culture that values respect, fairness, and inclusion. We invite you to be a part of our quest.

and/or

Our mission is ____. We understand we can't live up to that mission, or serve our customer base without providing you, our most important resource, a safe, comfortable, positive, and productive work environment. To that end, we give you our word that we are committed to providing a healthy work environment where you can effectively perform your job and where you can thrive — as an individual and as a valuable member of a supportive team.

and/or

Whereas some companies promise a "harassment-free workplace," our goals are much loftier than that. This isn't simply a guarantee that we won't violate the law. Our word to you is that we will not only do our part to prevent and resolve unlawful harassment, but that we are committed to creating and maintaining a diverse, inclusive, and professional environment.

2. Let employees and managers know the resources you'll provide to help them distinguish between severity of conduct (unlawful versus objectionable/offensive but not illegal), and guidance on how to make and receive reports of workplace concerns.

We are steadfast in our commitment to:

- *Provide relevant, practical, and continuous education about our behavioral expectations to all employees—behavior we find acceptable or unacceptable, regardless of whether it rises to the level of illegal harassment. We understand that conduct that might start out as minor or infrequent can, if left unaddressed, quickly turn into more serious misconduct.*
- *Provide employees, supervisors, and company leaders with resources, including helpful communication tools—including tools to object to inappropriate behavior as it occurs as well as tools to learn to report behavior to supervisors, HR, or through our company hotline.*

- *Create a safe and comfortable environment where employees and managers share concerns so that we have an opportunity to look into them and resolve them.*
- *Fairly and honestly investigate any reports of misconduct, allowing all parties to have a say.*
- *Implement appropriate and meaningful corrective measures in the event our investigation uncovers misconduct (in English, we promise to fix any problems we identify).*
- *Implement appropriate and meaningful consequences in an even-handed way and through the use of discipline that is commensurate with the wrongdoing uncovered by an independent investigation.*

3. Close your policy with uplifting language (or send similar language in an email distributing the policy, or put language like this in a preamble to an employee handbook):

What is most important to us is to start an honest dialogue about these issues. Though these topics (bias, harassment, racial strife, gender issues) might be difficult and sensitive, we want all our employees to feel comfortable asking questions and giving suggestions on how we can foster an atmosphere of trust and of mutual respect.

We want to reiterate that we are not simply reciting corporate speak when we say that you, our valued employees, are truly our most valuable resource. We mean it, and we know that we cannot succeed on any level if we don't have a workforce who trusts us, who views their role at the company (and their actual work) as meaningful, and who we can deploy as true-believing brand ambassadors. We hope this policy answers any questions you have about where we stand when it comes to these issues, but if you have any additional comments, please do not hesitate to contact any of us.

This is a lot. Perhaps you'll opt to put only some of this language in your formal policy. Or maybe you'll decide that you'll have a policy spelling out the legal issues, and have a separate policy or a separate handbook that has these messages. Regardless of which option you select, the important thing is that you're now on a clear path that will allow you to use policies to set expectations and to use as a vehicle to communicate with your employees.

More important, you're on your way to making your policies a key aspect on your trip to the top of the Healthy Workplace Culture Pyramid.

Harassment Prevention Policy Checklist[2]

This checklist will help you avoid the top 10 mistakes in harassment prevention policies. These suggestions will help you create an effective policy.

1. **Policy addresses the law, but focuses on more than the law.**
   - ☑ Policy contains required legal language:
     - ○ Definition of unlawful behavior (stated precisely, clearly, and succinctly)
     - ○ Examples of unlawful behavior
     - ○ Retaliation – all are protected by it, all are bound to follow it
     - ○ How to report, details on how reports will be handled
   - ☑ Policy goes beyond legal definitions, says all misconduct is unacceptable, especially if it has the effect of making employees feel excluded, demeaned, or disrespected.
   - ☑ Policy lists core values and these are woven into the entire policy—respect, inclusion, accountability, integrity, ethics.
   - ☑ Is the name of the policy clear or does it sound legal?
   - ☑ Is the policy too long?

2. **Zero-tolerance policy?**
   - ☑ Decide if want/need to include.
   - ☑ Consider renaming or rewriting policy to precisely define which behavior is intolerable and the consequence for engaging in that behavior.

3. **Provide supervisors with encouraging guidance to report misconduct.**
   - ☑ Policy should not be threatening or punitive.
   - ☑ Policy written to honor supervisor role as company eyes and ears.

---

[2]For a downloadable copy of this checklist as well as other useful resources to create a drama-free workplace, please go to www.emtrain.com/drama-free-workplace-book.

☑ Policy written to encourage reporting, and explain why that's so important.

☑ Policy written to set expectations, not written in legalese.

4. Reporting – encourage early reports.

☑ Policy welcomes complaints of misconduct, that is, conduct that excludes, belittles, or demeans; does not limit complaints to only those about unlawful conduct.

☑ Policy encourages speaking with a manager or HR if there is a concern that can be addressed and resolved early (even if no formal investigation is needed).

☑ Policy states the company's commitment to teach early conflict resolution skills so that drama can be nipped in the bud.

5. Reporting – make it easy and safe.

☑ Policy says employees are "invited to" or "encouraged" to report concerns, not "required to."

☑ Policy language makes it clear that company sees reports as an opportunity to make workplace better; to make culture healthier.

☑ Policy refers to company's commitment to educate employees and managers on how to address conflict early, but does not "require" that employee "confront" person engaged in misconduct before filing a complaint.

☑ Policy provides numerous avenues to lodge complaints; message to employees is "we welcome hearing from you."

6. Reporting – do not cause a chilling effect.

☑ Policy says company will investigate concerns brought in "good faith," not that company will discipline or fire employee if concerns are "malicious" or "frivolous."

☑ Concept of "good faith" is further explored in other policies that address ethics, expected professional conduct, integrity, and values.

7. Investigations – include broad language for what you will investigate.

☑ Policy language is broad, making it clear that the company will investigate concerns of misconduct.

☑ Policy includes commitment to a healthy culture, which means concerns are identified, investigated, and resolved early, long before they reach the level of unlawful harassment.

8. **Investigations – don't overpromise.**

☑ Policy refers to "limited confidentiality" or "discretion," not to a "confidential investigation."

☑ Policy indicates that the company will communicate with the main parties (complainant and accused) after the investigation to provide them conclusions and next steps, but does not guarantee that specific information or documents will be shared (policy explains that the company will be transparent but needs to exercise judgment and discretion).

9. **Conflict resolution – promise more than "We will fix problems only if harassment is found."**

☑ Policy clearly indicates that appropriate remedies will be taken if the investigation uncovers misconduct, *not* that action will *only* be taken *if* the conduct violates a policy or is found to be unlawful.

☑ Policy provides general statement indicating that remedial action taken after the investigation will vary and will be guided primarily by the severity of the misconduct.

☑ Policy emphasizes company's commitment to not only discipline when necessary, but to also learn from each investigation since goal is to make culture healthier.

10. **Make sure your discipline policy is precise and clear.**

☑ Policy on progressive discipline is clear, precise, and customized; it is not canned.

☑ Language on discipline makes it clear that investigations that uncover misconduct will include a step to determine the best remedial measure—one that aims to correct behavior and prevent it from happening again.

☑ Policy emphasizes the company's commitment to even-handedness when it comes to discipline.

10 | Your Step-by-Step Guide to Designing and Delivering Effective Workplace Training

Debates about harassment prevention training are all the rage. Does it work? What's the ROI? Who is best suited to design and deliver training? Will it help us change behavior? Will it reduce the risk of being sued?

In the wake of #MeToo, the issue of harassment prevention training has taken on a life of its own. Numerous state legislatures have passed mandatory training laws. These laws require harassment prevention training and though they vary in detail, what they have in common is that training, whether you love it or hate it, is seen as a necessary piece in the larger puzzle of harassment prevention.

So what's the best way to design and deliver training that has its intended effect?

First, let's take a look at why so many researchers, academics, and even lawmakers have determined that training hasn't achieved its intended

179

result—to move the needle in terms of improving workplace conduct. When you dig deeper into what the data show, you see that it's not that training is bad, it's that *bad training is bad.*

And once we've uncovered the reasons why training hasn't moved the needle, let's explore practical, easy-to-implement ways that can make your training program a cricital element to not only prevent misconduct but also to help make your environment drama-free.

The bottom line is that, while workplace training isn't the magic bullet that will alone create a healthy culture, when done well, it is an essential component of it.

What's Kept Training from Moving the Needle?

It's important to briefly cover what doesn't work, and why we know that certain efforts have been ineffective. I've identified four categories that fall under "what not to do":

1. *Check-the-box mentality:* Training has been ineffective because it has, for the most part, focused solely on issues related to legal compliance. When the message given to employees is, "We are only interested in complying with the minimum legal standards, but nothing else," the research shows that the training will not only be ineffective, it could actually have a backlash effect.

2. *Stand-alone training:* Harassment prevention training does not achieve the desired effect if it doesn't include necessary topics such as unconscious bias, diversity and equity, civility and respect training, bystander intervention training, communications training, and conflict resolution training. Since these topics can't be covered in a one- or two-hour course, they are usually simply ignored and all employees and managers learn is the legal language of unlawful harassment.

3. *Content:* Too many training courses stay within the lines of what is mandatory—legal definitions—rather than exploring issues such as root causes of bad behavior, examples of good behavior, and a focus on tools to make respectful conduct a no-brainer.

   a. *Tone:* If your content only covers legal definitions, scary stories, instructions on what not to do, and warnings of the myriad ways employees can cause harm, there is no chance that participants will learn key ways to identify, prevent, and resolve drama.

b. *Not focused on understanding and behavior change:* Put another way, if the goal of the training is to avoid lawsuits, rather than to persuade people to behave respectfully and inclusively, it will fail (it won't even help you avoid lawsuits). Research shows us that harassment that puts the blame on one side and fails to promote understanding, empathy, and clarity has zero effect on behavior.

c. *Unrealistic examples:* We hear over and over from employees and managers alike that workplace scenarios in most training courses are unrealistic, exaggerated, and show obvious examples of workplace misconduct. Words I've heard to describe this kind of training range from "boring" to "cheesy." Regardless of the words used to describe the training, the result is a failure to pay attention and therefore no learning.

4. *Walking the walk or just talking the talk?* As I've stated over and over, without authenticity, any program you implement that attempts to improve your workplace culture will fail. If employees sense that the training you offer does not line up with what they know to be true about the workplace, it will have no effect on understanding or behavior.

a. *Lack of authenticity:* People have to already believe that they work for an organization that values ethics, respect, and inclusion. Without that foundation, training is viewed as inauthentic and is therefore ineffective.

b. *View that reporting is futile:* Do you have a positive cycle of reporting-investigating-resolving? If not, employees will not believe that their complaints will be taken seriously. Training in this environment does nothing to move the needle.

What Does Work?

So now that we know the current state of affairs, let's turn our attention to why we're here—to find solutions. Solutions that will not only be effective, but also doable.

Starting with the last of the items in the "what not to do" list, the most important aspect of designing and developing an effective training program is to focus on fostering a positive, respectful, and inclusive workplace culture. Without that, training is a waste of time, energy, and other valuable resources. Most entities have been hyper-focused on unlawful harassment (the symptom), while ignoring the disease (an unhealthy workplace culture).

In order to get maximum effectiveness from your training program, make sure your "cure" to the disease of sexual harassment is in line with other pieces of the healthy workplace puzzle. Ask yourself these questions as you get started:

- ☑ Do your policies and practices focus solely on legal issues? If so, no amount of training will help create a feeling of safety and comfort when it comes to solving issues early and effectively.
- ☑ Are you embracing a culture of truth-telling? In a workplace that embraces the idea of being healthy, respectful, inclusive and productive, reports of possible misconduct are welcomed and seen as an opportunity to improve the workplace. Failure to welcome complaints and failure to address concerns doesn't make them go away, it simply robs you of the opportunity to address and resolve them.
- ☑ Are you teaching a new language/tools to communicate precisely and effectively? Today, most employees and managers approach issues of workplace conflict in a defensive and confrontational way. The employee is typically fed up by the time she complains and the person receiving the complaint is nervous that this will turn into a lawsuit. The root here is a mutual lack of trust. When we teach our employees and managers to use only legal language, it's reasonable that they don't have the tools and language necessary to report behavior at the point where it can be resolved as an employee relations issue rather than a public relations or legal issue. Providing employees and managers with precise and simple communication tools and training them on how to use those tools is key.
- ☑ Are you providing training opportunities for everyone? Before #MeToo, I'd often have conversations with leaders who resisted training all employees. "That's essentially providing a road map for how to sue us," they'd say. Nothing could be further from the truth. In fact, well-designed training does the opposite. Training that focuses

on defining what is legal (but might be objectionable) and what is illegal helps reduce claims since employees learn the importance of these distinctions. If they understand that some conduct needs to be addressed but shouldn't be labeled as "harassment" or "discrimination" then they're more likely to report their concerns precisely. And your organization is more likely to respond appropriately.

☑ Are you in a continuous learning mode or do you think harassment prevention training is a one-and-done effort? The answer, of course, is that simply deploying one training session will not move the needle (especially if it's one you're forced to deploy because your state law tells you to do so). What will help, then? Developing a training *program*, rather than deploying a training course. Employees and managers know when a company doesn't care about the workplace culture and understand that this type of compliance-only training isn't designed to affect behavior, it's only designed to check a box.

☑ Do you use a variety of methods to train? Micro learning, mini-lessons, guides, summaries, FAQs, sample scripts, checklists, articles, books, discussion questions …the list is endless. Don't let the learning stop when your employees walk out of the training room or log off the online training course. We need to supplement formal learning sessions with resources to reinforce what is taught in formal training.

☑ Are you relying on the best experts to design and deliver training? Make sure training is designed and delivered by experts who understand the nuances of the workplace. At a minimum, they must have an understanding of legal concepts (although that doesn't mean the expert has to be an attorney, just someone who understands legal concepts). But an expert in the design and delivery of effective harassment prevention training has to know a lot more than the law. She must also be well-versed in the development and enforcement of workplace policies and must have experience investigating and resolving allegations of misconduct. Ideally, the expert can draw on experience to answer questions, use real-life scenes that resonate with the learners, and has the ability to teach skills like communication, empathy, and conflict resolution. Finally, the content needs to be developed and delivered in a way that is easy to implement. You want your employees to say, "I can use these tools to communicate and reduce drama starting this afternoon."

☑   Is your training interactive and personalized? Make sure live training is engaging and allows learners to participate. In live training, interaction should occur naturally—not only in communication between trainer and trainee, but also among the learners themselves. I can honestly say that I learn from every live session I conduct because there is always at least one insightful question asked, or a comment made that helps me see things from a different vantage point.

☑   If you use online training, is it interactive? Interaction is harder to achieve via online training, but there are at least three things you should look for. First, make sure the training is *actually* interactive – simply pressing "play" won't work. Second, have a way for learners to ask questions, and get them answered. And make sure the answers aren't just legal jargon, but instead provide actual advice. In my experience, the questions asked at training sessions aren't the type employees will take to HR. Instead, they involve early onset of misconduct, which means that answering questions at this stage is critical to nipping drama in the bud. Finally, in order to replicate the feel of live training where learners often learn as much from each other as they do from the trainer, use an online solution that allows learners to have some form of interaction with their fellow learners—within and outside of their organization.

☑   Do you collect, analyze, and use data to continuously improve your training and your other prevention efforts? Prior to launching a training program, collect and analyze data that will guide you to what is right for your company. This will help you define training goals. Review feedback from prior training sessions and continuously evaluate to collect data and info. A question I'd ask clients when I was tasked with delivering live training was, "What do you want the participants to say as they walk out of the training room?" I would then work backwards to design a program to achieve that goal. Use a similar methodology *after* the training to continue to tweak, improve, and uncover possible hot spots. Ideal training programs include a way to track issues related to workplace concerns that can then be analyzed and used to create a positive cycle of reporting, investigating, and resolving issues early.

Step-by-Step Guide to Implementing a Successful Training Program

As more and more companies focus on training, particularly in states that now require harassment-prevention training for all employees, employers are wondering how to make it effective. The key is to be thoughtful and methodical in planning, designing, deploying, and tracking your work. It will take effort and commitment, but going through these steps will be well worth the journey since training done right will provide you with a critical component in your quest to become drama free.

So here are the steps:

1. Plan and set the tone.
2. Design a program for the areas you've identified are in need.
3. Work with subject matter and training experts to develop content.
4. Map out how the training will be delivered and who will deliver it.
5. Deploy, track, and celebrate the training.
6. Collect and use data to keep the learning loop uninterrupted (basically, shampoo, rinse, and repeat).

Step 1. Plan and Set the Tone

It will be vital for you to do some planning up front to make the training program successful. Equally important will be setting the tone so that your program flows with your other harassment prevention efforts. To accomplish that, you'll need to:

- Get buy-in from leadership.
- Collect and analyze information.
- Coordinate training with other efforts to improve your culture.

Buy-in From Leadership

Before designing your training program, you'll need to make sure the entire leadership team is on the same page about tone and content, and you must secure a budget for deploying the training. Use the skills of persuasion presented in Chapter 8 to make an indisputable case for why your training ideas are a necessary component to achieve a healthy culture and why the ROI will be good for the company.

Collect and Analyze Information

Collect any information you have; it could be in the form of hard data or anecdotal information.

Hard data might include:

- ☑ A chart showing the history of complaints received, the types received, and tracking whether the resolution of those complaints has alleviated issues.
  - o The number of complaints received might show a pattern. Have you received more and more complaints over the years? Fewer complaints? About the same over a period of time?
  - o Numbers aren't enough. Can you correlate any changes (an increase or decrease) to a tangible event—perhaps more complaints after a campaign to advertise your hotline, or after providing training that tells employees that you want to hear from them? Or perhaps fewer complaints after a well-known investigation resulted in no action taken against someone who behaved badly, perhaps sending a message that complaining is futile?
  - o Does your tracking show other important patterns? For example, perhaps the vast majority of complaints are about a particular type of issue (sexual harassment, bullying, unfairness in evaluations) making it clear that employees and managers need to learn more about these topics. Or perhaps they spike at one point and decrease at others. Or maybe the allegations are almost always against new managers, perhaps indicating a need for more training for that population.
- ☑ Other data that shows trends to guide you on what you need to include in your training program. Maybe data from an engagement survey or from a summary of exit interviews.

Anecdotal data might include comments you've heard. For example, I sometimes spoke with employees who told me in no uncertain terms that they felt their voice was not really heard by management. They would agree to speak with me for my investigation and would speak openly and candidly, but would also tell me they expected nothing to happen. These types of comments (or if you're lucky, positive comments) will help guide you to better plan what you need to highlight in your training.

Coordinate Training Efforts

Coordinate your training efforts to make sure they align with the other work you're doing to improve your workplace culture. For example, make sure there is a consistent message between policies and training. And, of course, make sure you're authentic and consistent when it comes to reporting and resolving claims of misconduct.

Step 2. Design the Program Based on What You've Learned from Step 1

Now that you have solid guidance about what you need to emphasize in your training program, it's time to roll up your sleeves and start designing it. Here are the questions you need to ask yourself first:

- What methodology will you use to train?
- Who will you train?
- How will you prioritize training?
- What other training topics will you cover?

Methodology

The first order of business is deciding whether to design our own training, hire consultants to provide live training, engage with an e-learning company to provide online training, or opt for a combination of these choices. This decision will mostly be based on your employee population size and whether you're planning to train all your employees, or only a subset.

Who to Train

I highly encourage organizations to train ALL employees, especially on the topics of harassment prevention, respect, inclusion, and communication.

Design a program that clearly distinguishes between illegal behavior and behavior that might be objectionable but isn't unlawful. And provide communication tools for employees and managers to address low-level drama long before it reaches the point of illegality. A great tool to incorporate is Emtrain's Workplace Color Spectrum (as discussed in Chapter 8).

Prioritize Order

Prioritizing the order in which you'll roll out training is critical. You need to be sure to start with topics you know need the most attention. Perhaps you'll start with a focus on issues related to communicating clearly and precisely, because you've identified that issue as an underlying cause of much of your workplace drama. Or maybe you've identified unconscious bias as the root that needs to be addressed before moving on to another topic. Use the information you've collected to make these decisions and it will make your training program impactful and relevant.

Other Topics

Address training topics (and populations) that are critical in your quest to have a drama-free workplace. For example, make sure that those who are tasked with receiving complaints, conducting investigations, and implementing measures to address drama are well versed on how best to do their job. And I don't mean a training session entitled "How to Make Your Investigations Bulletproof at Trial." This type of session only addresses the legal obligations and doesn't help investigators learn to sharpen the skills that are vital for their job. This includes developing curiosity, addressing any biases they might have so they can be truly impartial, developing a methodology for investigating that is equal parts structured and flexible, and honing interview and analysis skills to make it easier to find out the truth in all investigations.

Step 3. Design the Content

Create the content based on what is required (if you're in a state that requires training), what your workplace needs most, and what other skills will help you achieve a healthy culture. This will include looking at the following:

- If you're in a state that mandates training, what is the legally required content?
- What supplemental content will you include to make your program comprehensive and more likely to move the needle in terms of greater understanding and connection, and to have a positive impact on behavior?
- Are there other preliminary issues you need to analyze before developing the content?
- Begin collecting relevant examples that you know will resonate with your learner population.
- Make it interactive.

What Is Legally Required?

Yes, in some cases you'll have to check some compliance boxes. But don't stop there. Even if you're required to cover certain topics, weave in helpful learning lessons that are about the larger issue of respect so that the message is that compliance is a goal, but not the singular or most important goal.

Other Topics to Cover

Did your research uncover hot spots that need to be addressed? For example, you might know that managers have a hard time giving honest feedback and you've seen that this deficiency can lead to claims of unfairness. That means incorporating the how and why of evaluations is critical (or perhaps developing and deploying a separate course on evaluations). Or maybe your company has a long-standing tradition of not enforcing policies, or of selective enforcement. This is an opportunity to design content that not only addresses the need to be consistent, but also provides tangible tools for how that's achieved.

This step also allows you to map out supplemental content. What type of skills training should you prioritize? Once employees complete formal harassment prevention training, what other content should you develop? If you see that employees are afraid to intervene when they see bad behavior, teach them ways to do so. If you know that retaliation has been an issue in the past, create a micro lesson on that. If you've noticed that many in your organization lack emotional intelligence and know that's at the root of a significant percentage of your workplace conflict, then research and recommend books on EQ, along with a list of thoughtful questions about the content, for department managers to use.

Other Preliminary Issues

This is also the step during which you need to ask yourself a tough question: Do you have the internal team to develop this type of content, or should you look for help from the outside? (Or maybe another question is: Do you need to beef up your training team with more professionals who can develop content with this level of focus and detail?)

Make sure you develop material that is written in English, not legalese. Yes, the definition of unlawful harassment includes technical language, but break it down so that everyone understands precisely what you mean.

Use Helpful Examples

Now that you're ready to put together the content, make sure to incorporate relevant, nuanced, and interesting examples to drive home your main points. If you want to make sure your employees understand the distinction between unlawful and inappropriate behavior, use an example and have the audience give you feedback to explain the distinctions. If you want to make sure managers understand why it's important that they let you know if they observe or hear about misconduct, don't just tell them that "they're required to report." Instead, use an example that not only paints a realistic (not legalistic) picture for them, but an example that also provides usable instruction on how to handle difficult situations (including sample language they can use).

Make It Interactive

No matter the exact content or methodology, focus on interaction. This not only makes the training more engaging, it increases retention.

Here are some ways to make your training interactive, engaging, and compelling:

- ☑ Use quizzes or activities.
- ☑ The questions in quizzes should be thoughtful and nuanced, not obvious or scary.
- ☑ Develop a bank of activities to use and test them out to see which resonate most with your audience.

In some cases, I don't want people working individually on a quiz, so instead I use a small group activity. One of my favorites is one I call "Two Truths and Two Lies." Much like the well-known icebreaker, I give each small group four statements; two of the statements are true and two are lies. The object of the activity is not only to get the group discussing the right answer, but also expressing their views as to why they think a particular answer is right or wrong.

Make it fun; this increases interaction. I often will make my "Two Truths and Two Lies" activity into a competitive game. The group with the best answers and explanations wins gift cards or swag.

By using an activity up front, you not only get engagement and buy in, but you can go through a portion of your agenda in a seamless and natural way (rather than having a presentation deck that doesn't allow anyone else to talk until one hour into the training).

Use stories: Bring your stories to life by making them into an activity. Here's one I use (based, of course, on one of my actual investigations):

Start with a basic set of facts like:

Marianne complains that Thurston asked her why she didn't tell him his fly was open … twice. She says she finds this behavior "creepy" because he is old enough to be her father, because he talks about his preference to date young women all the time, and because she doesn't think it's her job to monitor his fly. Ginger investigates and finds no harassment. Her "fix" is to tell Thurston to "stop talking about his fly."

On the next slide, I ask what happens next and give the following options:

1. *Thurston says he learned a lot from the investigation. He learned he should stay away from Marianne who is clearly "hyper sensitive."*
2. *Thurston retaliates against Marianne by disciplining her for spending too much time chatting with coworkers and for arriving late to work.*
3. *Thurston stops talking about his fly.*
4. *Marianne leaves the company.*

In real life, all of these things happened. Using an example like this accomplishes so much.

First, it depicts a real-life and very relatable scenario. Many of us know a "Thurston" in our lives – someone who just doesn't get it.

Next, it is an excellent way to discuss the distinction between unlawful and unprofessional ("creepy") conduct. The initial facts don't give rise to a legal claim, but Thurston's actions cause Marianne reasonable distress. What can and should be done to address that?

The next part of the facts makes it clear that Ginger lost an opportunity to make the workplace better. By simply saying "no harassment" and "stop talking about your fly" she failed to let Thurston know that while his behavior wasn't unlawful, he needed to stop oversharing, and needed to realize that the impression he was creating of himself was not positive.

In the section with the answers, I emphasize the fact that by saying he "learned to stay away from Marianne," Thurston is revealing something incredibly important—he doesn't understand the impact his behavior has on others. This is a problem and will dictate the type of remedial measure you decide to implement after your investigations (see Chapter 11 for more on this). One of the answers also reveals the fact that while the initial conduct wasn't unlawful, by failing to fix the problem, Thurston has created a legitimate legal issue with his seemingly vengeful (retaliatory) behavior.

And finally, discussing the fact that Marianne left the company allows you to discuss the real-life tangible consequences of not dealing with drama effectively.

Be creative and resourceful. Find examples, research activities, learn about best methods for teaching and retaining these nuanced topics, read books and articles that inspire you—do whatever it takes to develop content that is engaging, informative, and interactive.[1]

Step 4. Map Out a Detailed Plan on How to Deliver the Content

Once you've decided on whether your training will be live, online, or a combination of both, it's time to develop an actual calendar and a methodology to track who will be trained and when. This work will include:

- Making decisions about deploying the training
- Deciding what type of supplemental training/education you'll include in your program

Deploying the Training

Decide who you will train and in what order you'll deploy the training. This might be influenced by legal requirements (in those states that mandate training).

Decide how often you'll train or in what intervals you'll deploy training. Again, this might be partially dictated by legal mandate, but go beyond what you have to do and develop a schedule that sends the strong message that you are embarking on a long-term program.

Put together a schedule for what you'll deploy after the initial, formal training. Will you deploy micro lessons? Will you develop discussion questions so that those lessons can be used at department meetings? Will you create a space on your company's internal site or a social media channel to provide continuous resources to managers and employees?

Other Ways to Provide Education

Be creative and consider all sorts of educational activities to incorporate into your schedule. Maybe you develop a calendar to email, on a regular basis, a workplace scene, a guide, an activity, a call to action, or anything else that puts

---

[1]Log on to www.emtrain.com/drama-free-workplace-book for additional ideas on how to make your training interactive, fun, and effective.

the issues of respect, civility, going from bystander to upstander, communication, conflict resolution, diversity, and inclusion top of mind and continues to reinforce the importance of these topics. And remember that "training" is really educating and raising awareness, so share stories, articles, books, and other resources that might not technically fall under the definition of training, but that will go a long way toward making it clear that you value these skills.

And, one final note, make sure you check in with the folks in operations to avoid scheduling conflicts. You don't want your training schedule to interfere with projects or priorities. You want to make sure that your schedule is conducive to employees paying attention and learning.

Step 5. Deploy, Track, and Celebrate

Too many companies miss all three of these critical points. Failing to establish a method to deploy the training, especially if you have a large workforce, will make your efforts infinitely harder and more confusing than they have to be. The failure to set up an easy way to track who has completed training sessions makes it that much harder to run reports that are critical to prove compliance, and also critical for measuring important components of your training efforts (such as which courses are the most popular, which are the least popular, which have been the ones employees have commented on the most, etc.). And celebrating milestones is also critical if you want to authentically present training as a core component of your quest to achieve a healthy workplace culture.

Deploy

Create a training calendar and start scheduling sessions or rolling out e-training. Stay mindful of deadlines for mandatory training and deploy it in a way that makes it easy for everyone to be trained on time.

Track

Make sure you have a way to track who has attended/taken training. And if you're in a state that requires a certain amount of time for training, make sure you can show compliance. Ideally, you'll be able to develop an electronic tracking system that will allow you to monitor any reports about attendance.

Also, set up a system to remind employees if your records show they have not yet taken training.

Celebrate

Not enough companies celebrate training. As a result, it's seen as a "must do" item rather than a "get to do" item. Set up a system to recognize a job well done. Consider giving a prize to the department who has the highest training attendance. Send out periodic updates about introspective questions you've received that you think everyone should read about. Involve employees and managers in the process and give them public praise for their help.

Step 6. Collect and Analyze Data to Keep the Training Loop Going

Track anything and everything related to training:

☑ Is there a trend in terms of the types of questions employees are asking, or issues they express confusion or concern about?

☑ If you have a system that asks polling questions, what information do the answers uncover?

☑ If you have a system that tracks how much time is spent on certain parts of the training, what does that tell you?

☑ Has there been an effect on other data points post-training? For example, have complaints gone up, down, or stayed steady? Have the nature of the complaints changed? Are people using the new language you've taught them and no longer resorting to legal language to report complaints? Are your investigations taking less time but getting better results?

☑ Are your employees giving you positive feedback that you should share?

☑ Is any of the information you collect helpful for starting the process again to develop better and more relevant content, to deploy in a more effective way, or to implement better ways to use supplemental training?

The bottom line with workplace training is this: While it's true that decades of designing and deploying bad or mediocre training has done almost nothing to rid our workplaces of drama, you now have a great opportunity to rewrite that script and make training a signature piece of your drama-free workplace puzzle.

A Checklist for Sexual Harassment Prevention Training[2]

Figure 10.1 shows a method of creating a training program for preventing sexual harassment in the workplace.

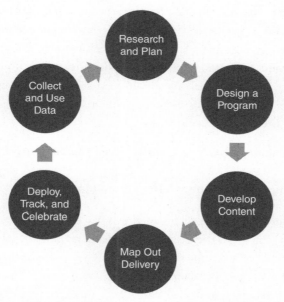

Figure 10.1 The Steps for Creating a Sexual Harassment Prevention Training Program

Step 1. Planning and Setting the Tone
- ☑ Get buy-in from leadership.
- ☑ Collect and analyze information:
  - ○ Data on investigations (types of claims, trends)
  - ○ Comments related to other harassment prevention efforts
- ☑ Coordinate training with other company efforts related to improving culture.

Step 2.   Design the Program Based on Information Obtained from Step #1

☑ Select a training methodology:
  ○ Live
  ○ Online
  ○ Combination of both
☑ Choose who will conduct the training.
☑ Develop a priority for rollout of training.
☑ Select topics to be covered in formal training and follow-up training.

Step 3.   Develop the Content

☑ Verify whether your state has legally mandated content.
☑ Select additional content geared toward increasing understanding and empathy, and positively affecting behavior.
☑ Verify whether the content can be developed with internal resources.
☑ Begin drafting content, including helpful and relevant examples that include real-life, nuanced situations.
☑ Make sure the training is interactive.
  ○ If live, develop activities, quizzes, and group exercises.
  ○ If online, make sure program requires interaction, allows for Q&A.

Step 4.   Map Out a Detailed Plan on How to Deliver the Content

☑ Develop a detailed plan on how you will deploy formal training.
☑ Develop a detailed plan on how you will deploy additional topics to be covered in the program.

Step 5.   Deploy, Track, and Celebrate

☑ Deploy the training.
☑ Develop a tracking system with reminders and that can easily produce reports.
☑ Celebrate a job well done.

**Step 6. Collect and Analyze Data to Keep the Training
            Loop Going**

☑ Are there trends based on employee questions asked during the training?

☑ Are there trends based on employee answers to polling questions, tests, or comments?

☑ Did you identify any hot spots that need to be taken care of?

☑ Does the data show opportunities for additional training?

☑ Use this information to improve the next round of training.

11

How to Effectively Investigate and Resolve Claims of Workplace Misconduct

Over the past few decades, organizations have embraced the need to receive, investigate, and resolve complaints of workplace misconduct. Unfortunately, despite all the attention placed on the importance of setting up ways to look into employee concerns, most companies still rely on antiquated systems. In many instances, investigations have become nothing more than obligatory exercises, meant to show that the organization took action, even if only to check the "There, we did it" box.

This is a huge missed opportunity since the failure to welcome reports, investigate complaints, and resolve those complaints is a leading cause of workplace drama.

The truth is that conducting investigations is hard work, but it is well worth the effort. The work involves following a number of general guidelines and establishing a set process, but injecting flexibility and independence since no two investigations are the same.

To top it off, the work is emotional. The parties making allegations (I'll call them complainants) are often upset or even distraught. The parties who are accused of wrongdoing (I'll call them the accused) often deny the allegations and feel hurt and insulted by them. Coworkers sometimes want to get involved, but oftentimes they are reluctant to do so.

An investigator is therefore given a tall order: To perform unbiased, complete work that will help address everyone's concerns and to do so in a way that is fair and thorough so that their work can uncover the evidence necessary to make a reasonable determination.

And then, the investigator is tasked with helping the individuals and the organization heal and learn from the investigation. And all of this work must be done quickly and investigators are expected to keep meticulous records.

It's a lot to ask, but this guide will provide you with a roadmap to make your work seamless.

Best Practices for Getting Started

Before outlining the various steps required to fully and fairly investigate complaints, a few words about best practices for approaching your work:

- Your ability to address issues and resolve problems is rooted in mutual trust. For a conflict-resolution system to be truly effective, there needs to be an atmosphere where employees trust that you will listen objectively and will take complaints as an opportunity to improve the workplace. Your goal should be to leave the workplace better than when you started your work.

- The goal of workplace investigations is clear: You should seek to uncover evidence that will show you whether the claims made are true. You should always approach investigations with a problem-solving mentality, not with a legal compliance mentality. Legal compliance is the floor, you should be reaching for higher than simply complying with the minimum.

- That said, there is a legal component. Your obligation is to not only take steps to prevent misconduct in the first place, it is also to nip problems in the bud—to resolve issues while they are still minor so they don't fester and turn into unlawful harassment. And although this is the legal rule, it makes a lot of sense from a business perspective, too. (See Chapter 2 for more information on how viewing "the law as your friend" is possible.)

- Workplace investigations are not about "protecting the company." In fact, the best way to "protect" the company is to perform an investigation that uncovers the truth and to resolve problems.

- There is no one-size-fits-all investigation. You will need to use your good judgment throughout the investigation process. Your job is to establish a standard methodology for how to conduct investigations (addressed here) with sufficient flexibility to address the issues that are specific to each individual investigation.

- Although investigations involve objectivity and a focus on facts, don't leave out humanity and empathy. Investigations involve emotions and your goal to be unbiased does not mean you should forget the human component.

- Before beginning your work, watch for unconscious biases you might have—against a specific person, department, position, or type of allegation. Make sure you begin your work with no preconceived notions about the parties or the allegation. It is critical that you conduct your investigation in an impartial and unbiased manner, and it is just as critical to take steps to avoid even the appearance of bias. (See Chapter 3 for a discussion on how to keep unconscious bias out of your investigations.)

Performed well, workplace investigations are a part of a positive workplace cycle (complaint-investigation-resolution-trust in system-comfort in reporting-complaint, etc.). Fair investigations instill trust and help create healthier workplace cultures.

The Qualities of an Excellent Workplace Sleuth

When thinking about the characteristics a workplace investigator needs to succeed, most people focus on hard skills like interviewing experience and an understanding of legal principles. These are helpful, but the job of an investigator requires more nuanced skills and abilities. The best investigators are authentic truth seekers and have the following traits:

- Workplace investigators should, above all, be genuinely curious and authentically open-minded. Genuine curiosity is something that all witnesses will sense, which makes for comfortable and open interviews. In this setting, witnesses are more willing to share all the information they know.

- Similar to curiosity is a desire to listen, learn, and help solve problems. If people sense that you're just there because you have to be, they'll clam up and your job will be infinitely harder.

- Good listening also means having the ability to absorb the information presented and quickly understand and, when necessary, restate what you've heard. This tells the witness you are listening and you take your role as a truth seeker very seriously.

- An investigator should make all witnesses feel comfortable and safe.

- An excellent investigator doesn't check compassion and humanity at the door. She uses emotional intelligence to conduct the work and make decisions. (See Chapter 8 to read more about emotional intelligence and communication.)

- A workplace sleuth must also have excellent research skills. (Investigating is like putting together a complicated jigsaw puzzle, sometimes with 100 pieces, sometimes with 1,000.) Also necessary: superb analytical skills and above-average writing skills.

- An investigator must be comfortable establishing and following investigation protocols, but be flexible enough to make changes on the fly, as necessary.

- To do good work, an investigator must be able to anticipate issues.

- A workplace investigator must have courage. She will often be tasked with making tough calls and having tough conversations.

- And though it's unlikely that an investigator will testify about the investigation, it could happen, so an investigator needs to be comfortable with the idea that one day she may need to explain to a mediator, judge, or jury how she did her work and why she reached certain conclusions.

- And finally, a good workplace sleuth has exceptional common sense and excellent judgment.

If you don't already have a staff that has these qualities, it's time to either level up your talent or focus on providing training to your existing staff. Your investigation staff is a key ingredient to keeping drama out of your workplace so a healthy investment in them is well worth it.

Determining Whether a Full Investigation Is Necessary

When must you conduct a formal investigation?

The legal answer to this question is that a company has a duty to investigate when it receives a complaint of harassment, discrimination, or other potential legal violation, either formally or informally, or when it becomes aware of any such conduct. It's important to note that the law assumes organizations will do what they can to correct misconduct *before* it rises to the level of unlawful harassment.

A better answer than the legal one is that an investigation is likely warranted when someone expresses a concern that should be addressed and resolved. If the behavior alleged excludes or demeans, that likely warrants some type of investigation. If you're serious about your core values of respect, inclusion, accountability, integrity, and ethics, then allegations related to someone failing to meet these standards, especially leaders who fail to do so, should be a cause for concern.

The bottom line is that if you're trying to create an environment that is open and comfortable, you need to take each and every complaint seriously. While not every complaint warrants a full-blown investigation, no complaint warrants you blowing it off. At the very least, validate the concerns raised and be clear about your next steps. If that next step isn't an investigation, tell the employee how you can and will help. (See Chapter 2 for suggestions on how you might set up a two-track system for "formal investigations" and less formal inquiries that still need your attention.)

Here's a tool to help you determine when a formal investigation is warranted. I'll also refer to this tool later when I provide insight on fixing issues. I call it the "Pyramid of Workplace Misconduct" (Figure 11.1) and in my view, any allegation that falls under this pyramid should be looked into—although sometimes the investigation will be relatively short.

I developed this pyramid after conducting a long and complicated investigation that involved multiple allegations of bullying against an executive director. One of the complainants believed her boss bullied her because

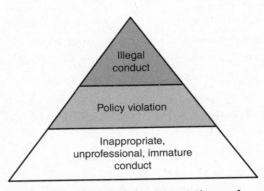

Figure 11.1   The Pyramid of Workplace Misconduct

This pyramid makes a distinction between bad behavior (unprofessional, immature), worse behavior (a violation of a set company policy), and the worst behavior (conduct that meets the definition of illegal).

of racial bias. The evidence indicated otherwise. This executive director was a bad boss, no doubt, but he didn't treat people differently because of race or any other protected category.

When I presented my findings to the complainant and I told her the evidence didn't support her claim of racial bias, she became upset and said "So you're telling me that his behavior is perfectly acceptable." I developed this tool then and have found it helpful to explain the varying degrees of bad workplace conduct since (and it did the trick in the investigation I was handling at the time—the employee understood the distinctions and appreciated that I took the time to explain them to her).

The pyramid has three sections: The bottom section describes behavior that is bad (immature, bad management, unprofessional), the middle section describes behavior that is worse (a workplace rule was violated), and the top section describes behavior that is the worst of all (unlawful behavior). All behavior in the pyramid needs to be addressed. If the behavior is relatively mild, it may not require a full-blown investigation, but it will require some action so that it does not escalate. And if the behavior is more serious, a formal investigation is warranted.

As I discussed in Chapter 2, consider developing a second track for lower-level complaints. For concerns that don't rise to the level of needing a formal investigation, establish a track that focuses on restorative justice operated by someone well-versed in the principles of workplace mediation. Having this second track helps you with legal compliance and, more important, will help keep drama out of your organization and create a healthier culture.

Conducting Investigations That Get to the Truth and Fix Problems: A Step-by-Step Guide

Investigations must be timely, fair, and thorough. They also need to be conducted in good faith and conclusions should be based on a reasonable interpretation of the evidence you diligently gathered. And while you'll need to use your good judgment when investigating complaints, it is helpful to have a framework and a general procedure to follow, including these steps:

1. Intake – Understanding What You're Investigating
2. Planning – Creating Your Roadmap
3. Evidence Gathering – Interviews, Document Analysis, and Other Investigatory Work
4. Analyzing the Evidence and Making Credibility Determinations
5. Reaching Factual Findings – Standards of Proof and Reasonableness
6. Reporting the Findings – Best Practices
7. Fixing the Problem
8. Closing the Loop – Learning Lessons and Next Steps

Step 1   Intake

The intake process is important since it sets the tone for your investigation. It's your best opportunity to tell employees that you welcome complaints. Here are a few important issues to consider as you start your work:

- Decide what "category" the allegation falls under so that you can start planning. A claim involving timesheet fraud will be a very different investigation from one involving allegations of sexually charged misconduct.
- If there is a need to take immediate action, make sure you do so.
  - If, for example, the allegations involve physical contact, you should consider a suspension of the accused during the investi-

gation. (One important note, if you are going to suspend, switch shifts, or move someone, be careful not to negatively affect the complainant since it could create an impression that she is being punished for raising a concern.)

o You might need to notify certain people (an executive, a department hear) if the allegations warrant notice.

o Decide whether you need to enlist the help of IT. For instance, if you need to access or freeze computer records.

■ You're required to do your work promptly, but sometimes investigations are delayed for reasons beyond your control (a key witness is on leave or vacation, for example). Do your best to start and finish your investigation promptly, and make notes of the reasons for any delays.

■ That said, you'll need to decide how quickly you need to start your work. A good rule of thumb (as stated by the EEOC) is to start the investigation within two business days from the time you receive the complaint, but in some instances you'll need to start immediately.

■ Decide whether there are documents you should start collecting or securing right away. This might include relevant policies, electronic records, and personnel file documents.

■ Finally, you need to decide who will conduct the investigation. An internal investigator should be unbiased, have no involvement in the claim, have the requisite skills and training, and have the time to dedicate to the project. If you opt to bring in a third-party investigator, be careful to choose someone with qualities beyond knowledge of the law (see the list of investigator qualities summarized above). And check your state laws regarding third-party investigators. Some states require that outside investigators be licensed (usually licensed private investigators or licensed attorneys).

Step 2   *Planning an Investigation Strategy*

Now that you have a general idea about the topic you're investigating, it's time to develop a plan. That includes making a number of decisions and taking some proactive steps:

■ Who will you interview? In what order? Where? How quickly? The answers will vary depending on the nature of the allegation, work schedules, and available resources.

- Immediately begin to communicate with witnesses to set up interviews. I typically send an email that says something like: "I'm tasked with conducting an independent investigation regarding concerns raised by one of your colleagues. The allegations are not related directly to you or your job, but you've been identified as someone who might have important information to share with me. I'll provide background and additional information when we meet, but for now, I'm contacting you to schedule a meeting. Please let me know when you're available." (This message is for witnesses. The message is different for the accused and a best practice would be to contact the accused by phone or in person if possible. But even then, hold off on going through the details of the allegations until you're meeting with the accused face-to-face.)

- As you start deciding whom to interview, take into consideration those people named by the main parties, but know that the decision about whom to interview is entirely yours. Explain this to the main parties. Ask for names and details about information those witnesses might have, but let the parties know that you will make an assessment and decide who you should interview. You typically want to speak with eyewitnesses, authors of important documents, and anyone else you deem relevant to your inquiry. And keep actual and perceived fairness in mind when making these decisions.

- Continue to identify relevant documents and begin your document review and analysis. Often, reviewing documents will also point you to additional witnesses and will help you develop detailed interview outlines.

Keep track of your work with a strategy document. It doesn't have to be formal and it will be a living and breathing document, but it will help you stay focused. (See the appendix for a sample.)

Step 3   Gathering and Analyzing the Evidence: Interviews, Documents, and More

Now that you've prepared and strategized, it's time to get started with the actual investigation. The bulk of the evidence gathering will come in the form of interviews and document analysis, but there are a few other actions you should consider as part of your investigation.

Interviews: Preliminary Issues

Before asking any questions, you'll need to consider a few issues:

- Draft an outline before each interview.
- Develop a way to address preliminary issues including confidentiality, scope of investigation, retaliation, and getting started. Here are some suggestions:
  - On confidentiality: "While I can't promise you complete confidentiality, I will be discreet and can promise a high level of confidentiality. I will share information only as needed, but understand that if I keep things secret, then I can't do my job."
  - A special note on confidentiality when speaking to the complainant: Be meticulous about letting the complainant know that you need to conduct a fair investigation and that means letting the accused party know about each allegation so he or she has a chance to respond. This doesn't mean you have to disclose the complainant's name or share the written complaint (if there is one), but you do need to provide details about every allegation and allow the accused to respond to each one.
  - The law goes back and forth regarding whether you can require employees to keep information confidential. A best practice is to request, but not mandate, discretion. You have more leeway with managers and supervisors, but even then, make sure you choose words that don't cause unnecessary fear or sound punitive.
  - On scope and process: Give witnesses a general road map. Provide a brief description of the work you'll be doing ("I'm looking into concerns raised by a colleague and I'll be speaking with you and others to find out what you know"). Let the witnesses know you are impartial and will analyze the totality of the evidence. Also let them know that your job is to put all that evidence together and to provide the company with conclusions based on your analysis of that evidence.
  - Be clear about the consequences of retaliation—make sure you don't just reiterate the policy. Be compassionate and empathetic. Retaliation is a real and legitimate fear and it often keeps employees from reporting or sharing information.

○ I often end each of these statements with, "is that clear," or "does that make sense," to make sure we're on the same page. In my experience, going through this process helps put witnesses at ease and increases trust because you're making it clear that you're there to get to the truth. (See the appendix for an interview cover sheet that has a checklist of these items.)

A final, and important, preliminary issue is deciding how to document your investigation interviews. While there are different schools of thought as to how to best do this, the bottom line is that you need to find a way that is accurate and reliable. While you might sometimes veer from your normal practice, it's best to develop a system that you use in most cases. Here are some choices:

- Witness statement written by the witness.
- Witness statement written by the investigator but reviewed by the witness.
- Notes taken by the investigator. These can be handwritten or typed.
- Tape recording interviews.

While there might be other choices, these are the four that are primarily used. Each one has advantages and disadvantages. Some investigators don't like having a witness write a statement because it might be incomplete. Others say that writing it for them is like putting words in their mouth. Some say you should write the statement but purposely put mistakes in there to see if the witness is really reading it (that sounds sneaky to me!). Some don't like to write their own notes because they feel they might be challenged as inaccurate. Some like to tape record to feel safer, but many still find that recording is cumbersome and reduces the comfort level.

Here is the truth about documenting interviews: If your investigation makes it to trial, the employee's attorney will likely find fault with your preferred method. That's the attorney's job. Since the probability that your investigation will end up being examined in a lawsuit is miniscule, don't let this unreasonable fear (criticism by an attorney) keep you from focusing on what matters. You need to document what you were told so that what you were told is clear, complete, and accurate. Any one of these methods can achieve that goal. Be careful to select the best method to reach this goal, but spend your time and energy learning to perfect the art of summarizing conversations, rather than wasting energy on worrying whether you've selected the right method.

Interviews: How to Best Elicit Information

There are a number of proven strategies to elicit as much information as possible during interviews. The most important is to create a comfortable environment and to express your authentic curiosity. By doing this, you'll have people telling you all they know, and sometimes even telling you more than you asked for!

Here are some tips for making the most of your interviews:

- Before you get started, acknowledge the difficulty of the situation and assure all parties that you aren't there to gossip or snoop, but that the interview might include some questions that are uncomfortable or may include a discussion of sensitive information. Witnesses appreciate you acknowledging this.
- Ask open-ended questions, not questions that require only a yes or no answer ("tell me what happened next . . .").
- Do not ask leading questions, that is, questions that point to a particular answer. Again, let the witnesses give you the information they have. (Say something like, "tell me how John reacted after Rachel made that statement.")
- Use the "funnel method" for interviewing. Start with general topics and get more and more detailed with each question.
- Repeat/rephrase questions to make sure you clearly understand what the witness is saying ("so if I heard you correctly, what you said was . . .")
- Ask follow-up questions and ask for more details if the initial answer doesn't provide enough information.
- Ask more than once if the witness isn't giving you a straight answer. Rephrase the question if necessary, but don't move on until you've gotten answers to your important questions.
- Use techniques to help witnesses remember things. It helps to have a calendar handy or to use other tools that might help them recall what happened.

- Allow witnesses to tell their story, but be mindful of the time and make sure you stay focused.
- Ask the witness to draw a picture if that will help explain what they're trying to tell you.
- Use tools to help the witness give you precise information.
  - For example, when I ask about overall environment, I ask the witness to give the workplace (or department) a movie rating from G to NC–17.
  - When someone describes behavior with imprecise words ("he gets angry"), I ask them to put the anger in a range from 1–10 (with 1 being slightly angry and 10 being a rage-filled person who throws things).
  - If the allegations center around events that occurred at specific times, begin writing a timeline and have the witness help you fill in the blanks. Be creative and learn to read the person you're interviewing.
- Perfect your personal power of persuasion. Don't be manipulative or disingenuous, but learn to speak in the language that motivates the witness to feel comfortable and safe enough to share important information with you. (For more on perfecting your powers of persuasion, see Chapter 8.)
- Ask the "Five Ws" questions: who, what, where, when, and why. Also ask about reactions to behavior, whether the complainant shared her experience with anyone, whether the parties spoke about the conduct, and whether other similar complaints have been previously lodged.
- Have the witness tell you the story using imagery, putting themselves back in the situation so they might better remember details.
- Ask the witness to tell you the story backwards. This might reveal additional facts, or it might reveal holes in the story.
- Make sure your questions are clear and concise. Don't ask questions that include judgments or assumptions.
- Stay away from legally charged language like "harassment" and "discrimination." (So rather than asking, "Did you see John sexually harass Maria?" you might ask, "I'm looking into a claim that John made sexually tinged comments to Maria at the meeting last Tuesday; did you hear those?")

- Do not shy away from asking difficult or even embarrassing questions. It might be difficult at first to ask about an alleged romantic affair, but it's critical that you ask specifics.
  - If the complainant or witnesses have shared specific statements made or words used, say those words during the interview to confirm whether anyone heard them.
  - If witnesses recall hearing specific words or phrases, write those as direct quotes in your notes since they will often be helpful in the conclusion and reporting phases of your work.
  - If the witness is reluctant to share information, do your best to make him or her feel comfortable and make it clear that you need to hear all evidence, even if it's hard to share. I often tell embarrassed witnesses that I've been doing this for long enough that it's unlikely they will say anything that will shock me or that I haven't heard before. This seems to put them at ease.
- End the interview with a reiteration of the issues you started with: confidentiality, retaliation, and process. Make sure the witness knows there is a chance you might need to speak with him or her again.

When you get to the analysis phase, you'll be making credibility determinations and also determining whether someone has a motive to be dishonest with you. Take this opportunity to ask any other questions that you believe will help you in making these two determinations. This doesn't imply being sneaky or manipulative, but rather requires creativity and customizing your questions so that you can more easily determine whether the allegations are credible.

Interviews with Main Parties

There are a few questions you should consider asking the main parties (the complainant and accused), including:

- Consider asking the complainant how she wants the situation resolved.
- If the accused denies the allegations, ask why he thinks the complainant is bringing these claims. Also ask whether there is something that he said or did that might have been misinterpreted.

- Consider asking the parties, especially the accused, what he learned during the process, or whether he would have done anything differently. (This could be very helpful if you need to impose discipline, as I'll discuss below in step #7.)
- Close the interviews with the main parties by letting them know that someone will be in contact at the end of the investigation to tell them about the findings—and then follow through to make sure that someone actually gets in touch with them after the investigation.

One last word about interviews. These are not cross-examinations. They do not involve sworn testimony. Although investigation interviews have a certain formality to them, the ideal interview is free-flowing and comfortable. Some investigators mistakenly take a combative approach and feel it's their job to pin witnesses to a certain story (as an attorney does in a deposition) or to get someone to confess. Remember that the goal is to get to the truth. An important mantra that I use about investigations is that, unlike in litigation, there is no such thing as a bad fact in an investigation. There is also no good fact. There are only facts.

Remember that throughout your investigation. There are no good facts, there are no bad facts. There are only facts and those facts will lead you to the truth and will help you fix problems.

Document Review and Analysis

Each investigation will require a review of a different set of documents. Base that decision on the nature of the allegations. If performance evaluations are at issue, review those. If the allegations involve times when people were at work, check timesheets, computer log-in records, security records, or videos showing when people arrived or left the building. If the allegations involve claims that inappropriate emails were sent, review all emails—and don't forget to check other computer records like internet search histories and calendars.

Other Investigation Work

Again, there is no one-size-fits-all approach for other investigation work, but make sure to explore all evidence necessary to reach reasonable conclusions.

In some cases all you need to do is conduct interviews and review documents. In other cases you might visit an important location. In some cases you'll take pictures or draw a layout of the location. Sometimes you'll need to review video, request receipts from the local bar where the events allegedly took place, or drive to a location to see if the markers identified by a witness are really there.

Once you feel comfortable that you've unearthed all the necessary information, it's time to start analyzing the evidence.

Step 4 *Analyzing the Evidence and Making Credibility Determinations*

I see the analysis phase as separate from the conclusion phase (step 5). Here's why: If you put those two steps together, investigators tend to skip the analysis and go straight to reaching conclusions without putting in the necessary work to show *why* they made a particular finding.

The analysis phase includes looking at the evidence to see if there are patterns, if the evidence corroborates or contradicts the allegations, and if it includes a credibility analysis.

Analysis

In some cases the analysis is easy because there are no disputed facts. For example, if two people agree that sexually charged jokes and comments were made, but one says it was appropriate and the other says it wasn't, it's your job to determine whether the behavior meets or falls below your expected behavioral standards.

If, by contrast, the evidence presents contradicting accounts, then your job is to look at the evidence critically and carefully and make determinations about credibility and reasonableness.

For example, if you have a "he said/she said" investigation, you should look at other evidence that might tend to prove or contradict the claim.

- What have other witnesses said?
- Do the documents provide insight? For example, were any texts sent or calls made during the relevant time period?

- Did the complainant share the experience with someone after it happened? If she says she did, did you interview that witness and did the witness corroborate that statement?
- Has the accused behaved in ways that makes the allegation more or less likely? A question I often ask witnesses is, "I know you weren't in the room when the behavior allegedly occurred, but does the description of the behavior sound like something Carl would do?" In my experience, the answers are never lukewarm. The witness either says, "Absolutely not, Carl would never behave that way," or she says, "Oh yeah, I wasn't there to witness this particular incident, but that sounds like Carl . . . he does that kind of thing all the time."

The point is that you need to spend time actually studying the information you've collected and putting together the jigsaw puzzle until a clear image emerges.

Credibility Determinations

If the facts are disputed, you'll need to make determinations about whose claim is more credible—the claim that the allegations occurred, or the denial.

Here are some factors you should consider when making credibility assessments:

- Is the story inherently plausible, or is the story itself simply unbelievable?
- Does one of the main parties have a reason to lie? If so, what is that reason?
- Does the additional evidence you collected corroborate or contradict what one of the parties has said? Perhaps a document proves that someone was at a place they said they were. Conversely, maybe an eyewitness disproves the person's alleged whereabouts.
- How well was the witness able to recall and describe the situation? This doesn't mean they have to remember every single detail, but were they able to provide you with credible descriptions of what happened?
- Is there a history of honesty or dishonesty that you should take into account?

- Has the person accused or been accused before? This isn't determinative but is a factor you should consider, especially when you decide how you're going to fix the situation.
- Did the person make any inconsistent statements during the course of the investigation?
- Some investigators also look at demeanor to make credibility assessments. My advice on this is that while this evidence is not irrelevant, be careful not to base your conclusions exclusively on this, or on a "gut feeling" that someone was either telling the truth or lying simply because of their demeanor at an interview.

Going through this careful analysis naturally guides you to a reasonable conclusion.

Step 5   Reaching Conclusions Based on the Evidence Collected

Once you've finished your analysis, it's time to reach conclusions. This will include:

- Determining whether there is sufficient proof to substantiate the actual claims made (the behavior described).
- If you determine that some or all of the alleged misconduct occurred, you'll need to identify what this means for your workplace. Did the misconduct violate an expected behavioral standard? Did it violate a specific policy?

The following sections offer some additional points to consider as you formulate your conclusions.

Standard of Proof

In reaching your findings, you first need to start with the right standard of proof. Novices mistakenly believe that the evidence must be "beyond a reasonable doubt" or "clear and convincing." In fact, the well-established rule for workplace investigations is that the evidence must show that it is "more likely than not" that the behavior did or didn't occur.

Reasonableness

Your findings should be reasonable. That means that if after your analysis the evidence points you in one direction, that's the direction you should go in. Sometimes, investigators do a great job of collecting evidence, but then reach a finding that is completely contrary to what the evidence indicates.

Additional Notes on Findings

No legal conclusions: The role of the investigator is to make factual determinations, not to reach legal conclusions. Your findings should never be that unlawful harassment did or didn't occur, or that someone did or did not engage in illegal discrimination. Instead, make a finding about the allegations themselves ("The evidence supports Smith's claim that Jones sent her sexually charged emails and gave her two unwanted back rubs"). You should also indicate what that means in terms of your organization's expectations ("By engaging in this behavior, Jones showed poor judgment and violated our code of conduct").

"Inconclusive" should be rare: When it comes to factual findings, watch out for this trap—the one where investigators throw up their hands and say "inconclusive" if there isn't eyewitness testimony about an event. As I described in the analysis section above, there are other ways to view the evidence and make a finding that the behavior likely did or did not happen. A finding of "inconclusive" should be a rarity. Often this finding indicates that you have more investigation work to do or you need to spend more time on the analysis of the evidence.

Failure to present your analysis makes your conclusions deficient: And finally, another trap that investigators often fall into is that they reach a conclusion with no analysis. Here's what I sometimes see: "Smith says Jones touched her lower back at a work event. Jones denies it. Therefore the claim is unsubstantiated." This is not a proper conclusion and is certainly not one that is well-analyzed. The conclusion must be supported with a well-articulated analysis ("The claim is unsubstantiated because, in addition to Jones's denial, 10 witnesses who were at the event deny seeing the alleged touching, there is no evidence that Jones has ever engaged in this type of behavior in the past, and a review of their email exchanges shows no change after the alleged event . . .").

The appendix includes a lengthy document with sample conclusion language. This should help you as you seek to state your findings in a clear and precise way. And keep in mind that at this stage, you can also rely on some of the tools I previously presented. If it's helpful, you should categorize the misconduct by using Emtrain's Workplace Color Spectrum® (Figure 8.1) or the Pyramid of Workplace Misconduct (Figure 11.1).

Step 6   Reporting the Findings

Now that you've reached conclusions, you will need to report your findings. That might mean writing an executive summary, perhaps with copies of interview notes attached, or it might mean writing a long and detailed report. Here are some points to guide you in that decision-making.

When Do You Draft a Report?

There is no specific hard and fast rule, but if you've conducted a formal investigation, you'll want to have a document outlining your investigation, your analysis, and your conclusions. If the conclusions will lead to disciplinary action, write a full report.

What Information Should a Report Include?

Again, while there is no one-size-fits-all way of reporting, generally speaking, a report should include:

- *An introduction*. This opening section should give helpful information, including a summary of the allegations or scope of the investigation. The introduction should also outline how you conducted the investigation (whom you spoke with and what documents you reviewed).
- *A summary of the facts*. Some investigators write summaries of each interview, others write a chronological account, and yet others summarize each allegation separately. No matter which method you use, make sure this section provides sufficient facts for a third-party reader to understand the evidence you found. This section should be written in an objective way.

- *Factual findings.* This section will detail your analysis and your factual conclusions. This section will also include credibility determinations if that's relevant. (See the appendix for sample language for findings.)
- *Conclusion section.* Once you've made factual determinations, you need to determine whether the behavior constitutes misconduct, and if so, the severity of the misconduct.

While this step ends the formal investigation process, the next two steps—fixing the problem and closing the loop—are vital.

Step 7   Fixing the Problem

Sometimes investigators conduct fair, thorough, and timely investigations, but their work is all for naught since they forget this critical last step: to fix the problem.

As I discussed in Chapter 7, savvy investigators use backward- and forward-looking accountability to fix problems.

Backward-Looking Accountability

While most companies understand this concept—the need to implement corrective measures to address the misconduct—most don't take the time to find a helpful solution. Follow these tips to become a master fixer.

1. *Keep two general principles in mind:* There are two well-recognized general rules of thumb to follow when deciding what discipline to impose:
   - Is the discipline equal to the wrongdoing?
   - Is the discipline designed to keep the behavior from occurring again?
2. *Rate the misconduct:* Use the various tools I've introduced here to put the behavior in an appropriate range. Measuring the misconduct guides you to the right level of discipline and keeps your discipline even-handed.
3. *Rate the bad actor on the "salvageability scale" to determine an effective solution:* A remedial measure that isn't customized according to the

facts, and what you know will send the right message will not solve the problem. Use the information you gathered during the investigation to determine what resolution will be most effective.

4. *Look to past actions:* Since allegations and facts differ, there may not be a past situation that exactly matches this situation, but make sure you're being consistent. This is another way to avoid uneven discipline and claims of unfairness.

5. *Be creative:* Too many companies go to the same short list of possible remedial measures: A meeting, a written warning, training, a last-chance agreement, or termination. This is hardly an exhaustive list of possible remedial measures. Use these tools and be creative to determine how to implement a measure that will fix the situation once and for all.

Most investigators are familiar with the first and fourth concepts, but the second, third, and fifth are likely new to you. Here's how those work.

Rate the Misconduct

- Pick a tool.
  - You can use Emtrain's Workplace Color Spectrum® (Figure 8.1) to rate the misconduct on a scale from light yellow to deep orange (since your investigation does not include reaching legal findings, the red rating should not apply, but you might find that the misconduct falls in the darkest part of the orange section).
  - Use the Pyramid of Workplace Misconduct (Figure 11.1) to similarly place the behavior in the bottom part or middle part of the pyramid.
  - Use a simple rating system like a scale of 1–10, with 1 being very mild misconduct and 10 being egregious misconduct.
- Rate the behavior.
  - If you use the color spectrum, rate the behavior by color, but be detailed. Maybe the behavior is dark yellow or light orange.
  - If you use the pyramid, also put it in a range within the category of inappropriate conduct or policy violation.

○ If you use a simple rating system, assign the behavior to a range. Maybe the behavior was somewhere between 1 and 3, or between 7 and 9.

○ Regardless of the tool you use, once you've rated the behavior, you've eliminated a whole host of possible remedial measures. After all, you shouldn't implement the same fix for behavior that is a 4 as you would behavior that's a 9, and you wouldn't choose the same fix for light yellow behavior that you would for burnt orange behavior.

○ This not only guides you in terms of the type of discipline you'll implement, it also keeps you honest. This all but eliminates the possibility of bias or a lack of even-handedness. If the CEO engaged in behavior that you rate a 9.9 and you've fired 100% of employees whose behavior you've rated as such, it becomes difficult to justify any other remedial measure.

○ Develop a list of remedial measures that match the rating you assign to the misconduct. This list will be developed over time and it will become more refined and therefore effective.

  ▪ Mild behavior might include "fixes" such as written discipline, targeted training, restorative justice (the issue might be solved with a simple apology), taking steps to increase emotional intelligence and communication skills, or improving leadership skills.

  ▪ Conduct that is somewhere between mild and egregious might warrant a demotion, a loss of pay, a loss of a bonus, a loss of title, removal from an important committee, removal from leadership, one-on-one training to address specific issues, a performance improvement plan, or anything else that will resonate.

  ▪ Egregious or severe conduct will warrant a detailed and specific last-chance agreement or termination.

Develop a System to Rate Whether the Bad Actor Is Salvageable

Once you've rated the behavior and know that there are certain types of remedial measures that are on the table, and others that aren't, it's time to drill down further.

When you asked the accused party what he learned from this situation, did he say, "I learned that none of this was my fault, this all happened because Suzie is hypersensitive" (these are exact words used by someone I interviewed). Or did he say, "I still disagree that what I did was wrong, but I've definitely learned that my words and actions can be easily misinterpreted, so I know I need to do better." Or perhaps he said, "I'm mortified. I never intended to make Suzie feel alienated or excluded. I don't know how this works, but if I'm able to sit down with her to apologize profusely, I'd welcome the chance to do so. I understand that even if my intentions weren't bad, Suzie is reasonable in thinking that what I did was unacceptable."

The answer to this question as well as other information you collected during the investigation will guide you as whether the bad actor is salvageable. The other information will include issues such as: Has the person engaged in the behavior before, making this a repeat allegation? Did the target of the conduct tell him to stop to no avail? Has the person taken his role seriously in the past— for example, has he enthusiastically attended and participated in training sessions, embraced the concepts of a healthy workplace culture? Also, you should have higher behavioral expectations of leaders. Taking a page from military language, I often deemed leaders' bad behavior as "conduct unbecoming of a leader in our organization." This doesn't mean you let nonmanagement employees off the hook for bad behavior, but it's fair to assume that leaders should set an example and behave in ways that honor your company's core values.

Once you've looked at this information, you can once again rate this person's salvageability on a scale of 1 to 10. If the person scores low, then a remedial measure that might work for someone with a high rating will likely not work for this person. So if, for instance, targeted training is on the list of potential remedial measures based on your misconduct rating, but the person doesn't accept responsibility for his actions and thinks training is useless, then you're spinning your wheels by sending him to training. If, on the other hand, you know this person is primarily motivated by money and power, then you'll send a much stronger and more effective message, and are more likely to impact behavior, if you take away a title, demote the person, or hit him in the pocketbook.

Be Creative

By going through this two-step process (rating the behavior and the actor), you'll be better able to select more creative remedial measures than simply choosing between doing nothing, providing training or firing the person. You'll begin to see that there are hundreds if not thousands of possible fixes and you'll get better and better at implementing the one that will have the desired effect: to fix problems in a fair and even-handed way.

Forward-Looking Accountability

Looking backwards is critical, but it's not the end of the story. As I outlined in Chapter 7, cutting-edge organizations should also incorporate forward-looking accountability when they're resolving claims of misconduct.

In addition to following the steps I outline above in relation to the bad actor himself, use the investigation process as an opportunity to positively affect the entire department, location, or organization. I have yet to conduct even one investigation that didn't have a learning lesson. Here are some common examples and ways you can use them to look into the future to make your culture healthier:

- Even if the allegation isn't substantiated, help people adjust their perceptions. Was the complainant's interpretation of the facts reasonable? If so, then you have work to do to change behavior that is causing reasonable angst. If not, you need to develop creative ways to help the employee understand why her view is not reasonable, without alienating her or breaking trust. (See Chapter 8 to learn to become a compassionate sharpshooter.)

- Look at whether there were environmental factors that caused this behavior to occur, or caused it to escalate. If you identify any, you need to fix them.

- Were there missed opportunities to stop the behavior or to prevent it from occurring in the first place? Maybe employees are still not comfortable intervening and are still passive bystanders. If so, what can you do to help them feel safe and comfortable speaking up?

- If there was an HR or management misstep, make your systems better. If, for example, the root of the issue was that the hiring manager didn't follow protocol and made a bad hire, do you need to improve the protocol or provide more resources on how to follow the protocol? If the underlying drama is related to evaluations that are viewed as unfair, follow a similar process to see if your procedures are clear and helpful, and if not, fix them.

- If an entire department needs to improve, implement ways to help.
- And, finally, ask whether the complainant needs to be made whole. Did your investigation uncover an evaluation that resulted in a less-than-deserved rating and salary increase? If so, you might need to review that person's raise. If you found evidence supporting the complainant's claim that a written warning was given vengefully, consider removing that unfair document from the employee's personnel file.

Over time, as you add this step into your investigation process, you'll see patterns. But more important, as you focus on not only implementing backward-looking accountability but also begin to authentically see the investigation process as a tool to make the workplace better, your culture will improve and there is a high likelihood that you'll need to conduct fewer and fewer formal investigations.

Step 8   *Closing the Loop*

After all this good work, you now need to close the loop. Two important issues to do so are recordkeeping practices and communicating with the parties.

Recordkeeping

In terms of recordkeeping, you should check to see if there are specific legal requirements about how long you need to keep records, but the most important aspect of recordkeeping is making sure that you keep all documents related to the investigation in a separate investigation file. Do not place an entire investigation file in a personnel file. That said, you might need to place specific documents into someone's personnel file. If for example, you implemented a remedial measure like a written warning, a demotion, a performance improvement plan, or something else related directly to the accused's job, that does need to be documented in the personnel file.

Following Up with Parties

The most basic step organizations miss is simply following-up with the main parties. While there is no obligation to share your report or to tell the parties everything about the investigation, you owe it to them to sit down to reassure them that you conducted an unbiased investigation and to talk about next steps.

And even when the investigator does follow-up, often the communication leaves a lot to be desired and ends up doing more harm than good. Here's the drill I've seen more often than I'd like:

- Based on fear that they aren't allowed to share "confidential information" the investigator usually tells the complainant something like: "Thank you for bringing your complaint to us. I conducted a thorough investigation and couldn't substantiate your claim that Bob was biased when he gave you your evaluation. Again, thanks for taking the time to come to us. We really appreciate it."
- The investigator thinks that by thanking the complainant at the beginning and the end, she won't notice that in the middle, nothing was really said.
- The investigator's message is lost for a simple reason: All the complainant hears the investigator say is, "I didn't believe a word you said."
- This may not be what the investigator said or may not even be what she meant, but it's what the complainant heard. I've heard this from enough complainants to know this is the truth.

Try this instead:

- "Thank you for bringing your complaint to us. Your concerns centered on your belief that you've been evaluated unfairly, and that the unfairness is rooted in bias because of your gender. I conducted a thorough investigation and didn't find evidence that gender, or any other characteristic, influenced decisions about your performance evaluation. What I did find though, is that your manager failed to give you timely and clear feedback. I can see why hearing criticism for the first time at your annual review caught you off guard. Your manager also expressed his concerns in a less than ideal way, and that clearly increased your belief that a lack of fairness was at play. That said, our plan is to improve our systems related to evaluations and to provide additional training on that topic. I hope that helps explain my findings and again, thanks so much for bringing your concerns to our attention."

- No confidential information shared. No admission of legal liability. Just simple, candid, precise, and compassionate language that the complainant will appreciate hearing.

This advice also applies to the accused party. If your investigation didn't substantiate the exact claims, there are still forward-looking learning lessons. Discuss those and make it clear that you intend to use what you learned from this and every investigation to continuously improve your culture.

Although there is rarely a reason to communicate directly with other witnesses, you might need to if you find that an entire department or location needs some extra attention to get them back on track.

And don't forget that the follow-up doesn't end with this conversation. Stay in touch with the parties to see if remedial measures are working, to make sure the complainant hasn't been retaliated against, and to make sure everyone got the message—that you take your role as an investigator seriously and that you are happy to hear about and investigate concerns.

. . .

By following these steps, you will send a strong message to your employees: We care about our culture more than we do about legal compliance. And since we want to have a healthy culture, know that we take complaints seriously and have set up systems to investigate and fix problems quickly and fairly.

Appendix

Supporting Documents for Conducting Investigations

This appendix includes checklists and worksheets that you can use to investigate and resolve claims of workplace misconduct. Included are:

1. An Investigation Strategy worksheet for keeping track of investigation steps.
2. An Interview Notes Cover Page that gives you a place to record information about a witness you are interviewing and a checklist of statements to make at the beginning and end of each interview.
3. Sample Conclusion Language. You can use the language found here to state your findings clearly and precisely.

INVESTIGATION STRATEGY

General Information

Matter Name: _____

Matter #: _____

Matter Type: _____

Investigator: _____

Immediate Remedial Action Taken: _____

_____

_____

Checklist

- ❑ Review written complaint or other written statements regarding allegations.
  Documents reviewed: _____
  _____

- ❑ Review relevant company policies and procedures.
  Policies reviewed: _____
  _____

- ❑ Review complainant's and alleged wrongdoer's personnel files.

Potential Witnesses

Name	Notes

Documents to Review

Documents	Notes

Other Notes

Action	Notes

INTERVIEW NOTES COVER PAGE

General Information

Witness's Name: _____

Documents Provided by Witness: ☐ Yes ☐ No

Date of Interview: _____

Interview Location: _____

Start Time/End Time: _____/_____

Investigator's Name: _____

Other Representatives Present (including relationship): _____
_____

Introduction

- ❑ Explain the investigation scope; disclose only necessary information about allegations.
- ❑ Explain the company policy on the subject matter, if applicable.
- ❑ Explain the investigation process.
- ❑ Explain your role in the investigation.
- ❑ Explain that witness cooperation is important.
- ❑ Address confidentiality and its limits.
- ❑ Stress retaliation prohibition: All are protected and bound.
- ❑ Explain the importance of being completely honest and open.

Witness Background

Position/Title: _____

Department: _____

Direct Supervisor:_____

Date of Hire/How Long with Company:_____

Witness's General Description of the Workplace:_____
_____
_____

SEE ATTACHED PAGES (___ pages in total) FOR DETAILED INTERVIEW QUESTIONS AND RELATED NOTES

Closing the Interview

Ask, "Is there anything else that we haven't discussed that you believe will be helpful to me?"

Stress that retaliation is strictly prohibited. Remind witness to report any retaliation.

Inform witness that s/he may need to be contacted for additional information.

Sample Conclusion Language

Though not intended to be a script for the formulation of a written conclusion to an investigation, this sample language is intended to be an illustra-
tion of the various ways in which conclusions can be drafted, depending on
the type of findings or severity of behavior found in an investigation. The
nuanced analysis will vary depending on the specific facts of and individuals
involved in the investigation.

Sample Conclusion Language

Finding	Practice Tips	Sample Language

Allegations Substantiated	This conclusion might be reached because there is proof that the behavior occurred (an admission by the wrongdoer; emails or other documents confirming the events/behavior; corroborating testimony, etc.) or because a careful and reasonable review of all the evidence (sometimes circumstantial) makes it more likely than not that the behavior in fact occurred. As is true with all conclusions, they should be stated as factual conclusions (not legal conclusions) and should be based on the evidence presented. (For easier reference, the sample language refers to "harassment" recognizing that this is the language used by many employees and often an analysis will be made using the policy. The use of those legal phrases does not imply illegality and, as suggested throughout this book, you should refrain from using legal language whenever possible.)	For "harassment" allegations (allegations of sexually charged misconduct):
		
		    ■ Though Roger Smith denies Lucy Warren's allegations, the evidence strongly suggests that Smith engaged in the behavior described. The witness testimony is consistent with Warren's recollection of events and the documentary evidence also substantiates her allegations. Therefore, it is more likely than not that the behavior occurred and by engaging in this behavior Smith fell below our company's behavioral expectation.
		
		For allegations involving a negative employment action ("discrimination"):
		
		    The totality of the evidence suggests that Joe Garcia took Marcie Daley's gender into consideration when making decisions about her employment. For example, Garcia admits he wondered whether Daley would be able to "handle" the duties associated with the director position for which she applied. Garcia admits he assumed that Daley, a single mother, may have been limited in her ability to perform the duties required since she has many time commitments outside of work. Additionally, Garcia admits he became angry after Daley applied for stress leave as a result of her belief that he (Garcia) was engaging in inappropriate behavior. Garcia says he suspended Daley a few hours after learning of her application for stress leave. As such, the evidence indicates that Garcia's decisions about Daley were infected with bias and that his actions to suspend her were vengeful and done in response to Daley's reasonable request to take time off.

(continued)

Sample Conclusion Language (continued)

Finding	Practice Tips	Sample Language
Allegations Unsubstantiated	In some instances, the allegations are not supported by the evidence. In this case, the complainant might have a reasonable belief of wrongdoing, but his/her perceptions are simply not supported by the evidence presented (note that this is very different than a "false claim"—that implies a complainant made up facts maliciously). In such a case, investigators need not directly attack the complainant, but rather base the conclusions on the fact that the objective evidence simply does not support his/her allegations.	■ For "harassment" allegations: Although Jerri McKay alleges that Jason Cameron has engaged in sexually charged and demeaning conduct on numerous occasions (verbally and in writing), the evidence (witness testimony and documentary evidence) shows that their communication was professional and appropriate and that Cameron treated McKay respectfully and professionally (in meetings, during one-on-one interaction, and in written communication). The evidence is therefore insufficient to prove Cameron behaved inappropriately towards McKay (or any other employee). ■ For allegations involving a negative employment action: While Charlie Kuo alleges that he was not promoted to manager of his department because Kristen Shaw, his department director, took his race into consideration, the evidence suggests otherwise. For example, though it is true that Shaw criticized Kuo's writing skills, the evidence shows that Shaw was equally critical of other employees with poor writing skills. Additionally, the evidence validates Shaw's testimony that in Kuo's position (HR supervisor), it is imperative that his writing be clear and concise. Finally, the evidence indicates Kuo often drafted documents with many factual errors—a deficiency Shaw says is unacceptable in any position, but particularly in Kuo's position, which often involves drafting letters to attorneys and governmental entities involving intricate details that must be recited accurately.

| Some Allegations Substantiated | Often the investigator will find that the evidence suggests that the complainant's allegations did not occur as reported but there still might be a finding that some of the allegations are substantiated and that the accused fell below the expected behavioral standard. In some cases, the investigator might find that the allegations occurred as stated (in fact, some investigations involve descriptions of events with no factual variations), but that perceptions and interpretations of the events diverge. (Of course, when any witness's credibility is called into question, this should be noted in the verbal and/or written conclusions.) | For "harassment" allegations:

Although there is insufficient evidence to substantiate all of Carol Smith's allegations of harassment against Bill Thompson (particularly the most egregious allegation of inappropriate physical touching) there is sufficient evidence, based on the testimony of several witnesses as well as a review of the email traffic between the two, to support Smith's allegations that Thompson has behaved inappropriately on several occasions (discussing details of his own and his subordinates' personal lives, forwarding emails with off-color [though not wholly inappropriate] content, for example). Thompson displayed poor judgment by engaging in this behavior and fell below the standards of conduct expected of someone in his position. While he may not have violated the letter of the harassment policy, he did violate the spirit of it. [This last sentence should only be included if your practice is to make a determination about whether a company policy was violated.]

For allegations involving a negative employment action:

Annie Sampson says that the decision to demote her (which occurred 10 days after her complaint of harassment against her coworker) was made in retaliation for her complaint. The evidence suggests that Sampson's performance issues (failing to meet quotas, failing to meet deadlines, failure to keep clients informed) had been informally discussed with her on numerous occasions before the demotion, and the documentary evidence shows the decision to demote was made by an independent committee two weeks before Sampson lodged her complaint. Despite |

(continued)

Sample Conclusion Language (continued)

Finding	Practice Tips	Sample Language
		this, Sampson's supervisor, George Glass, should have engaged in more formal and straightforward efforts to not only provide Sampson with clear feedback about her performance deficiencies, but also with a clear warning that failure to meet these expectations could lead to a demotion. Although the evidence does not suggest that anyone behaved in a vengeful manner, Sampson's perceptions of inappropriateness could have been avoided if Glass had implemented better HR practices related to performance evaluations.
"Inconclusive" Findings	Though it should be extremely rare, there will be an occasional situation where you simply do not have enough evidence (despite your best attempts to collect it) to allow you to reach a reasonable and fair conclusion. In this case, investigators should be meticulous about reciting the facts as presented by the various witnesses (and by the documentary evidence, if appropriate), but should also clearly state that the evidence is insufficient to reach a conclusion one way or the other.	■ For "harassment" allegations: Despite the numerous witnesses interviewed and documents reviewed, there is insufficient evidence to reach a definitive conclusion with respect to Sally Johnson's allegations of sexually charged misconduct against Trevor Jones. There are no witnesses who can corroborate Johnson's claims that Jones tried to kiss her after a company-sponsored event. The one witness who might have witnessed the incident is no longer with the company and could not be found, despite repeated attempts to do so. Therefore, I am unable to reach a definitive conclusion on the specific allegations. However, there are some important general observations and learning lessons that have been uncovered as a result of the investigation. ■ For allegations involving a negative employment action: After a careful review and analysis of the witness testimony and documentary evidence (described in detail earlier in this report), there is insufficient evidence to reach a definitive conclusion regarding

"Inconclusive" Findings	Randy Garcia's allegations of racial bias. Jae Chang, whom Garcia says engaged in the biased behavior, denies the allegation and there is insufficient evidence to make a determination in terms of the specific allegation. That said, the investigation did uncover reasons why Garcia might have perceived unfairness and those are covered in this report. ■ For "harassment" allegations: In addition to substantiating Katie Catan's allegations against Billy Jordan, the evidence uncovered during this investigation also shows that the culture in the accounting department is often too casual. The perception created is that employees are free to talk about sexually explicit topics, drink heavily at company events, and treat each other in an unprofessional manner as long as "everyone is okay with it." The employees in this department would likely benefit from additional training and additional monitoring to ensure that they understand that while it is acceptable to have a light environment, they must always exhibit professionalism and appropriateness, both on site and off site. For allegations involving a negative employment action: The investigation uncovered several missteps that might have avoided a perception of unfairness, including HR's failure to adequately review performance evaluation ratings for "inflation" and consistency, and the department managers' own inconsistent practices related to evaluations and discipline. Both of these problems provide some big-picture learning lessons regarding the importance of open and honest communication, including always providing timely and accurate performance feedback.
"Learning Lessons"	Regardless of the conclusion, almost all investigations present facts or circumstances that provide some learning lessons. Investigators should not be afraid to point out ways in which behavior, policies, or practices could be improved. For example, in some instances, even if there is insufficient evidence to support the allegations, individuals may benefit from coaching/training, or the business might benefit from the implementation of procedures to improve effectiveness and/efficiency or the company might benefit from the implementation of new or improved policies. Incorporating forward-looking accountability is a key way to keep drama out of the workplace. (For more on the concept of forward-looking accountability, see Chapter 5.)

Index